THE ETERNAL SEA

The Eternal Sea

AN ANTHOLOGY OF SEA POETRY

EDITED BY W. M. WILLIAMSON

DRAWINGS BY GORDON GRANT

Granger Index Reprint Series

BOOKS FOR LIBRARIES PRESS
FREEPORT, NEW YORK

Copyright, 1946, by Coward-McCann, Inc.
Reprinted 1969 by arrangement

STANDARD BOOK NUMBER:
8369-6092-0

LIBRARY OF CONGRESS CATALOG CARD NUMBER:
79-86804

MANUFACTURED
BY
HALLMARK LITHOGRAPHERS, INC.
IN THE U.S.A.

CONTENTS

INTRODUCTION		vii
1.	THE CALL OF THE SEA	1
2.	THE BUILDING OF THE SHIP	25
3.	OUTWARD BOUND	55
4.	STORMY SEAS	83
5.	CALM, SUNNY SEAS	123
6.	"ROLL ON, THOU DEEP AND DARK BLUE OCEAN, ROLL!"	143
7.	NAUTICA MYSTICA	167
8.	"LOVE STILL HAS SOMETHING OF THE SEA"	197
9.	HOMEWARD BOUND—MAKING PORT	219
10.	SAILOR TOWN	247
11.	SEA WINGS	269
12.	FISHERMEN	287
13.	NAVAL SONGS AND BALLADS	311
14.	"AH BLO-O-OWS!"	349
15.	PIRATES AND BUCCANEERS	375

16. NEPTUNE'S KINGDOM	395
17. GHOST SHIPS AND PHANTOMS	423
18. "SPIN A YARN, SAILOR!"	449
19. CHILD OF THE SEA	469
20. THE VOICE OF THE SEA	491
21. HAIL AND FAREWELL	513
ACKNOWLEDGMENTS	541
INDEXES	
AUTHORS AND TITLES	549
FIRST LINES	557

INTRODUCTION

In the rhythmic swing and heave of the sea, in its ceaseless ebb and flow, there surge for us overtones and intimations of the Eternal. Lord Byron, in his "Apostrophe to the Ocean," sings:

"Thou glorious mirror, where the Almighty's form
Glasses itself in tempests: in all time,
Calm or convulsed—in breeze, or gale, or storm,
Icing the pole, or in the torrid clime
Dark-heaving;—boundless, endless, and sublime—
The image of Eternity—the throne
Of the Invisible; even from out thy slime
The monsters of the deep are made; each zone
Obeys thee; thou goest forth, dread, fathomless, alone."

The poet, like the lookout at masthead, strains his vision from horizon to farther horizon. The sea is at once his inspiration and his despair. He seeks to interpret its mystery; there are times when he may look through

"—magic casements opening on the foam
Of perilous seas in faery lands forlorn"

but the sea still clings to the inscrutable secret of an ancient and solitary reign. Shelley sings:

> "Unfathomable Sea! whose waves are years!
>   Ocean of Time, whose waters of deep woe
> Are brackish with the salt of human tears!
>   Thou shoreless flood which in thy ebb and flow
> Claspest the limits of mortality,
> And, sick of prey, yet howling on for more,
> Vomitest thy wrecks on its inhospitable shore!
> Treacherous in calm, and terrible in storm,
>   Who shall put forth on thee,
>   Unfathomable Sea?"

Yet ever the sea tides strain at the heart of the poet; he must put forth in the good gray dawn. Little it matters to him whether his craft to cleave the blue be coracle or felucca, whaler or fisherman, barque or schooner, sloop or corvette. The sea calls! Before the last star pales in the west he must be out beyond the gleam of the farthest harbor light. He would fathom the secret of the deep, plumb the world below the brine, sail with the slim mast trucks writing a poem across the heavens, and explore the far-flung shores of the spirit. With no other instrument to guide him than the Stella Polaris of his own dreams' devising, he would reveal to us the awe and wonder, the sublimity and verities of the deep. That most unerring of instruments invented by man, John Harrison's chronometer, cannot equal in sensitivity the poet's intuition of the tide's turning in the great mystery and beauty of the waters of life.

Let's up anchor, lovers of the sea! All you will need is a duffle bag of memory to tuck away your favorite gems of sea poetry. There'll be a goodly crew—some fine shipmates to sing for us: Chaucer and Spenser, Milton and Shakespeare, Keats and Shelley, Falconer and Donne, Longfellow and Whittier, Kipling and Masefield, and many others who have sung of the sea. And what ho! Here's a letter from an old mariner friend—a poet, as well. He wants to sign on for one more voyage; says we can sail on his white-winged barque moored down at the Port o' Dreams. "Sometimes I wish that I had never left her," he writes, "for she was beautiful. She was my youth, my last ship, a lofty four-master—the loveliest ever to come from a shipbuilder's yard. I know what you say to that, shipmate. Your ship was loveliest, too. You had your dreams in her. You, I, Paddy, and Reuben and all of our breed. We each say the same thing. Each ship was loveliest. Such was the way with a sailor.

"D'ye mind the clear dawn at one in the morning, down south of the Horn in midsummer, with the gale at her swift heels? The albatross circling us, the bead-eyed cape pigeons, the cape hens and the mollyhawks; the great bergs around us, with the combers, the eighty foot combers roaring and thundering, the Old Man by the helmsman, life lines stretched taut from fo'c'sle to poop's break, hatches hid under the gray backs that rolled o'er her deck—*and somebody singing.*

"Or d'ye mind it in the winter? Pitch dark before five in the evening, two bells of the dog watch, outbound with the snow flying, ice on the shrouds and ratlines and sails and deck house, hove to with the gale in her teeth, black as the devil's own coal hole, pitch dark till nigh eight of the morning. So, day upon day, till six weeks are gone by. Sore handed we are, salt caked to the backbone, weary in mind and in sinew—*and somebody singing.*

"Or mind you the sunset, in latitude nothing? The sea a blue mirror, not a stir on the water, not a sound in the ship, all hands at the railing to watch the red sun dip, the ship's tall trucks gleaming, her white sails flat, the sky streamed with banners of amethyst, sapphire, topaz and opal. An old sailor speaking, low voiced, for all of us, a bright-eyed, white-headed man of the fo'c'sle who's followed the sea since he was a lad of fourteen. He preaches a sermon:

'Lord, sons, ain't that beautiful?'

"Or mind you that Christmas, outbound in the channel with the wind dead ahead, and the fog on the green sea? Mind you that rust sided clipper, homebound, how she raced from the fog and swept by us, racing for home under skysails? Mind you the man on the poop, how sudden he started his singing? And another joined in, and another, till all of the glad crowd were singing? And how then one of our young kid apprentices joined in the singing, and all of us followed so that all hands in both ships were singing:

'God rest you merry, gentlemen!
Let nothing you dismay!
For Jesus Christ our Saviour
Was born on Christmas Day!'"

Come aboard all you lovers of the sea—we're outbound to the blue!

—W. M. Williamson

1. The Call of the Sea

SEA-FEVER

I must down to the seas again, to the lonely sea and the sky,
And all I ask is a tall ship and a star to steer her by,
And the wheel's kick and the wind's song and the white sail's shaking,
And a grey mist on the sea's face and a grey dawn breaking.

I must down to the seas again, for the call of the running tide
Is a wild call and a clear call that may not be denied;
And all I ask is a windy day with the white clouds flying,
And the flung spray and the blown spume, and the sea-gulls crying.

I must down to the seas again to the vagrant gypsy life,
To the gull's way and the whale's way where the wind's like a whetted knife;
And all I ask is a merry yarn from a laughing fellow-rover,
And quiet sleep and a sweet dream when the long trick's over.

John Masefield

SEA-SHORE

I heard, or seemed to hear, the chiding Sea
Say: Pilgrim, why so late and slow to come?
Am I not always here?—thy summer home.
Is not my voice thy music, morn and eve?—
My breath thy healthful climate in the heats,
My touch thy antidote, my bay thy bath?
Was ever building like my terraces?
Was ever couch magnificent as mine?
Lie on the warm rock-ledges, and there learn
A little hut suffices like a town.
I make your sculptured architecture vain—
Vain beside mine. I drive my wedges home,
And carve the coastwise mountain into caves.
Lo! here is Rome and Nineveh and Thebes,
Karnak and Pyramid and Giant's Stairs
Half-piled or prostrate,—and my newest slab
Older than all thy race.
       Behold the Sea,
The opaline, the plentiful and strong,
Yet beautiful as is the rose in June,
Fresh as the trickling rainbow of July;
Sea full of food, the nourisher of kinds,
Purger of earth, and medicine of men;
Creating a sweet climate by my breath,
Washing out harms and griefs from memory,
And, in my mathematic ebb and flow,
Giving a hint of that which changes not.
Rich are the sea-gods:—who give gifts but they?
They grope the sea for pearls, but more than pearls:

They pluck Force thence, and give it to the wise.
For every wave is wealth to Dædalus,
Wealth to the cunning artist who can work
This matchless strength. Where shall he find, O waves!
A load your Atlas shoulders cannot lift?

I with my hammer pounding evermore
The rocky coast, smite Andes into dust,
Strewing my bed, and, in another age,
Rebuild a continent of better men.
Then I unbar the doors: my paths lead out
The exodus of nations: I disperse
Men to all shores that front the hoary main.
I, too, have arts and sorceries;
Illusion dwells forever with the wave.
I know what spells are laid. Leave me to deal
With credulous and imaginative man;
For, though he scoop my water in his palm,
A few rods off he deems it gems and clouds.
Planting strange fruits and sunshine on the shore,
I make some coasts alluring, some lone isle,
To distant men, who must go there, or die.
Ralph Waldo Emerson

THE SEA GIPSY

I am fevered with the sunset,
I am fretful with the bay,
For the wander-thirst is on me
And my soul is in Cathay.

There's a schooner in the offing,
  With her topsails shot with fire,
And my heart has gone aboard her
  For the Islands of Desire.

I must forth again tomorrow!
  With the sunset I must be
Hull down on the trail of rapture
  In the wonder of the Sea.

Richard Hovey

THE SECRET OF THE SEA

Ah! what pleasant visions haunt me
  As I gaze upon the sea!
All the old romantic legends,
  All my dreams, come back to me.

Sails of silk and ropes of sandal,
  Such as gleam in ancient lore;
And the singing of the sailors,
  And the answer from the shore!

Most of all, the Spanish ballad
  Haunts me oft, and tarries long,
Of the noble Count Arnaldos
  And the sailor's mystic song.

Like the long waves on a sea-beach,
  Where the sand as silver shines,

With a soft, monotonous cadence,
  Flow its unrhymed lyric lines;—

Telling how the Count Arnaldos,
  With his hawk upon his hand,
Saw a fair and stately galley,
  Steering onward to the land;—

How he heard the ancient helmsman
  Chant a song so wild and clear,
That the sailing sea-bird slowly
  Poised upon the mast to hear,

Till his soul was full of longing
  And he cried, with impulse strong,—
"Helmsman! for the love of heaven,
  Teach me, too, that wondrous song!"

"Wouldst thou,"—so the helmsman answered,
  "Learn the secret of the sea?
Only those who brave its dangers
  Comprehend its mystery!"

In each sail that skims the horizon,
  In each landward-blowing breeze,
I behold that stately galley,
  Hear those mournful melodies;

Till my soul is full of longing
  For the secret of the sea,
And the heart of the great ocean
  Sends a thrilling pulse through me.
          Henry Wadsworth Longfellow

EXILED

Searching my heart for its true sorrow,
  This is the thing I find to be:
That I am weary of words and people,
  Sick of the city, wanting the sea;

Wanting the sticky, salty sweetness
  Of the strong wind and shattered spray;
Wanting the loud sound and the soft sound
  Of the big surf that breaks all day.

Always before about my dooryard,
  Marking the reach of the winter sea,
Rooted in sand and dragging drift-wood,
  Straggled the purple wild sweet-pea;

Always I climbed the wave at morning,
  Shook the sand from my shoes at night,
That now am caught beneath great buildings,
  Stricken with noise, confused with light.

If I could hear the green piles groaning
  Under the windy wooden piers,
See once again the bobbing barrels,
  And the black sticks that fence the weirs,

If I could see the weedy mussels
  Crusting the wrecked and rotting hulls,
Hear once again the hungry crying
  Overhead, of the wheeling gulls,

Feel once again the shanty straining
  Under the turning of the tide,
Fear once again the rising freshet,
  Dread the bell in the fog outside,

I should be happy,—that was happy
  All day long on the coast of Maine!
I have a need to hold and handle
  Shells and anchors and ships again!

I should be happy, that am happy
  Never at all since I came here.
I am too long away from water.
  I have a need of water near.
                    Edna St. Vincent Millay

ODE TO THE MEDITERRANEAN

Of thee the Northman by his beachèd galley
Dreamt, as he watched the never-setting Ursa
And longed for summer and thy light, O sacred
            Mediterranean.

Unseen he loved thee; for the heart within him
Knew earth had gardens where he might be blessed,
Putting away long dreams and aimless, barbarous
            Hunger for battle.

The foretaste of thy languors thawed his bosom,
A great need drove him to thy caverned islands
From the gray, endless reaches of the outer
            Desert of ocean.

He saw thy pillars, saw thy sudden mountains
Wrinkled and stark, and in their crooked gorges,
'Neath peeping pine and cypress, guessed the torrent
    Smothered in flowers.

Thine incense to the sun, thy gathered vapours,
He saw suspended on the flanks of Taurus,
Or veiling the snowed bosom of the virgin
    Sister of Atlas.

He saw the luminous top of wide Olympus,
Fit for the happy gods; he saw the pilgrim
River, with rains of Ethiopia flooding
    Populous Egypt.

And having seen, he loved thee. His racked spirit,
By thy breath tempered and the light that clothes thee,
Forgot the monstrous gods, and made of Nature
    Mistress and mother.

The more should I, O fatal sea, before thee
Of alien words make echoes to thy music;
For I was born where first the rills of Tagus
    Turn to the westward,

And, wandering long, alas! have need of drinking
Deep of the patience of thy perfect sadness,
O thou that constant through the change of ages,
    Beautiful ever,

Never wast wholly young and void of sorrows,
Nor ever canst be old, while yet the morning

Kindles thy ripples, or the golden evening
    Dyes thee in purple.

Thee, willing to be tamed but still untamable,
The Roman called his own until he perished,
As now the busy English hover o'er thee,
    Stalwart and noble;

But all is naught to thee, while no harsh winter
Congeals thy fountains, and the blown Sahara
Chokes not with dreadful sand thy deep and placid
    Rock-guarded havens.

Thou carest not what men may tread thy margin;
Nor I, while from some heather-scented headland
I may behold thy beauty, the eternal
    Solace of mortals.

George Santayana

THE SEAFARER

A song I sing of my sea-adventure,
The strain of peril, the stress of toil,
Which oft I endured in anguish of spirit
Through weary hours of aching woe.
My bark was swept by the breaking seas;
Bitter the watch from the bow by night
As my ship drove on within sound of the rocks.
My feet were numb with the nipping cold,
Hunger sapped a sea-weary spirit,
And care weighed heavy upon my heart.

Little the land-lubber, safe on shore,
Knows what I've suffered in icy seas
Wretched and worn by the winter storms,
Hung with icicles, stung by hail,
Lonely and friendless and far from home.
In my ears no sound but the roar of the sea,
The icy combers, the cry of the swan;
In place of the mead-hall and laughter of men
My only singing the sea-mew's call,
The scream of the gannet, the shriek of the gull;
Through the wail of the wild gale beating the bluffs
The piercing cry of the ice-coated petrel,
The storm-drenched eagle's echoing scream.
In all my wretchedness, weary and lone,
I had no comfort of comrade or kin.
Little indeed can he credit, whose town-life
Pleasantly passes in feasting and joy,
Sheltered from peril, what weary pain
Often I've suffered in foreign seas.
Night shades darkened with driving snow
From the freezing north, and the bonds of frost
Firm-locked the land, while falling hail,
Coldest of kernels, encrusted earth.
Yet still, even now, my spirit within me
Drives me seaward to sail the deep,
To ride the long swell of the salt sea-wave.
Never a day but my heart's desire
Would launch me forth on the long sea-path,
Fain of far harbors and foreign shores.
Yet lives no man so lordly of mood,
So eager in giving, so ardent in youth,
So bold in his deeds, or so dear to his lord,

THE CALL OF THE SEA

Who is free from dread in his far sea-travel,
Or fear of God's purpose and plan for his fate.
The beat of the harp, and bestowal of treasure,
The love of woman, and worldly hope,
Nor other interest can hold his heart
Save only the sweep of the surging billows;
His heart is haunted by love of the sea.
Trees are budding and towns are fair,
Meadows kindle and all life quickens,
All things hasten the eager-hearted,
Who joyeth therein, to journey afar,
Turning seaward to distant shores.
The cuckoo stirs him with plaintive call,
The herald of summer, with mournful song,
Foretelling the sorrow that stabs the heart.
Who liveth in luxury, little he knows
What woe men endure in exile's doom.
Yet still, even now, my desire outreaches,
My spirit soars over tracts of sea,
O'er the home of the whale, and the world's expanse.
Eager, desirous, the lone sprite returneth;
It cries in my ears and it calls to my heart
To launch where the whales plough their paths
    through the deep.

*   Translated from the Anglo-Saxon*
*   by Prof. Charles W. Kennedy*

DREAMS OF THE SEA

I know not why I yearn for thee again,
   To sail once more upon thy fickle flood;
I'll hear thy waves wash under my death-bed,
   Thy salt is lodged forever in my blood.

Yet I have seen thee lash the vessel's sides
   In fury, with thy many tailèd whip;
And I have seen thee, too, like Galilee,
   When Jesus walked in peace to Simon's ship.

And I have seen thy gentle breeze as soft
   As summer's, when it makes the cornfields run;
And I have seen thy rude and lusty gale
   Make ships show half their bellies to the sun.

Thou knowest the way to tame the wildest life,
   Thou knowest the way to bend the great and proud:
I think of that Armada whose puffed sails,
   Greedy and large, came swallowing every cloud.

But I have seen the sea-boy, young and drowned,
   Lying on shore and, by thy cruel hand,
A seaweed beard was on his tender chin,
   His heaven-blue eyes were filled with common sand.

And yet, for all, I yearn for thee again,
   To sail once more upon thy fickle flood:
I'll hear thy waves wash under my death-bed,
   Thy salt is lodged forever in my blood.

W. H. Davies

MARINERS

Men who have loved the ships they took to sea,
   Loved the tall masts, the prows that creamed with
      foam,
Have learned, deep in their hearts, how it might be
   That there is yet a dearer thing than home.
The decks they walk, the rigging in the stars,
   The clean boards counted in the watch they keep—
These, and the sunlight on the slippery spars,
   Will haunt them ever, waking and asleep.

Ashore, these men are not as other men:
   They walk as strangers through the crowded street,
Or, brooding by their fires, they hear again
   The drone astern, where gurgling waters meet,
Or see again a wide and blue lagoon,
And a lone ship that rides there with the moon.
                              David Morton

THEY WHO POSSESS THE SEA

They who possess the sea within their blood
have blood that courses with an endless motion,
deep is its surging, like a tide at flood from out of the
   ocean.
They hold the blue spray-water in their veins
that hints no crimson torn from leaf or berry,
neither the flame of sumach nor the stain of the wild
   cherry.

To mariners the call of land is thinned
    to a reed's calling. They who know the sound
of surf have blood tempestuous as wind
    yet ever bound.

Marguerite Janvrin Adams

SEA HUNGER

The wail of a waking wind in a wide-flung wheat field,
    The lilt of a low-flown lark o'er a listless lea,
The sigh of the serried trees on a city street yield
    Nothing to me.

The sails of a schooner bending across bright billows,
    Bright billows with ruff of lace and a lap of green;
The stir of a wild, salt wind in the clinging willows,
    Boisterous, clean;

Great combers that crash, cream-crested, against gray
        granite;
    A tangle of tawny weed at the tidal mark;
The flame of an iris flower, a fallen planet
    Cooled to a spark;

Nasturtiums sheathing the shells in neat white-washed
        gardens
    And fish that is put to dry on a birch-pole flake;
Remembering these means hope to a heart that hardens
    Ready to break,

Remembering these uplifts and yet leaves me lonely
    And sick for the song, the sheen of the Summer sea.

The wheat field, the lark wake pleasure in landsmen
    only—
  Nothing in me.

John Hanlon Mitchell

AT THE EDGE OF THE BAY

What! After your six-month drowsing and indolent
    sleeping,
The old blood beats fast again?
And all because of April and the warm weeping
Of her slow rain?

You had been content enough all winter long
To dream of old seafarers valiant in song,
But now you cry for a way through the restless
    foaming,
The quest of a lifting prow toward misty shores,
And foreign roadsteads at the end of an earth-wide
    roaming
To the creak on tholes of your oars.

Now you walk by the shipyards and each tall mast
Moves a longing for the blue of the offshore swell,
And you find your love for the ocean and all of its
    vast
Expanse in the disquiet of each ebb-tide smell.

Ever since men launched the *Argo*, this has been so.
Men in this cool-breeze season have known as high

Anguish of dream birth as ever a poet will know,
Considering how this line will let waves slip by,
And how that sheer will give grace, and how spars will
    show,
Black against the same moon in an unsame sky.
                                    Thomas Caldecot Chubb

THE RETURN

I will go back to the great sweet mother,
  Mother and lover of men, the sea.
I will go down to her, I and none other,
  Close with her, kiss her and mix her with me;
Cling to her, strive with her, hold her fast;
O fair white mother, in days long past
Born without sister, born without brother,
  Set free my soul as thy soul is free.

O fair green-girdled mother of mine,
  Sea, that art clothed with the sun and the rain,
Thy sweet hard kisses are strong like wine,
  Thy large embraces are keen like pain.
Save me and hide me with all thy waves,
Find me one grave of thy thousand graves,
Those pure cold populous graves of thine,
  Wrought without hand in a world without stain.

I shall sleep, and move with the moving ships,
  Change as the winds change, veer in the tide;
My lips will feast on the foam of thy lips,
  I shall rise with thy rising, with thee subside;

Sleep, and not know if she be, if she were,
Filled full with life to the eyes and hair,
As a rose is fulfilled to the roseleaf tips
   With splendid summer and perfume and pride.

This woven raiment of nights and days,
   Were it once cast off and unwound from me,
Naked and glad would I walk in thy ways,
   Alive and aware of thy ways and thee;
Clear of the whole world, hidden at home,
Clothed with the green and crowned with the foam,
A pulse of the life of thy straits and bays,
   A vein in the heart of the streams of the sea.
Algernon Charles Swinburne

THE HERITAGE

From the drear North, a cold and cheerless land,
   Our fathers sprang,
They drove no flocks to crop the tender grass,
They gazed on lonely moor, on deep morass,
And wintry skies whence, to their viking band,
   The raven sang.

O'er flowerless lands the storm-tossed forests threw
   A gloomy pall.
On treacherous seas they raised their plundering sail,
Fought with the waves, outside the Northern gale,
High overhead the startled sea gulls flew
   With clamoring call.

They heard the breakers smite the quivering shore
  With thunder roll.
No songs they sang to greet the Harvest wain
In happy fields rich with the ripened grain;
Stern was their world, a sorrow stern they bore
  Deep in the soul.

Through countless years, faint memories of their times
  Will oft awake.
From waves and shifting sands, their resting place,
The Norsemen send us, offspring of their race,
Dimly remembered dreams, like minster chimes
  Heard o'er a lake.

So come dark moments, when in the green land
  Norsemen are we;
And crave the sorrow of the leafless wood,
Or seek some barren dune's gray solitude
To hear bleak winds go moaning down the sand,
  By the wild sea.

Edward Bliss Reed

SHORE ROADS OF APRIL

What do I see and hear of an April morning?
Many a ridge and furrow, headland and bay,
Many a ship bound seaward, white at dawning,
Many a young lad singing a ship away.

Faces I see, ah, there were a' many women!
All wreathed in their gossam hair, with waiting lips.

THE CALL OF THE SEA

And there were eyes ashine, and tears a-brimming,
And there were lads who followed the calling ships.

I see them yet, long roads by the sea cliffs wending,
I hear the songs of birds, sweet flowers I smell,
I hear a lad who whispers of love unending,
I hear the roll of the shoreward running swell.

A little silk scarf, a pair of earrings swinging,
A silver ring, an indolent peacock fan,
Down at the foreshore cold iron ship bells ringing,
And laughing lips on an outbound sailorman.

What do I see and hear of an April morning?
Many a ridge and furrow, headland and bay,
Many a ship bound seaward, bright at dawning,
Many a young lad singing a ship away.

Bill Adams

WHERE IS THE SEA?

Song of the Greek Islander in exile

A Greek Islander, being taken to the Vale of
Tempe, and called upon to admire its beauty,
only replied—*"The Sea—where is it?"*

Where is the sea?—I languish here—
Where is my own blue sea?
With all its barks in fleet career,
And flags, and breezes free.

I miss that voice of waves, which first
  Awoke my childhood's glee;
The measured chime—the thundering burst—
  Where is my own blue sea?

Oh! rich your myrtle's breath may rise,
  Soft, soft your winds may be;
Yet my sick heart within me dies—
  Where is my own blue sea?

I hear the shepherd's mountain flute—
  I hear the whispering trees;
The echoes of my soul are mute:
  —Where is my own blue sea?

Felicia Hemans

SEA-NURTURED

The gay sea-plants familiar were to her
  As daisies to the children of the land;
Red wavy dulse the sunburnt mariner
  Raised from its bed to glisten in her hand;
The vessel and the sea were her life's stage,
Her house, her garden, and her hermitage.

Green fields and inland meadows faded out
  Of mind, or with sea-images were linked;
And yet she had her childish thoughts about
  The country she had left, though indistinct
And faint as mist the mountain-head that shrouds,
Or dim through distance as Magellan's clouds.

And when to frame a forest-scene she tried,
　The ever-present sea would yet intrude;
And all her towns were by the water's side:
　It murmured in all moorland solitude,
Where rocks and the ribbed sand would intervene,
And waves would edge her fancied village green;

Because her heart was like an ocean shell,
　That holds, men say, a message from the deep:
And yet the land was strong, she knew its spell;
　And harbor-lights could draw her in her sleep;
And minster chimes from pierced towers that swim
Were the land angels making God a hymn.
　　　　　　　　　　　　　Jean Ingelow

HAKLUYT UNPURCHASED

Man is a fool and a bag of wind!
Or was it madness that stopped my buying
The old brown Hakluyt I chanced to find
At twelve and sixpence, dustily lying

With shilling shockers? And if 'twere here
I'd kick off shoes and pull on slippers
And settle back to my briar and beer
For a windy voyage with Hakluyt's skippers.

Up the blue sea and down the sky
To Java Head or warm Cipango,
With albatrosses floating by
And a wind that whistles of spice and mango.

Into the ice with Frobisher's men,
Or south with Raleigh to seek Guiana,
In the "*Jesus of Lubeck*" with Hawkins then
To plunder the dons of smug Habana,

And east... But my ale is dregs and lees,
My pipe won't draw, and I, besotted,
The sport of devils—I failed to seize
On the rich old tome till another got it.

And so instead of an offshore gale
And a tropical sea and a lion skipper,
I sit and blow at my mug of ale
And stare at a toe through a toeless slipper.
Franklin McDuffee

SPIRIT OF FREEDOM, THOU DOST LOVE THE SEA

Spirit of freedom, thou dost love the sea,
Trackless and storm-tost ocean wild and free,
Faint symbol of thine own eternity.
   The seagulls wheel and soar and fearless roam,
   The stormy petrel dashes through the foam;
The mighty billows heave, the tempests roar,
The diapason thunders shake the shore
And chant the song of freedom evermore.
Henry Nehemiah Dodge

2. The Building of the Ship

THE SHIP-BUILDERS

The sky is ruddy in the east,
  The earth is gray below,
And, spectral in the river-mist,
  The ship's white timbers show.
Then let the sounds of measured stroke
  And grating saw begin;
The broad-axe to the gnarlèd oak,
  The mallet to the pin!

Hark!—roars the bellows, blast on blast,
  The sooty smithy jars,
And fire-sparks, rising far and fast,
  Are fading with the stars.
All day for us the smith shall stand
  Beside that flashing forge;
All day for us his heavy hand
  The groaning anvil scourge.

From far-off hills, the panting team
  For us is toiling near;
For us the raftsmen down the stream
  Their island barges steer.
Rings out for us the axe-man's stroke
  In forests old and still,—
For us the century-circled oak
  Falls crashing down his hill.

Up!—up!—in nobler toil than ours
   No craftsmen bear a part:
We make of Nature's giant powers
   The slaves of human Art.
Lay rib to rib and beam to beam,
   And drive the treenails free;
Nor faithless joint nor yawning seam
   Shall tempt the searching sea!

Where'er the keel of our good ship
   The sea's rough field shall plough,—
Where'er her tossing spars shall drip
   With salt-spray caught below,—
That ship must heed her master's beck,
   Her helm obey his hand,
And seamen tread her reeling deck
   As if they trod the land.

Her oaken ribs the vulture-beak
   Of Northern ice may peel;
The sunken rock and coral peak
   May grate along her keel;
And know we well the painted shell
   We give to wind and wave,
Must float, the sailor's citadel,
   Or sink, the sailor's grave!

Ho!—strike away the bars and blocks,
   And set the good ship free!
Why lingers on these dusty rocks
   The young bride of the sea?

THE BUILDING OF THE SHIP

Look! how she moves adown the grooves,
   In graceful beauty now!
How lowly on the breast she loves
   Sinks down her virgin prow!

God bless her! wheresoe'er the breeze
   Her snowy wing shall fan,
Aside the frozen Hebrides,
   Or sultry Hindostan!
Where'er in mart or on the main,
   With peaceful flag unfurled,
She·helps to wind the silken chain
   Of commerce round the world!

Speed on the ship! But let her bear
   No merchandise of sin,
No groaning cargo of despair
   Her roomy hold within;
No Lethean drug for Eastern lands,
   Nor poison-draught for ours;
But honest fruits of toiling hands
   And Nature's sun and showers.

Be hers the Prairie's golden grain,
   The Desert's golden sand,
The clustered fruits of sunny Spain,
   The spice of Morning-land!
Her pathway on the open main
   May blessings follow free,
And glad hearts welcome back again
   Her white sails from the sea!

John Greenleaf Whittier

OLD SHIP RIGGERS

Yes, we did a heap o' riggin'
In those rampin' boomin' days,
When the wooden ships were buildin'
On their quaint old greasy ways;
Crafts of every sort an' fashion,
Big an' little, lithe an' tall,
Had their birthplace by the harbor,
An' we rigged 'em one and all.

Jacob's ladder wasn't in it
With the riggin' on those ships
From the trunnels and the keelson
To the pointed royal tips;
That old ladder was for angels
Comin' down from up aloft,
With their wings an' gleamin' garments,
An' their hands all white an' soft.

Our riggin' was for sailors,
Tough an' hardy Bluenose dogs,
With their hands as hard as leather,
An' their boots thick heavy clogs,
They were nuthin' much like angels,
But they'd learned their business right,
An' they trusted to our riggin'
When the sea was roarin' white.

Seemed like fittin' out a maiden
For her happy weddin' day,
When we rigged a noble vessel,

THE BUILDING OF THE SHIP

Where she calm at anchor lay;
All her gear was new an' shiny,
Every ribbon taut an' trim,
An' she stood, when she was finished,
Tall an' handsome, straight an' slim.

When at last she slipped her moorin's,
An' slow-footed down the stream,
With her riggin' all aglowin',
An' her canvas all agleam,
How we cheered her to the echo,
An' our hearts thrilled high with pride,
As the ocean strode to meet her
For his own sea-royal bride.

Some came back just as they left us,
Trim an' spotless, buoyant, free;
Others crept up into harbor,
Scarred an' broken out at sea;
These we nursed like tender mothers,
Mendin' canvas, rope an' spar,
Till we had 'em all ashinin'
Like some twinklin' mornin' star.

But our riggin' days are over,
An' the past seems like a dream,
As we view the mighty changes
Brought about by wizard steam.
We are needed here no longer,
For there's nuthin' we can do—
Maybe there'll be work for riggers,
In the Port, beyond the blue.

H. A. Cody

THE OLD FIGUREHEAD CARVER

I have done my bit of carving,
Figureheads of quaint design,
For the Olives and the Ruddocks,
And the famous Black Ball Line.
Brigantines and barques and clippers,
Brigs and schooners, lithe and tall,
But the bounding *Marco Polo*
Was the proudest of them all.

I can see that white-winged clipper
Reeling under scudding clouds,
Tramping down a hazy sky-line,
With a Norther in her shrouds.
I can feel her lines of beauty,
See her flecked with spume and brine,
As she drives her scuppers under,
And that figurehead of mine.

'Twas of seasoned pine I made it,
Clear from outer bark to core,
And the finest piece of timber
From the mast-pond on Straight Shore.
Every bite of axe or chisel,
Every ringing mallet welt,
Brought from out that block of timber
All the spirit that I felt.

I had read of Marco Polo
Till his daring deeds were mine

And I saw them all aglowing
In that balsam-scented pine;
Saw his eyes alight with purpose,
Facing every vagrant breeze;
Saw him lilting, free and careless,
Over all the Seven Seas,

That was how I did my carving;
Beat of heart and stroke of hand
Blended into life and action
All the purpose that I planned;
Flowing robes and wind-tossed tresses,
Forms of beauty, strength, design—
Saw them all, and strove to carve them
In those figureheads of mine.

I am old, my hands are feeble,
And my outward eyes are dim,
But I see again those clippers
Lifting o'er the ocean's rim;
Great white fleet of reeling rovers,
Wind above, the surf beneath,
And the *Marco Polo* leading
With my carving in her teeth.

H. A. Cody

THE BUILDING OF THE SHIP

"Build me straight, O worthy Master!
  Stanch and strong, a goodly vessel,
That shall laugh at all disaster,
  And with wave and whirlwind wrestle!"

The merchant's word
Delighted the Master heard;
For his heart was in his work, and the heart
Giveth grace unto every Art.

A quiet smile played round his lips,
As the eddies and dimples of the tide
Play round the bows of ships,
That steadily at anchor ride.
And with a voice that was full of glee,
He answered, "Erelong we will launch
A vessel as goodly, and strong, and stanch,
As ever weathered a wintry sea!"
And first with nicest skill and art,
Perfect and finished in every part,
A little model the Master wrought,
Which should be to the larger plan
What the child is to the man,
Its counterpart in miniature;
That with a hand more swift and sure
The greater labor might be brought
To answer to his inward thought.
And as he labored, his mind ran o'er
The various ships that were built of yore,
And above them all, and strangest of all

Towered the *Great Harry*, crank and tall,
Whose picture was hanging on the wall,
With bows and stern raised high in air,
And balconies hanging here and there,
And signal lanterns and flags afloat,
And eight round towers, like those that frown
From some old castle, looking down
Upon the drawbridge and the moat.
And he said with a smile, "Our ship, I wis,
Shall be of another form than this!"

It was of another form, indeed;
Built for freight, and yet for speed,
A beautiful and gallant craft;
Broad in the beam, that the stress of the blast,
Pressing down upon sail and mast,
Might not the sharp bows overwhelm;
Broad in the beam, but sloping aft
With graceful curve and slow degrees,
That she might be docile to the helm,
And that the currents of parted seas,
Closing behind, with mighty force,
Might aid and not impede her course.

In the ship-yard stood the master,
  With the model of the vessel,
That should laugh at all disaster,
  And with wave and whirlwind wrestle!

Covering many a rood of ground,
Lay the timber piled around;
Timber of chestnut, and elm, and oak,
And scattered here and there, with these,

The knarred and crooked cedar knees;
Brought from regions far away,
From Pascagoula's sunny bay,
And the banks of the roaring Roanoke!
Ah! what a wondrous thing it is
To note how many wheels of toil
One thought, one word, can set in motion!
There's not a ship that sails the ocean,
But every climate, every soil,
Must bring its tribute, great or small,
And help to build the wooden wall!

The sun was rising o'er the sea,
And long the level shadows lay,
As if they, too, the beams would be
Of some great, airy argosy,
Framed and launched in a single day.
That silent architect, the sun,
Had hewn and laid them every one,
Ere the work of man was yet begun.
Beside the master, when he spoke,
A youth, against an anchor leaning,
Listened, to catch his slightest meaning.
Only the long waves, as they broke
In ripples on the pebbly beach,
Interrupted the old man's speech.

Beautiful they were, in sooth,
The old man and the fiery youth!
The old man, in whose busy brain
Many a ship that sailed the main
Was modelled o'er and o'er again;—

The fiery youth, who was to be
The heir of his dexterity,
The heir of his house, and his daughter's hand,
When he had built and launched from land
What the elder head had planned.

"Thus," said he, "will we build this ship!
Lay square the blocks upon the slip,
And follow well this plan of mine.
Choose the timbers with greatest care;
Of all that is unsound beware;
For only what is sound and strong
To this vessel shall belong.
Cedar of Maine and Georgia pine
Here together shall combine.
A goodly frame, and a goodly fame,
And the *Union* be her name!
For the day that gives her to the sea
Shall give my daughter unto thee!"

The Master's word
Enraptured the young man heard;
And as he turned his face aside,
With a look of joy and a thrill of pride,
Standing before
Her father's door,
He saw the form of his promised bride.
The sun shone on her golden hair,
And her cheek was glowing fresh and fair,
With the breath of morn and the soft sea air.
Like a beauteous barge was she,
Still at rest on the sandy beach,

Just beyond the billow's reach;
But he
Was the restless, seething, stormy sea!

Ah, how skilful grows the hand
That obeyeth Love's command!
It is the heart, and not the brain,
That to the highest doth attain,
And he who followeth Love's behest
Far excelleth all the rest!

Thus with the rising of the sun
Was the noble task begun,
And soon throughout the ship-yard's bounds
Were heard the intermingled sounds
Of axes and of mallets, plied
With vigorous arms on every side;
Plied so deftly and so well,
That, ere the shadows of evening fell,
The keel of oak for a noble ship,
Scarfed and bolted, straight and strong,
Was lying ready, and stretched along
The blocks, well placed upon the slip.
Happy, thrice happy, every one
Who sees his labor well begun.
And not perplexed and multiplied,
By idly waiting for time and tide!

And when the hot, long day was o'er,
The young man at the master's door
Sat with the maiden, calm and still.
And within the porch, a little more

THE BUILDING OF THE SHIP

Removed beyond the evening chill,
The father sat, and told them tales
Of wrecks in the great September gales,
Of pirates coasting the Spanish Main,
And ships that never came back again,
The chance and change of a sailor's life,
Want and plenty, rest and strife,
His roving fancy, like the wind,
That nothing can stay and nothing can bind,
And the magic charm of foreign lands,
With shadows of palms, and shining sands,
Where the tumbling surf,
O'er the coral reefs of Madagascar,
Washes the feet of the swarthy Lascar,
As he lies alone and asleep on the turf.
And the trembling maiden held her breath
At the tales of that awful, pitiless sea,
With all its terror and mystery,
The dim, dark sea, so like unto death,
That divides and yet unites mankind!
And whenever the old man paused, a gleam
From the bowl of his pipe would awhile illume
The silent group in the twilight gloom,
And thoughtful faces, as in a dream;
And for a moment one might mark
What had been hidden by the dark,
That the head of the maiden lay at rest,
Tenderly, on the young man's breast!

Day by day the vessel grew,
With timbers fastened strong and true,
Stemson and keelson and sternson-knee,

Till, framed with perfect symmetry,
A skeleton ship rose up to view!
And around the bows and along the side
The heavy hammers and mallets plied,
Till after many a week, at length,
Wonderful for form and strength,
Sublime in its enormous bulk,
Loomed aloft the shadowy hulk!
And around it columns of smoke, upwreathing,
Rose from the boiling, bubbling, seething
Caldron, that glowed,
And overflowed
With the black tar, heated for the sheathing.
And amid the clamors
Of clattering hammers,
He who listened heard now and then
The song of the master and his men:—

"Build me straight, O worthy Master,
  Stanch and strong, a goodly vessel,
That shall laugh at all disaster,
  And with wave and whirlwind wrestle!"

With oaken brace and copper band,
Lay the rudder on the sand,
That, like a thought, should have control
Over the movement of the whole;
And near it the anchor, whose giant hand
Would reach down and grapple with the land,
And immovable and fast
Hold the great ship against the bellowing blast.
And at the bows an image stood,

By a cunning artist carved in wood,
With robes of white, that far behind
Seemed to be fluttering in the wind.
It was not shaped in a classic mould,
Nor like a Nymph or Goddess of old,
Or Naiad rising from the water,
But modelled from the master's daughter!
On many a dreary and misty night,
'T will be seen by the rays of the signal light,
Speeding along through the rain and the dark,
Like a ghost in its snow-white sark,
The pilot of some phantom bark,
Guiding the vessel, in its flight,
By a path none other knows aright!

Behold, at last,
Each tall and tapering mast
Is swung into its place;
Shrouds and stays
Holding it firm and fast!

Long ago,
In the deer-haunted forests of Maine,
When upon mountain and plain
Lay the snow,
They fell,—those lordly pines!
Those grand, majestic pines!
'Mid shouts and cheers
The jaded steers,
Panting beneath the goad,
Dragged down the weary, winding road
Those captive kings so straight and tall,

To be shorn of their streaming hair,
And, naked and bare,
To feel the stress and the strain
Of the wind and the reeling main,
Whose roar
Would remind them forevermore
Of their native forests they should not see again.

And everywhere
The slender, graceful spars
Poise aloft in the air,
And at the mast-head,
White, blue, and red,
A flag unrolls the stripes and stars.
Ah! when the wanderer, lonely, friendless,
In foreign harbors shall behold
That flag unrolled,
'T will be as a friendly hand
Stretched out from his native land,
Filling his heart with memories sweet and endless!

All is finished! and at length
Has come the bridal day
Of beauty and of strength.
To-day the vessel shall be launched!
With fleecy clouds the sky is blanched,
And o'er the bay,
Slowly, in all his splendors dight,
The great sun rises to behold the sight.
The ocean old,
Centuries old,
Strong as youth, and as uncontrolled,

Paces restless to and fro,
Up and down the sands of gold.
His beating heart is not at rest;
And far and wide,
With ceaseless flow,
His beard of snow
Heaves with the heaving of his breast.
He waits impatient for his bride.
There she stands,
With her foot upon the sands,
Decked with flags and streamers gay,
In honor of her marriage day,
Her snow-white signals fluttering, blending,
Round her like a veil descending,
Ready to be
The bride of the gray old sea.

On the deck another bride
Is standing by her lover's side.
Shadows from the flags and shrouds,
Like the shadows cast by clouds,
Broken by many a sunny fleck,
Fall around them on the deck.

The prayer is said,
The service read,
The joyous bridegroom bows his head;
And in tears the good old Master
Shakes the brown hand of his son,
Kisses his daughter's glowing cheek
In silence, for he cannot speak,
And ever faster

Down his own the tears begin to run.
The worthy pastor—
The shepherd of that wandering flock,
That has the ocean for its wold,
That has the vessel for its fold,
Leaping ever from rock to rock—
Spake, with accents mild and clear,
Words of warning, words of cheer,
But tedious to the bridegroom's ear.
He knew the chart
Of the sailor's heart,
All its pleasures and its griefs,
All its shallows and rocky reefs,
All those secret currents, that flow
With such resistless undertow,
And lift and drift, with terrible force,
The will from its moorings and its course.
Therefore he spake, and thus said he:—
"Like unto ships far off at sea,
Outward or homeward bound, are we.
Before, behind, and all around,
Floats and swings the horizon's bound,
Seems at its distant rim to rise
And climb the crystal wall of the skies,
And then again to turn and sink,
As if we could slide from its outer brink.
Ah! it is not the sea,
It is not the sea that sinks and shelves,
But ourselves
That rock and rise
With endless and uneasy motion,
Now touching the very skies,

THE BUILDING OF THE SHIP

Now sinking into the depths of ocean.
Ah! if our souls but poise and swing
Like the compass in its brazen ring,
Ever level and ever true
To the toil and the task we have to do,
We shall sail securely, and safely reach
The Fortunate Isles, on whose shining beach
The sights we see, and the sounds we hear,
Will be those of joy and not of fear!"

Then the Master,
With a gesture of command,
Waved his hand;
And at the word,
Loud and sudden there was heard,
All around them and below,
The sound of hammers, blow on blow,
Knocking away the shores and spurs.
And see! she stirs!
She starts,—she moves,—she seems to feel
The thrill of life along her keel,
And, spurning with her foot the ground,
With one exulting, joyous bound,
She leaps into the ocean's arms!

And lo! from the assembled crowd
There rose a shout, prolonged and loud,
That to the ocean seemed to say,
"Take her, O bridegroom, old and gray,
Take her to thy protecting arms,
With all her youth and all her charms!"

How beautiful she is! How fair
She lies within those arms, that press
Her form with many a soft caress
Of tenderness and watchful care!
Sail forth into the sea, O ship!
Through wind and wave, right onward steer!
The moistened eye, the trembling lip,
Are not the signs of doubt or fear.

Sail forth into the sea of life,
O gentle, loving, trusting wife,
And safe from all adversity
Upon the bosom of that sea
Thy comings and thy goings be!
For gentleness and love and trust
Prevail o'er angry wave and gust;
And in the wreck of noble lives
Something immortal still survives!

Thou, too, sail on, O Ship of State!
Sail on, O *Union*, strong and great!
Humanity with all its fears,
With all the hopes of future years,
Is hanging breathless on thy fate!
We know what Master laid thy keel,
What Workmen wrought thy ribs of steel,
Who made each mast, and sail, and rope,
What anvils rang, what hammers beat,
In what a forge and what a heat
Were shaped the anchors of thy hope!
Fear not each sudden sound and shock,
'T is of the wave and not the rock;

'T is but the flapping of the sail,
And not a rent made by the gale!
In spite of rock and tempest's roar,
In spite of false lights on the shore,
Sail on, nor fear to breast the sea!
Our hearts, our hopes, are all with thee,
Our hearts, our hopes, our prayers, our tears,
Our faith triumphant o'er our fears,
Are all with thee,—are all with thee!
     Henry Wadsworth Longfellow

THE ARK

At length a reverend sire among them came,
And of their doings great dislike declar'd,
And testify'd against their ways; he oft
Frequented their assemblies, whereso met,
Triumphs, or festivals, and to them preach'd
Conversion and repentance, as to souls
In prison under judgments imminent:
But all in vain: which when he saw, he ceas'd
Contending, and remov'd his tents far off:
Then from the mountain hewing timber tall,
Began to build a vessel of huge bulk,
Measur'd by cubit, length, and breadth, and height,
Smear'd round with pitch, and in the side a door
Contriv'd, and of provisions laid in large
For man and beast: when lo, a wonder strange!
Of every beast, and bird, and insect small,
Came sevens, and pairs, and enter'd in, as taught

Their order: last the sire and his three sons
With their four wives; and God made fast the door.
Meanwhile the south wind rose, and, with black wings
Wide hovering, all the clouds together drove
From under heaven; the hills to their supply
Vapour, and exhalation dusk and moist,
Sent up amain: and now the thicken'd sky
Like a dark ceiling stood; down rush'd the rain
Impetuous, and continu'd till the earth
No more was seen; the floating vessel swum
Uplifted, and secure with beaked prow
Rode tilting o'er the waves; all dwellings else
Flood overwhelm'd, and them with all their pomp
Deep under water roll'd; sea cover'd sea,
Sea without shore, and in their palaces,
Where luxury late reign'd, sea-monsters whelp'd
And stabled; of mankind, so numerous late,
All left in one small bottom swum imbark'd.
John Milton

RIVETS

My grandfather's hands were wise and hard
For he swung his adze in a Salem yard
And thumbed his planks and drove his nails
Till he learned his trade from strake to rails
And could dream a ship till he saw her whole
With royals set, and feel her roll
And lift her bows like a dripping blade
In the spacious swells of the India Trade.
...He's long been dead, and his ships are junk,
All rotting askew, or stripped or sunk.
But when they were loosed and took their slide

THE BUILDING OF THE SHIP

And squared away on the greasy tide,
He hitched up his belt, and "By God," said he,
"No sweeter ship has sailed the sea;
And she's all mine, yes, every inch,
From the spring of her heel to the swell of her winch!"
And he dusted his hands and wiped his face
And stood up his sledge in its proper place.
... And I swing here on a plank in a bight
Catching hot rivets from morning till night.
They've never told me who planned the craft
Or where they'll route the riveted raft:
Perhaps she'll do a tourist turn
And pack high hats with money to burn,
Or carry cargo of frozen meat
For Argentine, or hides or wheat.
They don't tell me; but I hear the clang
Of the hammers going, and see the gang
Ahoisting beams like a skyscraper frame
And bolting them in, and always the same
And all day long. I do my stunt
Of rackety rack and buntity bunt.
It's got to be so, for it's part of the plan
But I wonder some if I'm really a man.
... She'll soon be done and I'll be through.
They'll give me my time when my time is due.
I s'pose I've done my share of the trick,
They treat me right, and I shouldn't kick.
So I'll shed my jeans and I'll count my pay
And call it the end of a perfect day.
But all I'll own of the old man's pride
Are rows of rivets along her side.

N. S. Olds

THE BUILDING OF THE LONG SERPENT

Thorberg Skafting, master-builder,
  In his ship-yard by the sea,
Whistling, said, "It would bewilder
Any man but Thorberg Skafting,
  Any man but me!"

Near him lay the Dragon stranded,
  Built of old by Raud the Strong,
And King Olaf had commanded
He should build another Dragon,
  Twice as large and long.

Therefore whistled Thorberg Skafting,
  As he sat with half-closed eyes,
And his head turned sideways, drafting
That new vessel for King Olaf
  Twice the Dragon's size.

Round him busily hewed and hammered
  Mallet huge and heavy axe;
Workmen laughed and sang and clamored;
Whirred the wheels, that into rigging
  Spun the shining flax!

All this tumult heard the master,—
  It was music to his ear;
Fancy whispered all the faster,
"Men shall hear of Thorberg Skafting
  For a hundred year!"

THE BUILDING OF THE SHIP

Workmen sweating at the forges
  Fashioned iron bolt and bar,
Like a warlock's midnight orgies
Smoked and bubbled the black caldron
  With the boiling tar.

Did the warlocks mingle in it,
  Thorberg Skafting, any curse?
Could you not be gone a minute
But some mischief must be doing,
  Turning bad to worse?

'T was an ill wind that came wafting,
  From his homestead words of woe;
To his farm went Thorberg Skafting,
Oft repeating to his workmen,
  Build ye thus and so.

After long delays returning
  Came the master back by night;
To his ship-yard longing, yearning,
Hurried he, and did not leave it
  Till the morning's light.

"Come and see my ship, my darling!"
  On the morrow said the King;
"Finished now from keel to carling;
Never yet was seen in Norway
  Such a wondrous thing!"

In the ship-yard, idly talking,
  At the ship the workmen stared:

Some one all their labor balking,
Down her sides had cut deep gashes,
  Not a plank was spared!

"Death be to the evil-doer!"
  With an oath King Olaf spoke;
"But rewards to his pursuer!"
And with wrath his face grew redder
  Than his scarlet cloak.

Straight the master-builder, smiling,
  Answered thus the angry King:
"Cease blaspheming and reviling,
Olaf, it was Thorberg Skafting
  Who has done this thing!"

Then he chipped and smoothed the planking,
  Till the King, delighted, swore,
With much lauding and much thanking,
"Handsomer is now my Dragon
  Than she was before!"

Seventy ells and four extended
  On the grass the vessel's keel;
High above it, gilt and splendid,
Rose the figure-head ferocious
  With its crest of steel.

Then they launched her from the tressels,
  In the ship-yard by the sea;
She was the grandest of all vessels,
Never ship was built in Norway
  Half so fine as she!

The Long Serpent was she christened,
  'Mid the roar of cheer on cheer!
They who to the Saga listened
Heard the name of Thorberg Skafting
  For a hundred year!
         Henry Wadsworth Longfellow

THE PINE TO THE MARINER

"O man of little wit,
  What meanes this frantick fit
To make thy ship of mee
  That am a slender Tree,
Whome eurie blast that blowes
  Full lightly ouerthrowes?
Doth this not moue thy minde
  That rage of roring winde
Did beate my boughes agood
  When earst I grue in Wood?
How can I here auoyde
  The foe that there anoyde?
Thinkst thou now I am made
  A Vessel for thy trade
I shall be more at ease
  Amid the flashing Seas?
I fear if Aeole frowne
  Both thou and I shall drowne."

    *   *   *

"For thee is all my grief,
  For lightly I shall swim:
Though top and tackel all be torne,
  Yet I aloft the surge am borne."
         George Turberville

SONG OF THE MARINER'S NEEDLE

Ho! burnish well, ye cunning hands,
    A palace-home for me,
For I would ride in royal state
    Across the briny sea.
Bring ivory from the Indian main,
    To pave my mystic floor,
And build my dome of crystal sheen,
    My walls of shining ore.

The lone Enchantress of the Deep,
    I rule its boisterous realm;
Watch ye my lithe and quivering wand,
    To guide your straining helm.
Ay, bend your anxious gaze on me!
    The polar star is dim,
And waves and tempests fill the night
    With ocean's awful hymn.

And sapient eyes have watched me long,
    And science has grown gray,
And still ye dream not how or why
    I keep my wondrous way.
Ye know me as ye know the storm
That heaps your heaving path;
Ye love me, though, since mine is not
    The mystery of wrath!

C. R. Clarke

3. Outward Bound

A PASSER-BY

Whither, O splendid ship, thy white sails crowding,
   Leaning across the bosom of the urgent West,
That fearest nor sea rising, nor sky clouding,
   Whither away, fair rover, and what thy quest?
   Ah! soon, when Winter has all our vales opprest,
When skies are cold and misty, and hail is hurling,
   Wilt thou glide on the blue Pacific, or rest
In a summer haven asleep, thy white sails furling.

I there before thee, in the country that well thou knowest,
   Already arrived am inhaling the odorous air:
I watch thee enter unerringly where thou goest,
   And anchor queen of the strange shipping there,
   Thy sails for awnings spread, thy masts bare;
Nor is aught from the foaming reef to the snow-capped, grandest
   Peak, that is over the feathery palms more fair
Than thou, so upright, so stately, and still thou standest.

And yet, O splendid ship, unhailed and nameless,
   I know not if, aiming a fancy, I rightly divine
That thou hast a purpose joyful, a courage blameless,
   Thy port assured in a happier land than mine.
   But for all I have given thee, beauty enough is thine,

As thou, aslant with trim tackle and shrouding,
  From the proud nostril curve of a prow's line
In the offing scatterest foam, thy white sails crowding.
Robert Bridges

COLUMBUS

Behind him lay the gray Azores,
  Behind the Gates of Hercules;
Before him not the ghost of shores,
  Before him only shoreless seas.
The good mate said: "Now must we pray,
  For lo! the very stars are gone.
Brave Admiral, speak, what shall I say?"
  "Why, say, 'Sail on! sail on! and on!'"

"My men grow mutinous day by day;
  My men grow ghastly wan and weak."
The stout mate thought of home; a spray
  Of salt wave washed his swarthy cheek.
"What shall I say, brave Admiral, say,
  If we sight naught but seas at dawn?"
"Why, you shall say at break of day,
  'Sail on! sail on! sail on! and on!'"

They sailed and sailed, as winds might blow,
  Until at last the blanched mate said:
"Why, now not even God would know
  Should I and all my men fall dead.
These very winds forget their way,
  For God from these dread seas is gone.
Now speak, brave Admiral, speak and say"—
  He said: "Sail on! sail on! and on!"

They sailed. They sailed. Then spake the mate:
  "This mad sea shows his teeth tonight.
He curls his lip, he lies in wait,
  With lifted teeth, as if to bite!
Brave Admiral, say but one good word:
  What shall we do when hope is gone?"
The words leapt like a leaping sword:
  "Sail on! sail on! sail on! and on!"

Then, pale and worn, he kept his deck,
  And peered through darkness. Ah, that night
Of all dark nights! And then a speck—
  A light! A light! A light! A light!
It grew, a starlit flag unfurled!
  It grew to be Time's burst of dawn.
He gained a world; he gave that world
  Its grandest lesson: "On! sail on!"
Joaquin Miller

IN THE TRADES

Ho, let her rip—with her royal clew a-quiver,
  And the long miles reeling out behind—
For the Trade's got a hold of her and every rope's a-shiver
  With the strong and steady urging of the wind.

All the gleaming white of her, all the sun and shade
  Leaning, swaying to the seas,
All up the height of her the South-east Trade
  Humming like a swarm of bees.

Underneath the heel of her the white wake flying,
  Tumbled and trampled into snow—
Down below the keel of her the lost ships lying
  In the weed and the coral, far below...

C. Fox Smith

A LIFE ON THE OCEAN WAVE

A life on the ocean wave,
  A home on the rolling deep,
Where the scattered waters rave,
  And the winds their revels keep:
Like an eagle caged, I pine
  On this dull, unchanging shore:
Oh! give me the flashing brine,
  The spray and the tempest's roar!

Once more on the deck I stand
  Of my own swift-gliding craft:
Set sail! farewell to the land!
  The gale follows fair abaft.
We shoot through the sparkling foam
  Like an ocean-bird set free;—
Like the ocean-bird, our home
  We'll find far out on the sea.

The land is no longer in view,
  The clouds have begun to frown;
But with a stout vessel and crew,
  We'll say, Let the storm come down!

And the song of our hearts shall be,
> While the winds and the waters rave,
A home on the rolling sea!
> A life on the ocean wave!
>> *Epes Sargent*

From ULYSSES

There lies the port; the vessel puffs her sail;
There gloom the dark, broad seas. My mariners,
Souls that have toil'd, and wrought, and thought with
> me,—
That ever with a frolic welcome took
The thunder and the sunshine, and opposed
Free hearts, free foreheads,—you and I are old;
Old age hath yet his honor and his toil.
Death closes all; but something ere the end,
Some work of noble note, may yet be done,
Not unbecoming men that strove with Gods.
The lights begin to twinkle from the rocks;
The long day wanes; the slow moon climbs; the deep
Moans round with many voices. Come, my friends.
'T is not too late to seek a newer world.
Push off, and sitting well in order smite
The sounding furrows; for my purpose holds
To sail beyond the sunset, and the baths
Of all the western stars, until I die.
It may be that the gulfs will wash us down;
It may be we shall touch the Happy Isles,
And see the great Achilles, whom we knew.
Tho' much is taken, much abides; and tho'

We are not now that strength which in old days
Moved earth and heaven, that which we are, we are,—
One equal temper of heroic hearts
Made weak by time and fate, but strong in will
To strive, to seek, to find, and not to yield.
Alfred, Lord Tennyson

TACKING SHIP OFF SHORE

The weather leech of the topsail shivers,
   The bowlines strain and the lee shrouds slacken,
The braces are taut, the lithe boom quivers,
   And the waves with the coming squall-cloud blacken.

Open one point on the weather bow
   Is the light-house tall on Fire Island head;
There's a shade of doubt on the captain's brow,
   And the pilot watches the heaving lead.

I stand at the wheel and with eager eye
   To sea and to sky and to shore I gaze,
Till the muttered order of *"FULL AND BY!"*
   Is suddenly changed to *"FULL FOR STAYS!"*

The ship bends lower before the breeze,
   As her broadside fair to the blast she lays;
And she swifter springs to the rising seas,
   As the pilot calls, *"STAND BY FOR STAYS!"*

It is silence all, as each in his place,
  With the gathered coils in his hardened hands,
By tack and bowline, by sheet and brace,
  Waiting the watchword impatient stands.

And the light on Fire Island head draws near,
  As, trumpet-winged, the pilot's shout
From his post on the bowsprit's heel I hear,
  With the welcome call of *"READY! ABOUT!"*

No time to spare! It is touch and go,
  And the captain growls, *"DOWN HELM! HARD DOWN!"*
As my weight on the whirling spokes I throw,
  While heaven grows black with the storm-cloud's frown.

High o'er the knight-heads flies the spray,
  As we meet the shock of the plunging sea;
And my shoulder stiff to the wheel I lay,
  As I answer, *"AYE, AYE, SIR! HA-A-R-D A-LEE!"*

With the swerving leap of a startled steed
  The ship flies fast in the eye of the wind,
The dangerous shoals on the lee recede,
  And the headland white we have left behind.

The topsails flutter, the jibs collapse
  And belly and tug at the groaning cleats,
The spanker slats, and the mainsail flaps,
  And thunders the order, *"TACKS AND SHEETS!"*

'Mid the rattle of blocks and the tramp of the crew,
  Hisses the rain of the rushing squall;
The sails are aback from clew to clew,
  And now is the moment for *"MAINSAIL, HAUL!"*

And the heavy yards like a baby's toy
  By fifty strong arms are swiftly swung;
She holds her way, and I look with joy
  For the first white spray o'er the bulwarks flung.

"LET GO AND HAUL!" 'Tis the last command,
  And the head-sails fill to the blast once more;
Astern and to leeward lies the land,
  With its breakers white on the shingly shore.

What matters the reef, or the rain, or the squall?
  I steady the helm for the open sea;
The first mate clamors, *"BELAY THERE, ALL!"*
  And the captain's breath once more comes free.

And so off shore let the good ship fly;
  Little care I how the gusts may blow,
In my fo'castle bunk in a jacket dry,—
  Eight bells have struck, and my watch is below.

Walter Mitchell

WHERE LIES THE LAND
TO WHICH YON SHIP MUST GO?

Where lies the Land to which yon Ship must go?
Fresh as a lark mounting at break of day,
Festively she puts forth in trim array;

Is she for tropic suns, or polar snow?
What boots the inquiry?—Neither friend nor foe
She cares for; let her travel where she may,
She finds familiar names, a beaten way
Ever before her, and a wind to blow.
Yet still I ask, what haven is her mark?
And, almost as it was when ships were rare,
(From time to time, like Pilgrims, here and there
Crossing the waters) doubt, and something dark,
Of the old Sea some reverential fear,
Is with me at thy farewell, joyous Bark!
                             William Wordsworth

STOWAWAY

I crossed the gangway in the winter's raining,
Late in the night, when it was dreary dark;
The only sounds the rain's hiss, and complaining
Of chafing hawsers holding that lean barque.

She sailed before the dawn. The evening found me
A sea-sick nipper, hidden in spare sails.
I feared they'd drag me out, and maybe drown me,—
The barque was trembling, dipping both her rails.

Soon I crept forth. Her long lee rail was sweeping.
A homing ship drove by with hurrying feet,
A school of porpoises all round her leaping,
While stars dipped low, her dizzied spars to greet.

"Three cheers!" they cried, and I could hear their
    voices,

And the sharp beating of her clanged iron bells;
Her musics faded, merged in the sea's noises,
And she was gone, loud cheering down the swells.

And in me then a something seemed to waken,
And I was mazed. It was as though the sea,
Or the big topsails by the night wind shaken
Had cast a sort of magic over me.

The mast heads reeled. In the bright North the Dipper
Hung dazzling diamonds round her sails, ghost white,
The seas were dim, and the deep breathing clipper
Quivered her feet, and shook with sheer delight.

It's long ago, my first night on the sea,
And I'm grown old, and sailing days are sped.
And I am waiting, waiting patiently,
Till other topsails gleam above my head.

There'll be a wharf, I know, where I am going,
There'll be a gangway for the likes o' me;
There'll be some lofty packet seaward blowing,—
They'll be fine ships on that eternal sea.

Bill Adams

A WET SHEET AND A FLOWING SEA

A wet sheet and a flowing sea,
   A wind that follows fast,
And fills the white and rustling sail
   And bends the gallant mast;

And bends the gallant mast, my boys,
    While, like the eagle free,
Away the good ship flies, and leaves
    Old England on the lee.

O for a soft and gentle wind!
    I heard a fair one cry;
But give to me the snoring breeze
    And white waves heaving high;
And white waves heaving high, my lads,
    The good ship tight and free—
The world of waters is our home,
    And merry men are we.

There's tempest in yon hornèd moon,
    And lightning in yon cloud;
But hark the music, mariners!
    The wind is piping loud;
The wind is piping loud, my boys,
    The lightning flashes free—
While the hollow oak our palace is,
    Our heritage the sea.
Allan Cunningham

THE CLIPPER

Her sails are strong and yellow as the sand,
    Her spars are tall and supple as the pine,
    And, like the bounty of a generous mine,
Sun-touched, her brasses flash on every hand.

Her sheer takes beauty from a golden band,
　　Which, sweeping aft, is taught to twist and twine
　　Into a scroll, and badge of quaint design
Hang on her quarters. Insolent and grand
　　She drives. Her stem rings loudly as it throws
The hissing sapphire into foamy waves,
　　While on her weather bends the copper glows
In burnished splendor. Rolling down she laves
　　Her high black sides until the scupper flows,
Then pushing out her shapely bow she braves
　　The next tall sea, and, leaping, onward goes.

Thomas Fleming Day

MY BRIGANTINE

　　　　My brigantine!
Just in thy mould and beauteous in thy form,
Gentle in roll and buoyant on the surge,
Light as the sea-fowl rocking in the storm,
In breeze and gale thy onward course we urge,
　　　　My water-queen!

　　　　Lady of mine!
More light and swift than thou none thread the sea,
With surer keel or steadier on its path;
We brave each waste of ocean-mystery
And laugh to hear the howling tempest's wrath,
　　　　For we are thine!

　　　　My brigantine!
Trust to the mystic power that points thy way,
Trust to the eye that pierces from afar,

Trust the red meteors that around thee play,
And, fearless, trust the Sea-Green Lady's Star,
    Thou bark divine!
                James Fenimore Cooper

DUE NORTH

Enough: you have the dream, the flame;
   Free it henceforth:
The South has given you a name;—
   Now for the North.

Unsheathe your ship from where she lies,
   In narrow ease;
Fling out her sails to the tall skies,
   Flout the sharp seas.

Beyond bleak headlands wistful burn
   Warm lights of home;
In-shutting darkness frays astern,
   Far-spun, the foam.

Come wide sea-dawns, that empty are
   Of wet sea sand;
Come eves, that lay beneath a star
   No lull of land.

And whether on faint iris wings
   Of fancy borne,
Or blown and breathed, the south wind brings
   So much to mourn!

The deep wood-shadows, they that drew
    So softly near;
The violets all veined with blue,—
    Be strong, and steer!

There is a silence to be found,
    And rested in;
A stillness out of thought, where sound
    Can never win.

There is a peace, beyond the stir
    Of wind or wave;
A sleeping, where high stars confer
    Over the brave.

The south winds come, the south winds go,
    Caressing, dear;
Northward is silence, and white snow,—
    Be strong, and steer!

For in that silence, waiting, lies,
    Untroubled, true;—
Oh, eager, clear-like love in eyes—
    The soul of you.

Benjamin R. C. Low

SAILING AT DAWN

One by one the pale stars die before the day now,
    One by one the great ships are stirring from their sleep,

OUTWARD BOUND

Cables all are rumbling, anchors all aweigh now,
  Now the fleet's a fleet again, gliding toward the deep.
    Now the fleet's a fleet again, bound upon the old ways,
    Splendor of the past comes shining in the spray,
    Admirals of old time, bring us on the bold ways!
    Souls of all the sea-dogs, lead the line today!

Far away behind us tower and town are dwindling,
  Home becomes a fair dream faded long ago;
Infinitely glorious the height of heaven is kindling,
  Infinitely desolate the shoreless sea below.
    Now the fleet's a fleet again, bound upon the old ways,
    Splendor of the past comes shining in the spray,
    Admirals of old time, bring us on the bold ways!
    Souls of all the sea-dogs, lead the line today!

Once again with proud hearts we make the old surrender,
  Once again with high hearts serve the age to be,
Not for us the warm life of Earth, secure and tender,
  Ours the eternal wandering and warfare of the sea.
    Now the fleet's a fleet again, bound upon the old ways,
    Splendor of the past comes shining in the spray,
    Admirals of old time, bring us on the bold ways!
    Souls of all the sea-dogs, lead the line today!
                                      Sir Henry Newbolt

THE DEEPER SEAS

For now are wider ways, profounder tides:
I feel an even wind against my face—
Infinite, level wind from clear sea-space,
And longer rhythms as the free ship rides
The slower surge of foam against her sides.—
The very moon-sail feels the steady race
Of blue cross-currents from some alien place,
And sweeps its lofty arc with greater strides.

These are the deeper seas—the lonelier roads—
Where only the far-sailing ships go out
Alone—the stronger ships, that sailing free
Of little voyages and little loads,
Go boldly on with no land-looking doubt
Through the increasing seas to yet more sea.
Henry Bellamann

SOUTHWARD SIDONIAN HANNO

Southward Sidonian Hanno lashed his slaves
Farther than mortal barks had dared before,
Around a sphinx shaped cape that looked at stars,—
Then north they labored at the salty oar.

Northward and westward, till they saw at morn
A peak that vaulted upward into light,
Catching the crescent moon upon its horn,
An ivory tusk set in the jaw of night.

OUTWARD BOUND

Under the stars a dream was born in mist,
While clouds streamed from the nipples of low hills,
Leaving the slopes below pale amethyst,
Veined with the silver lightning of the rills.

High as the peak itself, a lark began
And each as in a shell could faintly hear
The voice of ocean from a far-off beach,
Whisper its hoary secret at his ear.

Behind the line of water upward smote
The petaled tangents of the rising sun,
Till straight from boat to sun, from sun to boat,
The liquid glory of his face had run.

And in the gardens underneath the keel
They saw the orange spiders on the corals,
Fiddling a demon music for the reel
Of gold-eyed serpents in vermillion quarrels.

The scent of woods rolled to them from the land,
While magiced at the oars they listless lay,
Mixed with a whiff of cresses on the cliff
And upland orchards redolent of May

Each thought that he alone beheld the dream,
Fearful that if he spoke it would be gone,
Until a thousand mast-lengths overhead
The sunrise leaped from lawn to gilded lawn.

Then with a throaty "ha" at every stroke
They walked the leaking ship toward the strand,
Making her weedy prow break into smoke
That drifted like an incense to the land.

Yet never might they find a place to beach;
At noon they beat their shields, but mocking hails
Blent with a god-like laughter out of reach,
Answered the friendly wafture of their sails.

It seemed a land where mortals had no part,
Red, ringed about with granite-teeth and foam,
With fiery-glinted pastures where Melcart
Or Baal with all his sons might be at home.

So, till the sun plunged into molten brass,
When horns of inland cities hailed the moon;
Down cliffs, all night, across a sea of glass,
Toppled the talking timbrel's toneless tune.

And from the ooze the dead-faced krakens came
To peer with lidless eyes into the ship,
Or dive beneath through clouds of milky flame,
In arctic light that streamed from fin and lip.

Until the quaking crew began to fret
And murmur, saying one had left his sire,
And one his wife and babe,—so Hanno set
His bow into the Bear and steered for Tyre.

Glad were his bearded men; with steady stroke
They sank the peak below the ocean-stream,
And afterwards of many lands they spoke,
But always of the island as a dream.

Hervey Allen

TO SEA, TO SEA!

To sea, to sea! The calm is o'er;
   The wanton water leaps in sport,
And rattles down the pebbly shore;
   The dolphin wheels, the sea-cows snort,
And unseen Mermaids' pearly song
Comes bubbling up, the weeds among.
   Fling broad the sail, dip deep the oar:
   To sea, to sea! the calm is o'er.

To sea, to sea! our wide-winged bark
   Shall billowy cleave its sunny way,
And with its shadow, fleet and dark,
   Break the caved Triton's azure day,
Like mighty eagle soaring light
O'er antelopes on Alpine height.
   The anchor heaves, the ship swings free,
   The sails swell full. To sea, to sea!
                  Thomas Lovell Beddoes

THE MAIN-SHEET SONG

Rushing along on a narrow reach,
   Our rival under the lee,
The wind falls foul of the weather leach,
   And the jib flaps fretfully.
The skipper casts a glance along,
   And handles his wheel to meet—
Then sings in the voice of a stormy song,
   "All hands get on that sheet!"

Yo ha! Yo ho! Then give her a spill
  With a rattle of blocks abaft.
Yo ha! Yo ho! Come down with a will
  And bring the main-sheet aft.

Rolling the foam up over the rail
  She smokes along and flings
A spurt of spray in the curving sail,
  And plunges and rolls and springs;
For a wild, wet spot is the scuppers' sweep,
  As we stand to our knees along—
It's a foot to make and a foot to keep
  As we surge to the bullie's song.

Yo ha! Yo ho! Then give her a spill
  With a rattle of blocks abaft.
Yo ha! Yo ho! Come down with a will
  And bring the main-sheet aft.

Muscle and mind are a winning pair
  With a lively plank below,
That whether the wind be foul or fair
  Will pick up her heels and go;
For old hemp and hands are shipmates long—
  There's work whenever they meet—
So here's to a pull that's steady and strong,
  When all hands get on the sheet.

Yo ha! Yo ho! Then give her a spill
  With a rattle of blocks abaft.
Yo ha! Yo ho! Come down with a will
  And bring the main-sheet aft.

Thomas Fleming Day

ALL HANDS UNMOOR!

... A thundering sound
He hears, and thrice the hollow decks rebound;
Upstarting from his couch on deck he sprung,
Thrice with shrill note the boatswain's whistle rung:
All hands unmoor! proclaims a boisterous cry,
All hands unmoor! the cavern'd rocks reply:
Roused from repose aloft the sailors swarm,
And with their levers soon the windlass arm:
The order given, up springing with a bound,
They fix the bars, and heave the windlass round;
At every turn the clanging pauls resound;
Up-torn reluctant from its oozy cave
The ponderous anchor rises o'er the wave.
High on the slippery masts the yards ascend,
And far abroad the canvas wings extend.
William Falconer

PEG-LEG'S FIDDLE

I've a pal called Billy Peg-leg, with one leg a wood leg,
And Billy he's a ship's cook, and lives upon the sea;
And, hanging by his griddle,
Old Billy keeps a fiddle,
For fiddling in the dog-watch, when the moon is on the sea.

We takes our luck wi' tough ships, wi' fast ships, wi' free ships,
We takes our luck wi' any ship to sign away for sea;
We takes our trick wi' the best o' them,

And sings our song wi' the rest o' them,
When the bell strikes the dog-watch, and the moon is on the sea.

You'd ought to see them tops'ls, them stays'ls, them stuns'ls,
When the moon's a-shinin' on them along a liftin' sea;
Hear the dandy bosun say,
"Peg-leg, make that fiddle play
And we'll dance away the dog-watch, while the moon is on the sea."

Then it's fun to see them dancin', them bow-legged sailors dancin',
To the tune o' Peg-leg's fiddle, a-fiddlin' fast and free;
It's fun to watch old Peg-leg,
A-waltzin' wi' his wood leg,
When bosun takes the fiddle, so Peg can dance wi' me.

The moon is on the water, the dark moon-glimmered water,
The night-wind pipin' plaintively along a liftin' sea;
There ain't no female wimmen,
No big beer glasses brimmen',
There's just the great sea's glory, an' Billy Peg an' me.

We takes our luck wi' tough ships, wi' fast ships, wi' free ships,
We takes our luck wi' any ship to sign away to sea:
We takes our luck wi' the best o' them,
And sings our songs wi' the rest o' them,
When the bell strikes the dog-watch and the moon is on the sea.

Bill Adams

WHERE LIES THE LAND?

Where lies the land to which the ship would go?
Far, far ahead, is all her seamen know.
And where the land she travels from? Away,
Far, far behind, is all that they can say.

On sunny noons upon the deck's smooth face,
Linked arm in arm, how pleasant here to pace;
Or, o'er the stern reclining, watch below
The foaming wake far widening as we go.

On stormy nights when wild northwesters rave,
How proud a thing to fight with wind and wave!
The dripping sailor on the reeling mast
Exults to bear, and scorns to wish it past.

Where lies the land to which the ship would go?
Far, far ahead, is all her seamen know.
And where the land she travels from? Away,
Far, far behind, is all that they can say.
Arthur Hugh Clough

GODSPEED

The great ship spreads her wings, her plumes are flying;
   Music sweeps down the deck, and chiming laughter;
She climbs the green crest of the shining surges,
   The shadow of the chasing surge climbs after.

Ah, never overtake her, mighty shadow!
  Spirits of fire and air, attend upon her;
In cloud by day and fire by night possess her;
  Sacred her charge, and sacred be her honor!

Far in the mid-waste of the weltering waters,
  Furrowed with dark and day and dark returning,
Fly, fly, good ship, easting with every dawning,
  To hail your beacon in the billows burning!

And though you toss where never breath of blossom
  Blows, nor sweeps round the mast the swift sea swallow,
Yet with you still, all storm, all space, defying,
  On her untiring wing my love shall follow!

Harriet Prescott Spofford

A LIFE

I heard my ancient sea-blood say,
  And wise in youth it counselled me—
'When women lure, when men betray,
  Break topsails for the open sea.'

I crowded sail on spar and mast,
  And half the world I left behind;
But in my breast I held it fast,
  That truth in men I still should find.

I set my life on swords of three,
  My back against my castle wall;
Now should I cry, 'A moi, amis!'
  It is three ghosts would come at call.

Alone upon the 'Far Away,'
  And nothing human sails with me;
My bare poles dip, through sun and spray,
  The dim marge of God's outer sea.
George Edward Woodberry

SONG OF THE ARGONAUTS

O bitter sea, tumultuous sea,
Full many an ill is wrought by thee!—
Unto the wasters of the land
Thou holdest out thy wrinkled hand;
And when they leave the conquered town,
Whose black smoke makes thy surges brown,
Driven betwixt thee and the sun,
As the long day of blood is done,
From many a league of glittering waves
Thou smilest on them and their slaves.
  Now, therefore, O thou bitter sea,
With no long words we pray to thee,
But ask thee, hast thou felt before
Such strokes of the long ashen oar?
And has thou yet seen such a prow
Thy rich and niggard waters plough?
  Nor yet, O sea, shalt thou be cursed,
If at thy hands we gain the worst,
And, wrapt in water, roll about
Blind-eyed, unheeding song or shout,
Within thine eddies far from shore,
Warmed by no sunlight any more.
  Therefore, indeed, we joy in thee,

And praise thy greatness, and will we
Take at thy hands both good and ill,
Yea, what thou wilt, and praise thee still,
Enduring not to sit at home,
And wait until the last days come,
When we no more may care to hold
White bosoms under crowns of gold,
And our dulled hearts no longer are
Stirred by the clangorous noise of war,
And hope within our souls is dead,
And no joy is remembered.

    So, if thou hast a mind to slay,
Fair prize thou hast of us today;
And if thou hast a mind to save,
Great praise and honour shalt thou have;
But whatso thou wilt do with us,
Our end shall not be piteous,
Because our memories shall live
When folk forget the way to drive
The black keel through the heaped-up sea,
And half dried up thy waters be.

William Morris

4. Stormy Seas

BALLAD OF THE TEMPEST

We were crowded in the cabin,
Not a soul would dare to sleep,—
It was midnight on the waters,
And a storm was on the deep.

'T is a fearful thing in winter
To be shattered in the blast,
And to hear the rattling trumpet
Thunder, "Cut away the mast!"

So we shuddered there in silence,—
For the stoutest held his breath,
While the hungry sea was roaring,
And the breakers talked with Death.

As thus we sat in darkness,
Each one busy in his prayers,—
"We are lost!" the captain shouted,
As he staggered down the stairs.

But his little daughter whispered,
As she took his icy hand,
"Isn't God upon the ocean,
Just the same as on the land?"

Then we kissed the little maiden,
And we spoke in better cheer,

And we anchored safe in harbor
When the morn was shining clear.

James T. Fields

ROUNDING THE HORN
(From "Dauber")

Then came the cry of "Call all hands on deck!"
The Dauber knew its meaning; it was come:
Cape Horn, that tramples beauty into wreck,
And crumples steel and smites the strong man dumb.
Down clattered flying kites and staysails: some
Sang out in quick, high calls: the fair-leads skirled,
And from the south-west came the end of the
    world....

"Lay out!" the Bosun yelled. The Dauber laid
Out on the yard, gripping the yard, and feeling
Sick at the mighty space of air displayed
Below his feet, where mewing birds were wheeling.
A giddy fear was on him; he was reeling.
He bit his lip half through, clutching the jack.
A cold sweat glued the shirt upon his back.

The yard was shaking, for a brace was loose.
He felt that he would fall; he clutched, he bent,
Clammy with natural terror to the shoes
While idiotic promptings came and went.
Snow fluttered on a wind-flaw and was spent;
He saw the water darken. Someone yelled,
"Frap it; don't stay to furl! Hold on!" He held.

STORMY SEAS

Darkness came down—half darkness—in a whirl;
The sky went out, the waters disappeared.
He felt a shocking pressure of blowing hurl
The ship upon her side. The darkness speared
At her with wind; she staggered, she careered,
Then down she lay. The Dauber felt her go;
He saw his yard tilt downwards. Then the snow

Whirled all about—dense, multitudinous, cold—
Mixed with the wind's one devilish thrust and shriek,
Which whiffled out men's tears, deafened, took hold,
Flattening the flying drift against the cheek.
The yards buckled and bent, man could not speak.
The ship lay on her broadside; the wind's sound
Had devilish malice at having got her downed.

* * * * *

How long the gale had blown he could not tell,
Only the world had changed, his life had died.
A moment now was everlasting hell.
Nature an onslaught from the weather side,
A withering rush of death, a frost that cried,
Shrieked, till he withered at the heart; a hail
Plastered his oilskins with an icy mail....

"Up!" yelled the Bosun; "up and clear the wreck!"
The Dauber followed where he led: below
He caught one giddy glimpsing of the deck
Filled with white water, as though heaped with snow.
He saw the streamers of the rigging blow
Straight out like pennons from the splintered mast,
Then, all sense dimmed, all was an icy blast

Roaring from nether hell and filled with ice,
Roaring and crashing on the jerking stage,
An utter bridle given to utter vice,
Limitless power mad with endless rage
Withering the soul; a minute seemed an age.
He clutched and hacked at ropes, at rags of sail,
Thinking that comfort was a fairy-tale

Told long ago—long, long ago—long since
Heard of in other lives—imagined, dreamed—
There where the basest beggar was a prince
To him in torment where the tempest screamed,
Comfort and warmth and ease no longer seemed
Things that a man could know: soul, body, brain,
Knew nothing but the wind, the cold, the pain.
John Masefield

CHRISTMAS AT SEA

The sheets were frozen hard, and they cut the naked hand;
The decks were like a slide, where a seaman scarce could stand;
The wind was a nor'-wester, blowing squally off the sea;
And cliffs and spouting breakers were the only things a-lee.

They heard the surf a-roaring before the break of day;
But 'twas only with the peep of light we saw how ill we lay.

We tumbled every hand on deck instanter, with a
    shout,
And we gave her the maintops'l, and stood by to go
    about.

All day we tacked and tacked between the South Head
    and the North;
All day we hauled the frozen sheets, and got no further
    forth;
All day as cold as charity, in bitter pain and dread,
For very life and nature we tacked from head to head.

We gave the South a wider berth, for there the tide-
    race roared;
But every tack we made brought the North Head close
    aboard:
So's we saw the cliffs and houses, and the breakers
    running high,
And the coastguard in his garden, with his glass against
    his eye.

The frost was on the village roofs as white as ocean
    foam;
The good red fires were burning bright in every 'long
    shore home;
The windows sparkled clear, and the chimneys vol-
    leyed out;
And I vow we sniffed the victuals as the vessel went
    about.

The bells upon the church were rung with a mighty
    jovial cheer;
For it's just that I should tell you how (of all days in
    the year)

This day of our adversity was blessèd Christmas morn
And the house above the coastguard's was the house where I was born.

O well I saw the pleasant room, the pleasant faces there,
My mother's silver spectacles, my father's silver hair;
And well I saw the firelight, like a flight of homely elves,
Go dancing round the china plates that stand upon the shelves.

And well I knew the talk they had, the talk that was of me,
Of the shadow on the household and the son that went to sea;
And O the wicked fool I seemed, in every kind of way,
To be here and hauling frozen ropes on blessèd Christmas Day.

They lit the high sea-light, and the dark began to fall.
"All hands to loose topgallant sails," I heard the captain call.
"By the Lord, she'll never stand it," our first mate, Jackson, cried.
... "It's the one way or the other, Mr. Jackson," he replied.

She staggered to her bearings, but the sails were new and good,
And the ship smelt up to windward, just as though she understood.

As the winter's day was ending, in the entry of the
    night,
We cleared the weary headland, and passed below the
    light.

And they heaved a mighty breath, every soul on board
    but me,
As they saw her nose again pointing handsome out to
    sea;
But all that I could think of, in the darkness and the
    cold,
Was just that I was leaving home and my folks were
    growing old.
                                    Robert Louis Stevenson

SHORTENING SAIL

As the proud horse with costly trappings gay,
Exulting, prances to the bloody fray;
Spurning the ground he glories in his might,
But reels tumultuous in the shock of fight:
E'en so, caparison'd in gaudy pride,
The bounding vessel dances on the tide.
   Fierce and more fierce the gathering tempest grew,
South, and by west, the threatening demon blew;
Auster's resistless force all air invades,
And every rolling wave more ample spreads:
The ship no longer can her top-sails bear;
No hopes of milder weather now appear.
Bow-lines and halyards are cast off again,

Clue-lines haul'd down, and sheets let fly amain:
Embrail'd each top-sail, and by braces squared,
The seamen climb aloft, and man each yard;
They furl'd the sails, and pointed to the wind
The yards, by rolling tackles then confined,
While o'er the ship the gallant boatswain flies;
Like a hoarse mastiff through the storm he cries,
Prompt to direct the unskilful still appears,
The expert he praises, and the timid cheers.
Now some, to strike top-gallant-yards attend,
Some, travellers up the weather-back-stays send,
At each mast-head the top-ropes others bend:
The parrels, lifts, and clue-lines soon are gone,
Topp'd and unrigg'd, they down the back-stays run;
The yards secure along the booms were laid,
And all the flying ropes aloft belay'd:
Their sails reduced, and all the rigging clear,
Awhile the crew relax from toils severe;
Awhile their spirits with fatigue opprest,
In vain expect the alternate hour of rest—
But with redoubling force the tempests blow,
And watery hills in dread succession flow:
A dismal shade o'ercasts the frowning skies,
New troubles grow; fresh difficulties rise;
No season this from duty to descend,
All hands on deck must now the storm attend.

  His race perform'd, the sacred lamp of day
Now dipt in western clouds his parting ray:
His languid fires, half lost in ambient haze,
Refract along the dusk a crimson blaze;
Till deep immerged the sickening orb descends,
And cheerless night o'er heaven her reign extends:

STORMY SEAS

Sad evening's hour, how different from the past!
No flaming pomp, no blushing glories cast,
No ray of friendly light is seen around;
The moon and stars in hopeless shade are drown'd.
 The ship no longer can whole courses bear,
To reef them now becomes the master's care;
The sailors, summon'd aft, all ready stand,
And man the enfolding brails at his command:
But here the doubtful officers dispute,
Till skill, and judgment, prejudice confute:
For Rodmond, to new methods still a foe,
Would first, at all events, the sheet let go;
To long-tried practice obstinately warm,
He doubts conviction, and relies on form.
This Albert and Arion disapprove,
And first to brail the tack up firmly move:
"The watchful seaman, whose sagacious eye
On sure experience may with truth rely,
Who from the reigning cause foretells the effect,
This barbarous practice ever will reject;
For, fluttering loose in air, the rigid sail
Soon flits to ruins in the furious gale;
And he, who strives the tempest to disarm,
Will never first embrail the lee yard-arm."
So Albert spoke; to windward, at his call,
Some seamen the clue-garnet stand to haul—
The tack's eased off, while the involving clue
Between the pendent blocks ascending flew;
The sheet and weather-brace they now stand by,
The lee clue-garnet, and the bunt-lines ply:
Then, all prepared, Let go the sheet! he cries—
Loud rattling, jarring, through the blocks it flies!

Shivering at first, till by the blast impell'd;
High o'er the lee yard-arm the canvas swell'd;
By spilling lines embraced, with brails confined,
It lies at length unshaken by the wind.
The fore-sail then secured with equal care,
Again to reef the main-sail they repair;
While some above the yard o'er-haul the tye,
Below, the down-haul tackle others ply;
Jears, lifts, and brails, a seaman each attends,
And down the mast its mighty yard descends:
When lower'd sufficient they securely brace,
And fix the rolling tackle in its place;
The reef-lines and their earings now prepared,
Mounting on pliant shrouds they man the yard:
Far on the extremes appear two able hands,
For no inferior skill this task demands—
To windward, foremost, young Arion strides,
The lee yard-arm the gallant boatswain rides:
Each earing to its cringle first they bend,
The reef-band then along the yard extend;
The circling earings round the extremes entwined,
By outer and by inner turns they bind;
The reef-lines next from hand to hand received,
Through eyelet-holes and roban-legs were reeved;
The folding reefs in plaits inroll'd they lay,
Extend the worming lines, and ends belay.

  Hadst thou, Arion! held the leeward post
While on the yard by mountain billows tost,
Perhaps oblivion o'er our tragic tale
Had then for ever drawn her dusky veil;
But ruling Heaven prolong'd thy vital date,
Severer ills to suffer, and relate.

STORMY SEAS

    For, while aloft the order those attend
To furl the main-sail, or on deck descend;
A sea, upsurging with stupendous roll,
To instant ruin seems to doom the whole:
O friends, secure your hold! Arion cries—
It comes all dreadful! down the vessel lies
Half buried sideways; while, beneath it tost,
Four seamen off the lee yard-arm are lost:
Torn with resistless fury from their hold,
In vain their struggling arms the yard enfold;
In vain to grapple flying ropes they try,
The ropes, alas! a solid gripe deny:
Prone on the midnight surge with panting breath
They cry for aid, and long contend with death;
High o'er their heads the rolling billows sweep,
And down they sink in everlasting sleep.
Bereft of power to help, their comrades see
The wretched victims die beneath the lee,
With fruitless sorrow their lost state bemoan,
Perhaps a fatal prelude to their own!
    In dark suspense on deck the pilots stand,
Nor can determine on the next command:
Though still they knew the vessel's armed side
Impenetrable to the clasping tide;
Though still the waters by no secret wound
A passage to her deep recesses found;
Surrounding evils yet they ponder o'er,
A storm, a dangerous sea, and leeward shore!
"Should they, though reef'd, again their sails extend,
Again in shivering streamers they may rend;
Or, should they stand, beneath the oppressive strain,
The down-press'd ship may never rise again;

Too late to weather now Morea's land,
And drifting fast on Athens' rocky strand."—
Thus they lament the consequence severe,
Where perils unallay'd by hope appear:
Long pondering in their minds each fear'd event,
At last to furl the courses they consent;
That done, to reef the mizzen next agree,
And try beneath it sidelong in the sea.

   Now down the mast the yard they lower away,
Then jears and topping-lift secure belay;
The head, with doubling canvas fenced around,
In balance near the lofty peak they bound;
The reef enwrapp'd, the inserting knittles tied,
The halyards throt and peak are next applied—
The order given, the yard aloft they sway'd,
The brails relax'd, the extended sheet belay'd;
The helm its post forsook, and, lash'd a-lee,
Incline the wayward prow to front the sea.

William Falconer

FRANKIE'S TRADE

Old Horn to All Atlantic said:
  (A-hay O! To me O!)
'Now where did Frankie learn his trade?
For he ran me down with a three-reef mains'l.'
  (All round the Horn!)

Atlantic answered:—'Not from me!
You better ask the cold North Sea,
For he ran me down under all plain canvas.'
  (All round the Horn!)

STORMY SEAS

The North Sea answered:—'He's my man,
For he came to me when he began—
Frankie Drake in an open coaster.
 (All round the Sands!)

'I caught him young and I used him sore,
So you never shall startle Frankie more,
Without capsizing Earth and her waters.
 (All round the Sands!)

'I did not favor him at all.
I made him pull and I made him haul—
And stand his trick with the common sailors.
 (All round the Sands!)

'I froze him stiff and I fogged him blind,
And kicked him home with his road to find
By what he could see in a three-day snowstorm.
 (All round the Sands!)

'I learned him his trade o' winter nights,
'Twixt Mardyk Fort and Dunkirk lights
On a five-knot tide with the forts a-firing.
 (All round the Sands!)

'Before his beard began to shoot,
I showed him the length of the Spaniard's foot—
And I reckon he clapped the boot on it later.
 (All round the Sands!)

'If there's a risk which you can make,
That's worse than he was used to take
Nigh every week in the way of his business;
 (All round the Sands!)

'If there's a trick that you can try,
Which he hasn't met in time gone by,
Not once or twice, but ten times over;
  (*All round the Sands!*)

'If you can teach him aught that's new,
  (*A-hay O! To me O!*)
I'll give you Bruges and Niewport too,
And the ten tall churches that stand between 'em,'
  Storm along my gallant Captains!
    (*All round the Horn!*)

                                    Rudyard Kipling

NIGHT STORM

This tempest sweeps the Atlantic!—Nevasink
  Is howling to the Capes! Grim Hatteras cries
Like thousand damnèd ghosts, that on the brink
  Lift their dark hands and threat the threatening skies;
Surging through foam and tempest, old Román
  Hangs o'er the gulf, and, with his cavernous throat,
  Pours out the torrent of his wolfish note,
And bids the billows bear it where they can!
Deep calleth unto deep, and, from the cloud,
  Launches the bolt, that, bursting o'er the sea,
Rends for a moment the thick pitchy shroud,
  And shows the ship the shore beneath her lee:
Start not, dear wife, no dangers here betide,-
And see, the boy still sleeping at your side!

                              William Gilmore Simms

REEFING TOPSAILS

Three hand-spike raps on the forward hatch,
   A hoarse voice shouts down the fo'castle dim,
Startling the sleeping starboard watch,
Out of their bunks, their clothes to snatch,
   With little thought of life or limb.

"All hands on deck! d'ye hear the news?
   Reef topsails all—'tis the old man's word.
Tumble up, never mind jackets or shoes!"
Never a man would dare refuse,
   When that stirring cry is heard.

The weather shrouds are like iron bars,
   The leeward backstays curving out.
Like steely spear-points gleam the stars
From the black sky flecked with feathery bars,
   By the storm-wind swerved about.

Across the bows like a sheeted ghost,
   Quivers a luminous cloud of spray,
Flooding the forward deck, and most
Of the waist; then, like a charging host,
   It rolls to leeward away.

"Mizzen topsail, clew up and furl;
   Clew up your main course now with a will!"
The wheel goes down with a sudden whirl.
"Ease her, ease her, the good old girl,
   Don't let your head sails fill!"

"Ease off lee braces; round in on the weather;
   Ease your halyards; clew down, clew down;
Haul out your reef tackles, now together!"
Like an angry bull against his tether,
   Heave the folds of the topsails brown.

"Haul taut your buntlines, cheerly, men, now!"
   The gale sweeps down with a fiercer shriek;
Shock after shock on the weather bow
Thunders the head sea, and below
   Throbbing timbers groan and creak.

The topsail yards are down on the caps;
   Her head lies up in the eyes of the blast;
The bellying sails, with sudden slaps,
Swell out and angrily collapse,
   Shaking the head of the springing mast.

Wilder and heavier comes the gale
   Out of the heart of the Northern Sea;
And the phosphorescent gleamings pale
Surge up awash of the monkey rail
   Along our down pressed lee.

"Lay aloft! lay aloft, boys, and reef,
   Don't let my starbolines be last,"
Cries from the deck the sturdy chief;
"Twill take a man of *muscle and beef*
   To get those ear-rings passed!"

Into the rigging with a shout,
   Our second and third mates foremost spring;

STORMY SEAS

Crackles the ice on the ratlines stout,
As the leaders on the yards lay out,
   And the footropes sway and swing.

On the weather end of the jumping yard,
   One hand on the lift, and one beneath,
Grasping the cringle, and tugging hard,
 Black Dan, our third, grim and scarred,
   Clutches the ear-ring for life or death.

"Light up to windward!" cries the mate,
   As he rides the surging yardarm end;
And into the work we throw our weight,
Every man bound to emulate,
   The rush of the gale, and the sea's wild send.

"Haul out to leeward," comes at last,
   With a cheering from the fore and main;
"Knot your reef-points, and knot them fast!"
Weather and lee are the ear-rings passed,
   And over the yard we bend and strain.

"Lay down men, all; and now with a will,
   Swing on your topsail halyards, and sway;
Ease your braces and let her fill,
There's an hour below of the mid-watch still,
   Haul taut your bowlines—well all—belay!"
                               Walter Mitchell

WHAT THE OLD MAN SAID
A Yarn of Dan's

"Don't you take no sail off 'er," the Ol' Man said....
Wind an' sea rampagin' fit to wake the dead....

Thrashin' through the Forties in the sleet an' hail,
Runnin' down the Eastin' under all plain sail!

"She's loggin' seventeen, an' she's liftin' to it grand,
So I'm goin' down below for a stretch off the land.

"An' if it's getting worse, Mister, come an' call me—
But—don't you take no sail off 'er," said the Ol' Man, said 'e.

*   *   *   *   *

Them was the times, sonnies, them was the men,
Them was the ships as we'll never see again.

Ah, but it was somethin' then to be alive,
Thrashin' under royals south o' Forty-five!

When it was—"Don't you take no sail off 'er," the Ol' Man'd say,
Beard an' whiskers starin' stiff wi' frozen spray.

"She's loggin' seventeen an' she's liftin' to it grand,
An' I mean to keep 'er goin' under all she'll stand.

"An' if it's getting worse, Mister, come an' call me,
But—don't you take no sail off 'er," said the Ol' Man, said 'e.

C. Fox Smith

SAILOR'S CONSOLATION

One night came on a hurricane,
  The sea was mountains rolling,
When Barney Buntline turned his quid,
  And said to Billy Bowling:
"A strong nor-wester's blowing, Bill:
  Hark! Don't ye hear it roar now?
Lord help 'em! How I pities all
  Unhappy folks on shore now!

"Fool-hardy chaps who live in towns,
  What danger they are all in,
And now lie quaking in their beds,
  For fear the roof should fall in;
Poor creatures! How they envies us,
  And wishes, I've a notion,
For our good luck, in such a storm
  To be upon the ocean!

"And as for them who are out all day
  On business from their houses,
And late at night are coming home,
  To cheer their babes and spouses;
While you and I, Bill, on the deck
  Are comfortably lying,
My eyes! What tiles and chimney-pots
  About their heads are flying!

"And very often have we heard
  How men are kill'd and undone,
By overturns of carriages,
  By thieves, and fires in London.

We know what risks all landsmen run,
  From noblemen to tailors;
Then, Bill, let us thank Providence
  That you and I are sailors!"

William Pitt

THE *THREE BELLS*

Beneath the low-hung night cloud
  That raked her splintering mast
The good ship settled slowly,
  The cruel leak gained fast.

Over the awful ocean
  Her signal guns pealed out.
Dear God! was that thy answer
  From the horror round about?

A voice came down the wild wind,
  "Ho! ship ahoy!" its cry:
"Our stout *Three Bells* of Glasgow
  Shall lay till daylight by!"

Hour after hour crept slowly,
  Yet on the heaving swells
Tossed up and down the ship-lights,
  The lights of the *Three Bells!*

And ship to ship made signals,
  Man answered back to man,
While oft, to cheer and hearten,
  The *Three Bells* nearer ran;

And the captain from her taffrail
  Sent down his hopeful cry:
"Take heart! Hold on!" he shouted,
  "The *Three Bells* shall lay by!"

All night across the waters
  The tossing lights shone clear;
All night from reeling taffrail
  The *Three Bells* sent her cheer.

And when the dreary watches
  Of storm and darkness passed,
Just as the wreck lurched under,
  All souls were saved at last.

Sail on, *Three Bells*, forever,
  In grateful memory sail!
Ring on, *Three Bells* of rescue,
  Above the wave and gale!

Type of the Love eternal,
  Repeat the Master's cry,
As tossing through our darkness
  The lights of God draw nigh!
                        John Greenleaf Whittier

HIGH O'ER THE POOP
THE AUDACIOUS SEAS ASPIRE

High o'er the poop the audacious seas aspire,
Uproll'd in hills of fluctuating fire;
With labouring throes she rolls on either side,

And dips her gunnels in the yawning tide;
Her joints unhinged in palsied languors play,
As ice-flakes part beneath the noon-tide ray:
The gale howls doleful thro' the blocks and shrouds,
And big rain pours a deluge from the clouds;
From wintry magazines that sweep the sky,
Descending globes of hail impetuous fly;
High on the masts, with pale and livid rays,
Amid the gloom portentous meteors blaze;
The ethereal dome in mournful pomp array'd
Now buried lies beneath impervious shade,
Now, flashing round intolerable light,
Redoubles all the horror of the night—
Such terror Sinai's trembling hill o'erspread,
When heaven's loud trumpet sounded o'er its head:
It seem'd the wrathful angel of the wind
Had all the horrors of the skies combined,
And here, to one ill-fated ship opposed,
At once the dreadful magazine disclosed:
And lo! tremendous o'er the deep he springs,
The inflaming sulphur flashing from his wings;
Hark! his strong voice the dismal silence breaks,
Mad chaos from the chains of death awakes:
Loud, and more loud, the rolling peals enlargé,
And blue on deck the fiery tides discharge;
There all aghast the shivering wretches stood,
While chill suspense and fear congeal'd their blood;
Wide bursts in dazzling sheets the living flame,
And dread concussion rends the ethereal frame;
Sick earth convulsive groans from shore to shore,
And nature, shuddering, feels the horrid roar.

William Falconer

THE EQUINOX
(From "Seaweed")

When descends on the Atlantic
  The gigantic
Storm-wind of the equinox,
Landward in his wrath he scourges
  The toiling surges,
Laden with seaweed from the rocks:

From Bermuda's reefs; from edges
  Of sunken ledges,
In some far-off, bright Azore;
From Bahama, and the dashing,
  Silver-flashing
Surges of San Salvador;

From the tumbling surf, that buries
  The Orkneyan skerries,
Answering the hoarse Hebrides;
And from wrecks of ships, and drifting
  Spars, uplifting
On the desolate, rainy seas;—

Ever drifting, drifting, drifting
  On the shifting
Currents of the restless main;
Till in sheltered coves, and reaches
  Of sandy beaches,
All have found repose again.
                    Henry Wadsworth Longfellow

THE TORNADO

Whose eye has marked his gendering? On his throne
He dwells apart in roofless caves of air,
Born of the stagnant, blown of the glassy heat
O'er the still mere Sargasso. When the world
Has fallen voluptuous, and the isles are grown
So bold they cry, God sees not!—as a rare
Sunflashing iceberg towers on high, and fleet
As air-ships rise, by upward currents whirled,
Even so the bane of lustful islanders
Wings him aloft. And scarce a pinion stirs.

There gathering hues, he stoopeth down again,
Down from the vault. Locks of the gold-tipped cloud
Fly o'er his head; his eyes, Saint Elmo flames;
His mouth, a surf on a red coral reef.
Embroidered is his cloak of dark blue stain
With lightning jags. Upon his pathway crowd
Dull Shudder, wan-faced Quaking, Ghastly-dreams.
And after these, in order near their chief,
Start, Tremor, Faint-heart, Panic and Affray,
Horror with blanching eyes, and limp Dismay

Unroll a grey-green carpet him before
Swathed in thick foam: thereon adventuring, bark
Need never hope to live; that yeasty pile
Bears her no longer; to the mast-head plunged
She writhes and groans, careens, and is no more.
Now, prickt by fear, the man-devourer shark,
Gale-breasting gull and whale that dreams no guile
Till the sharp steel quite to the life has lunged,

Before his pitiless, onward-hurling form
Hurry toward land for shelter from the storm.

In vain. Tornado and his pursuivants,
Whirlwind of giant bulk, and Water-spout,—
The gruesome, tortuous devil-fish of rain—
O'ertake them on the shoals and leave them dead.
Doomsday has come. Now men in speechless trance
Glower unmoved upon the hideous rout,
Or, shrieking, fly to holes, or yet complain
One moment to that lordly face of dread
Before he quits the mountain of his wave
And strews for all impartially their grave.
Charles de Kay

HYDROGRAPHIC REPORT

Off Portland: wind east, visibility eight,
sea smooth, the air
not too warm, storm due
from some quarter: watch.
A fellow from the Ice Patrol turned up
at the bar last night and said they'd named and charted
a thousand bergs that didn't go back up
east of Greenland with the Gulf Drift.

Off Gloucester: they've got to warn the traffic lanes,
those fellows. Sea choppy, wind southeast and chang-
   ing;
visibility ten; and what I think is—
Arctic and Gulf Streams 're arguing like hell.
Sea choppy; wind east by north; clouds.

Off Nantucket: visibility eight,
sea smooth and wind northeast, no squalls,
rain three days from now.
But fog's blown up; sea easy; wind southwest;
start all horns and subterranean bells.

Off Sandy Hook: wind south by west, gale force;
visibility ten, sea rising; what?
Shut up and haul sail; pull your fool head down;
ma, you'd better get your wash in; mister,
stoke the engines; cooky, take the lookout.

Off Hatteras: who's got the trick? Oh, you.
Hold on. Visibility eight, sea going
somewhere between America and Europe.
Wind east, wind southeast, wind northeast,
wind west, wind south by west,
wind north by west, wind east by—
hold on.

Off America, east: visibility—
barometer—
latitude—
longitude—
gulf stream—
labrador current—
the damned Atlantic's changing.

Hold on:
off the coast,
glass falling.

Frances Frost

THE WAY OF CAPE RACE

Lion-hunger, tiger-leap!
The waves are bred no other way;
It was their way when the Norseman came,
It was the same in Cabot's day:
A thousand years will come again,
When a thousand years have passed away—
Galleon, frigate, liner, plane,
The muster of the slain.

They have placed the light, fog-horn, and bell
Along the shore: the wardens keep
Their posts—they do not quell
The roar; they shorten not the leap.
The waves still ring the knell
Of ships that pass at night,
Of dreadnought and of cockle-shell:
They do not heed the light,
The fog-horn and the bell—
Lion-hunger, tiger-leap!

E. J. Pratt

STORM SONG

The clouds are scudding across the moon;
    A misty light is on the sea;
The wind in the shrouds has a wintry tune,
    And the foam is flying free.

Brothers, a night of terror and gloom
  Speaks in the cloud and gathering roar;
Thank God, He has given us broad sea-room,
  A thousand miles from shore.

Down with the hatches on those who sleep!
  The wild and whistling deck have we;
Good watch, my brothers, tonight we'll keep,
  While the tempest is on the sea!

Though the rigging shriek in his terrible grip,
  And the naked spars be snapped away,
Lashed to the helm, we'll drive our ship
  In the teeth of the whelming spray!

Hark! how the surges o'erleap the deck!
  Hark! how the pitiless tempest raves!
Ah, daylight will look upon many a wreck
  Drifting over the desert waves.

Yet, courage, brothers! we trust the wave,
  With God above us, our guiding chart.
So, whether to harbor or ocean-grave,
  Be it still with a cheery heart!

Bayard Taylor

WATERSPOUT

And oft, while wonder thrill'd my breast, mine eyes
To heaven have seen the watery columns rise,
Slender at first the subtle fume appears,
And, writhing round and round, its volume rears:

STORMY SEAS

Thick as a mast the vapour swells its size;
A curling whirlwind lifts it to the skies:
The tube now straitens, now in width extends,
And in a hovering cloud its summit ends:
Still gulph on gulph in sucks the rising tide,
And now the cloud, with cumbrous weight supplied,
Full-gorg'd, and black'ning, spreads, and moves more slow,
And, waving, trembles to the waves below.
Thus when, to shun the summer's sultry beam,
The thirsty heifer seeks the cooling stream,
The eager horse-leech fixing on her lips,
Her blood, with ardent throat, insatiate sips,
Till the gorg'd glutton, swell'd beyond her size,
Drops from her wounded hold, and, bursting, dies.
So bursts the cloud, o'erloaded with its freight,
And the dash'd ocean staggers with the weight.
But say, ye sages, who can weigh the cause,
And trace the secret springs of nature's laws;
Say, why the wave, of bitter brine erewhile,
Should to the bottom of the deep recoil,
Robb'd of its salt, and from the cloud distil
Sweet as the waters of the limpid rill?
Ye sons of boastful wisdom, fam'd of yore,
Whose feet unwearied wander'd many a shore,
From nature's wonders to withdraw the veil,
Had you with us unfurl'd the daring sail,
Had view'd the wondrous scenes mine eyes survey'd,
What seeming miracles the deep display'd,
What secret virtues various nature show'd,
Oh! with what a fire your page had glow'd!

Luis Camoens

THE STORM

The south and west winds joined, and, as they blew,
Waves like a rolling trench before them threw.
Sooner than you read this line, did the gale,
Like shot, not feared till felt, our sails assail;
And what at first was called a gust, the same
Hath now a storm's, anon a tempest's name.
Jonas, I pity thee, and curse those men,
Who, when the storm raged most, did wake thee then;
Sleep is pain's easiest salve, and doth fulfill
All offices of death, except to kill.
But when I waked, I saw that I saw not;
Ay, and the sun, which should teach me, had forgot
East, west, day, night, and I could only say,
If the world had lasted, now it had been day.
Thousands our noises were, yet we 'mongst all
Could none by his right name, but thunder call.
Lightning was all our light, and it rained more
Than if the sun had drunk the sea before.
Some coffin'd in their cabins lie, equally
Grieved that they are not dead, and yet must die;
And as sin-burdened souls from graves will creep
At the last day, some forth their cabins peep,
And tremblingly ask, "What news?" and do hear so,
Like jealous husbands, what they would not know.
Some, sitting on the hatches, would seem there
With hideous gazing to fear away fear.
Then note they the ship's sicknesses, the mast
Shaked with this ague, and the hold and waist
With a salt dropsy clogged, and all our tacklings

Snapping, like too-high-stretched treble strings,
And from our tattered sails rags drop down so,
As from one hanged in chains a year ago.
Even our ordnance placed for our defence,
Strives to break loose, and 'scape away from thence.
Pumping hath tired our men, and what's the gain?
Seas into seas thrown, we suck in again;
Hearing hath deaf'd our sailors, and if they
Knew how to hear, there's none knows what to say.
Compared to these storms death is but a qualm,
Hell somewhat lightsome, the Bermudas calm.
Darkness, light's elder brother, his birthright
Claims o'er this world, and to heaven hath chased light.
All things are one, and that one none can be,
Since all forms uniform deformity
Doth cover; so that we, except God say
Another Fiat, shall have no more day:
So violent, yet long these furies be.

John Donne

THE WRECK OF THE *HESPERUS*

It was the schooner *Hesperus*,
   That sailed the wintry sea;
And the skipper had taken his little daughter,
   To bear him company.

Blue were her eyes as the fairy-flax,
   Her cheeks like the dawn of day,
And her bosom white as the hawthorn buds,
   That ope in the month of May.

The skipper he stood beside the helm,
   His pipe was in his mouth,
And he watched how the veering flaw did blow
   The smoke now West, now South.

Then up and spake an old Sailòr,
   Had sailed to the Spanish Main,
"I pray thee, put into yonder port,
   For I fear a hurricane.

"Last night, the moon had a golden ring,
   And tonight no moon we see!"
The skipper, he blew a whiff from his pipe,
   And a scornful laugh laughed he.

Colder and louder blew the wind,
   A gale from the Northeast,
The snow fell hissing in the brine,
   And the billows frothed like yeast.

Down came the storm, and smote amain
   The vessel in its strength;
She shuddered and paused, like a frightened steed,
   Then leaped her cable's length.

"Come hither! come hither! my little daughter,
   And do not tremble so;
For I can weather the roughest gale
   That ever wind did blow."

He wrapped her warm in his seaman's coat
   Against the stinging blast;
He cut a rope from a broken spar,
   And bound her to the mast.

"O father! I hear the church-bells ring,
  O say, what may it be?"
" 'T is a fog-bell on a rock-bound coast!"—
  And he steered for the open sea.

"O father! I hear the sound of guns,
  O say, what may it be?"
"Some ship in distress, that cannot live
  In such an angry sea!"

"O father! I see a gleaming light,
  O say, what may it be?"
But the father answered never a word,
  A frozen corpse was he.

Lashed to the helm, all stiff and stark,
  With his face turned to the skies,
The lantern gleamed through the gleaming snow
  On his fixed and glassy eyes.

Then the maiden clasped her hands and prayed
  That savèd she might be;
And she thought of Christ, who stilled the wave,
  On the Lake of Galilee.

And fast through the midnight dark and drear
  Through the whistling sleet and snow,
Like a sheeted ghost, the vessel swept
  Tow'rds the Reef of Norman's Woe.

And ever the fitful gusts between
  A sound came from the land;
It was the sound of the trampling surf
  On the rocks and the hard sea-sand.

The breakers were right beneath her bows,
  She drifted a dreary wreck,
And a whooping billow swept the crew
  Like icicles from her deck.

She struck where the white and fleecy waves
  Looked soft as carded wool,
But the cruel rocks, they gored her side
  Like the horns of an angry bull.

Her rattling shrouds, all sheathed in ice,
  With the masts went by the board;
Like a vessel of glass, she stove and sank,
  Ho! ho! the breakers roared!

At daybreak, on the bleak sea-beach,
  A fisherman stood aghast,
To see the form of a maiden fair,
  Lashed close to a drifting mast.

The salt sea was frozen on her breast,
  The salt tears in her eyes;
And he saw her hair, like the brown sea-weed,
  On the billows fall and rise.

Such was the wreck of the *Hesperus,*
  In the midnight and the snow!
Christ save us all from a death like this,
  On the reef of Norman's Woe!

Henry Wadsworth Longfellow

THE WINTER STORM AT SEA

  View now the winter storm! Above—one cloud
Black and unbroken, all the skies o'ershroud:
The unwieldy porpoise through the day before
Had rolled in view of boding men on shore,
And sometimes hid and sometimes showed his form,
Dark as the cloud and furious as the storm.
  All where the eye delights, yet dreads to roam,
The breaking billows cast the flying foam
Upon the billows rising. All the deep
Is restless change—the waves so swelled and steep,
Breaking and sinking, and the sunken swells,
Nor one, one moment, in its station dwells.
But nearer land you may the billows trace
As if contending in their watery chase;
May watch the mightiest till the shoal they reach,
Then break and hurry to their utmost stretch;
Curled as they come, they strike with furious force
And then reflowing take their grating course
Raking the rounded flints which, ages past,
Rolled by their rage and shall to ages last.
    Far off the petrel in the troubled way
Swims with her brood or flutters in the spray;
She rises often, often drops again,
And sports at ease on the tempestuous main.
  High o'er the restless deep, above the reach
Of gunner's hope, vast flocks of wild-duck stretch.
Far as the eye can glance on either side,
In a broad space and level line they glide;

All in their wedge-like figures from the north,
Day after day, flight after flight, go forth.
Inshore their passage, tribes of sea-gulls urge,
And drop for prey within the sweeping surge;
Oft in the rough opposing blast they fly
Far back, then turn and all their force apply—
While to the storm they give their weak complaining
  cry
Or clap the sleek white pinion to the breast,
And in the restless ocean dip for rest.

  Darkness begins to reign—the louder wind
Appals the weak and awes the firmer mind;
But frights not him whom evening and the spray
In part conceal—yon prowler on his way;
Lo! he has something seen. He runs apace
As if he feared companion in the chase.
He sees his prize. And now he turns again,
Slowly and sorrowing—"Was your search in vain?"
Gruffly he answers, "'Tis a sorry sight!
A seaman's body! There'll be more tonight!"
                                         George Crabbe

BLACK SAILOR'S CHANTY

Yo ho, ma hahties, da's a hurricane a-brewin',
Fo' de cook he hasn't nuffin fo' de sailah-men
  a-stewin',—
He am skulkin' in his bunk, am dat niggah of a cook,
An his chaowdah 'm in de ocean while de pot am on
  de hook.

STORMY SEAS

Yo can chaw a chunk o' hahd-tack mos' as tendah as a brick,
But d'aint no smokin' possum when de cook am lyin' sick.

Ah remembah in de cane-fiel' we hed pone-cakes eb'ry day:
Slack yo line a bit ma hahties!—pull away! pull away!

An' Ah 'low Ah'm feelin' homesick, jes' t' mention ob ma honey,—
She's a libbin' at de cabin an she's out o' clo'es an' money.
While we chaw a chunk o' hahd-tack mos' as tendah as a brick,
But d'aint no smokin' possum while de cook am lyin' sick.

O ma po' neglected Liza an' her picanniny Jo,
Ah's ben roamin' sence Ah left her case Ah wanted fo' to go!
Ah's ben hustlin' roun' de islands, navigatin' all de sea,
While ma honey specs a hungry shark done stuff hisself wid me.

While we chaw a chunk o' hahd-tack mos' as tendah as a brick,
But d'aint no smokin' possum while de cook am lyin' sick.

Charles Keeler

NOR'EASTER

Out in a dark, lost kingdom of their own,
Sea and nor'east weather
Range the beach together

Spilling on foaming, windward shores
The booty of the deep...
Breaking across the sleep

Of gull and child and land-wise men,
Shaking roof and rafter,
In wild laughter

Threatening rows of wind-swept cottages...
Roaring pirate tunes
On down the dunes.

Bianca Bradbury

5. Calm, Sunny Seas

THE SEA—IN CALM

Look what immortal floods the sunset pours
    Upon us! Mark how still (as though in dreams
    Bound) the once wild and terrible Ocean seems!
How silent are the winds! No billow roars,
But all is tranquil as Elysian shores;
    The silver margin which aye runneth round
    The moon-enchanted sea hath here no sound:
Even Echo speaks not on these radiant moors.
What! is the giant of ocean dead,
    Whose strength was all unmatched beneath the sun?
    No: he but rests. Now that his toils are done,
    More quiet than the babbling brooks is he.
So mightiest powers by deepest calms are fed,
    And sleep, how oft, in things that gentlest be.
                      Barry Cornwall

A TROPICAL MORNING AT SEA

Sky in its lucent splendor lifted
    Higher than cloud can be;
Air with no breath of earth to stain it,
    Pure on the perfect sea.

Crests that touch and tilt each other,
  Jostling as they comb;
Delicate crash of tinkling water,
  Broken in pearling foam.

Plashings—or is it the pinewood's whispers,
  Babble of brooks unseen,
Laughter of winds when they find the blossoms,
  Brushing aside the green?

Waves that dip, and dash, and sparkle;
  Foam-wreaths slipping by,
Soft as a snow of broken roses
  Afloat over mirrored sky.

Off to the East the steady sun-track
  Golden meshes fill—
Webs of fire, that lace and tangle,
  Never a moment still.

Liquid palms but clap together,
  Fountains, flower-like, grow—
Limpid bells on stems of silver—
  Out of a slope of snow.

Sea-depths, blue as the blue of violets—
  Blue as a summer sky,
When you blink at its arch sprung over
  Where in the grass you lie.

Dimly an orange bit of rainbow
  Burns where the low west clears,
Broken in air, like a passionate promise
  Born of a moment's tears.

Thinned to amber, rimmed with silver,
   Clouds in the distance dwell,
Clouds that are cool, for all their color,
   Pure as a rose-lipped shell.

Fleets of wool in the upper heavens
   Gossamer wings unfurl;
Sail so high they seem but sleeping
   Over yon bar of pearl.

What would the great world lose, I wonder—
   Would it be missed or no,—
If we stayed in the opal morning,
   Floating forever so?

Swung to sleep by the swaying water,
   Only to dream all day—
Blow, salt wind from the north upstarting,
   Scatter such dreams away!

Edward Rowland Sill

MAY-DAY AT SEA

How do you know that May has come,
   You long sea-lanes of crested blue?
For you no lark has ever sung,
   No hawthorn burst its bud for you.

But sure as ever hawthorn lane,
   Or field where happy lark has sung,
Has quickened through soft April rain
   To flower beneath the warm May sun,

Your hidden gardens of the sea
  Have heard the secret call of May,
And decked their lapis-lazuli
  With crests as white as hawthorn spray.
                              John F. Finerty

SUNRISE AT SEA

    The quick sea shone
And shivered like spread wings of angels blown
By the sun's breath before him; and a low
Sweet gale shook all the foam-flowers of thin snow
As into rainfall of sea-roses shed
Leaf by wild leaf on that green garden-bed
Which tempests till and sea-winds turn and plough
For rosy and fiery round the running prow
Fluttered the flakes and feathers of the spray,
And bloomed like blossoms cast by God away
To waste on the ardent water; swift the moon
Withered to westward as a face in swoon
Death-stricken by glad tidings: and the height
Throbbed and the centre quivered with delight
And the depth quailed with passion as of love,
Till like the heart of some new-mated dove
Air, light, and wave seemed full of burning rest,
With motion as of one God's beating breast.
                      Algernon Charles Swinburne

SONG OF THE GULF STREAM

'Twas Yesterday He made me and Tomorrow I shall die,
An azure ribbon roaming in my course beneath the sky—
The tomb of old sea rovers, where their bones commingled lie.

You're standing out of Boston, Gloucester, any Eastern town—
The spray's akissing rigging and the rollers wash you down?
The tops'ls cracking like a gun?—It's time for you to bear
For the stream of purple bubbles and the glories waiting there.

My babes are always frolicking and skim the surf along;
The dolphins—twins and triplets—join in Ocean's mighty song.
And flashing schools of flying fish the surface deftly clear
When the bow proclaims a holiday and proudly ventures near.

With my wandering purple mountains capped with peaks of fleecy snow,
And the sunset peering through them, it is then the roamers know

Of the land of June eternal and the ballads of the sea—
Little whisperings and beckonings with a spindrift melody.

Where the rolling sun-kissed wool-packs rim the gold horizon 'round,
Sending snowy towers and battlements to the zenith with a bound,
Where the mellow notes of conches hail the sportive water throng
And the roamer's soul is softened by the siren's honeyed song—

Then you're sailing in my kingdom and your soul-strings do I own,
For although you leave my winey flow, you won't be coursing Home
Till you're warming to my heart again and choristers unseen
Give you Welcome to the Glories with the Song of the Gulf Stream.

Francis Alan Ford

THE CLIPPER LOITERED SOUTH
(From "Dauber")

Out of the air a time of quiet came,
Calm fell upon the heaven like a drouth;
The brass sky watched the brassy water flame.
Drowsed as a snail the clipper loitered south
Slowly, with no white bone across her mouth;

No rushing glory, like a queen made bold,
The Dauber strove to draw her as she rolled.

There the four leaning spires of canvas rose,
Royals and skysails lifting, gently lifting,
White like the brightness that a great fish blows
When billows are at peace and ships are drifting;
With mighty jerks that set the shadows shifting,
The courses tugged their tethers: a blue haze
Drifted like ghosts of flocks come down to graze.

There the great skyline made her perfect round,
Notched now and then by the sea's deeper blue;
A smoke-smutch marked a steamer homeward
   bound,
The haze wrought all things to intenser hue.
In tingling impotence the Dauber drew
As all men draw, keen to the shaken soul
To give a hint that might suggest the whole.
John Masefield

CALM MORNING AT SEA

Midocean like a pale blue morning-glory
   Opened wide, wide;
The ship cut softly through the silken surface;
   We watched the white sea-birds ride
Unrocking on the holy virgin water
   Fleckless on every side.
Sara Teasdale

WHITE-CAPPED WAVES

White-capped waves far round the Ocean,
 Leaping in thanks or leaping in play,
All your bright faces, in happy commotion,
 Make glad matins this summer day.

The rosy light through the morning's portals
 Tinges your crest with an August hue,
Calling on us, thought-prisoned mortals,
 Thus to live in the moment too:

For, graceful creatures, you live by dying,
 Save your life when you fling it away,
Flow through all forms, all forms defying,
 And in wildest freedom strict rule obey.

Show us your art, oh genial daughters
 Of solemn Ocean, thus to combine
Freedom and force of rolling waters
 With sharp observance of law divine.
James Freeman Clarke

A CALM SEA

Bright shine the golden summits in the light
Of the noon sun, and lovelier far by night
Their moonlight glories o'er the sea they shed;
Fair is the dark-green deep; by night and day
Unmoved with storms, the peaceful billows play;

The firmament above is bright and clear,
The sea-fowl, lords of water, air, and land,
Joyous alike upon the wing appear
Or when they side the waves, or walk the land;
Beauty and light and joy are everywhere,
There is no sorrow and no sadness here!
Robert Southey

TRANQUIL SEA

Sunlight falls happily upon this sea,
And evening marks it with no deeper stain
Than petals of the moon dropped carelessly
To where the drifting pools of kelp have lain,
And it is hard to quite believe the tale
Of tragic storm and wreck the years have brought
To those who barter life for sea and sail;
For now there is so much of beauty wrought,
So much of quiet beauty... neither you
Nor I shall ever hope to understand
What is His plan to shape the waters through;
The you, whose fate is water, never land;
The I, whose destiny it is to wait
Always a ship... and pray the winds abate.
Claire Aven Thomson

FIVE DEGREES SOUTH

I love all waves and lovely water in motion,
That wavering iris in comb of the blown spray:
Iris of tumbled nautilus in the wake's commotion,
Their spread sails dipped in a marmoreal way
Unquarried, wherein are green bubbles blowing
Plumes of faint spray, cool in the deep
And lucent seas, that pause not in their flowing
To lap the southern starlight while they sleep.
These I have seen, these I have loved and known:
I have seen Jupiter, that great star, swinging
Like a ship's lantern, silent and alone
Within his sea of sky, and heard the singing
Of the south trade, that siren of the air,
Who shivers the taut shrouds, and singeth there.
Francis Brett Young

THE GULF STREAM

They say a tropic river threads the seas
Bearing the strangest things to northern lands:
Vermilion fish, like flowers, with silver bands,
And bronze sea-weed from scarlet coral keys.
Green birds that mock the moon from tall palm trees
Where ghost-gray monkeys hang by cunning hands,
Follow the thinning blue to alien strands
And there among the black pines scream and freeze.

The while this ardent current chills and fails,
Splendors of ice drift slowly south, each one
A frozen torch of borealic fire,
Each one a fairy ship with rainbow sails,
Sinking and fading as it nears the sun
In this relentless river of desire.

Henry Bellamann

UPON THE SHORE

Who has not walked upon the shore,
And who does not the morning know,
The day the angry gale is o'er,
The hour the wind has ceased to blow?

The horses of the strong south-west
Are pastured round his tropic tent,
Careless how long the ocean's breast
Sob on and sigh for passion spent.

The frightened birds, that fled inland
To house in rock and tower and tree,
Are gathering on the peaceful strand,
To tempt again the sunny sea;

Whereon the timid ships steal out
And laugh to find their foe asleep,
That lately scattered them about,
And drave them to the fold like sheep.

The snow-white clouds he northward chased
Break into phalanx, line, and band:
All one way to the south they haste,
The south, their pleasant fatherland.

From distant hills their shadows creep,
Arrive in turn and mount the lea,
And flit across the downs, and leap
Sheer off the cliff upon the sea;

And sail and sail far out of sight.
But still I watch their fleecy trains,
That piling all the south with light,
Dapple in France the fertile plains.

Robert Bridges

SUNRISE AT SEA

When the mild weather came,
  And set the sea on flame,
How often would I rise before the sun,
  And from the mast behold
  The gradual splendors of the sky unfold
Ere the first line of disk had yet begun,
Above the horizon's arc,
  To show its flaming gold,
Across the purple dark!

One perfect dawn how well I recollect,
When the whole east was flecked
With flashing streaks and shafts of amethyst,
While a light crimson mist

Went up before the mounting luminary,
And all the strips of cloud began to vary
Their hues, and all the zenith seemed to ope
As if to show a cope beyond the cope!
  How reverently calm the ocean lay
    At the bright birth of that celestial day!
How every little vapor, robed in state,
Would melt and dissipate
  Before the augmenting ray,
Till the victorious Orb rose unattended,
And every billow was his mirror splendid!
Epes Sargent

A SUMMER NOON AT SEA

A holy stillness, beautiful and deep,
  Reigns in the air and broods upon the ocean;
The worn-out winds are quieted to sleep,
  And not a wave is lifted into motion.

The fleecy clouds hang on the soft blue sky,
  Into fantastic shapes of brilliance moulded,
Pillowed on one another broad and high,
  With the sun's dazzling tresses interfolded.

The sea-bird skims along the glassy tide,
  With sidelong flight and wing of glittering whiteness
Or floats upon the sea, outstretching wide
  A sheet of gold in the meridian brightness.

Our vessel lies, unstirred by wave or blast,
  As she were moored to her dark shadow seeming,
Her pennon twined around the tapering mast,
  And her loose sails like marble drapery gleaming.

How, at an hour like this, the unruffled mind
  Partakes the quiet that is shed around us!
As if the Power that chained the impatient wind
  With the same fetter of respose had bound us!

Epes Sargent

TO THE AFTERNOON MOON, AT SEA

Take care, O wisp of a moon,
Vague on the sunny blue above the sea,
Or the gull flying across you
Will pierce your veil-thin shape with a sharp wing!

Take care, or the wind will wilt you,
As he does the clouds snowily drifting by you,
And diffuse you over the sky, a silvery mist,
To give more cool to the day.

Take care, so near the horizon,
Or a phantom skipper, one who has long been
    drowned,
Will reach above it and seize you
And make you his sail to circle the world for ever!

Take care, take care! for frailty
Is the prey of the strong, and you, a wraith of it,
Have yet a long while to go before nightfall
Brings you to sure effulgence!

Cale Young Rice

CALM

So tame, so languid looks this drowsing sea,
With lazy clouds sprawled in the blue above,
One might proclaim the salt immensity
The soul of peace and love.

So tame, so languid! Can one then believe
Rumors of storms that riot down the night?
Of splintering reefs? and hulls that list and heave
And settle out of sight?

So tame, so languid! Yet as forth we glide
On paths no foamy surges agitate,
I see, like warnings on the vessel's side,
The lifeboats poised in wait!

Stanton A. Coblentz

TROPICAL WEATHER

Now we're afloat upon the tropic sea:
   Here Summer holdeth a perpetual reign.
How flash the waters in their bounding glee!
   The sky's soft purple is without a stain.

Full in our wake the smooth, warm trade-winds
    blowing,
  To their unvarying goal still faithful run;
And, as we steer, with sails before them flowing,
  Nearer the zenith daily climbs the sun,
The startled flying-fish around us skim,
  Glossed like the humming-bird, with rainbow
    dyes;
And, as they dip into the water's brim,
Swift in pursuit the preying dolphin hies.
All, all is fair; and gazing round, we feel
  Over the yielding sense the torrid languor steal.

Epes Sargent

SUNRISE AT SEA

The interminable ocean lay beneath,
At depth immense,—not quiet as before,
For a faint breath of air, e'en at the height
On which I stood scarce felt, play'd over it;
Waking innumerous dimples on its face,
As though 'twere conscious of the splendid guest
That e'en then touched the threshold of heaven's gates,
And smiled to bid him welcome. Far away,
On either hand, the broad-curved beach stretched on;
And I could see the slow-paced waves advance
One after one, and spread upon the sands,
Making a slender edge of pearly foam
Just as they broke; then softly falling back,
Noiseless to me on that tall head of rock,
As it had been a picture, clear descried
Through optic tube, leagues off.

A tender mist
Was round th' horizon and along the vales;
But the hill-tops stood in a crystal air,
The cope of heaven was clear and deeply blue,
And not a cloud was visible. Toward the east
An atmosphere of golden light, that grew
Momently brighter, and intensely bright,
Proclaim'd th' approaching sun. Now, now he comes:
A dazzling point emerges from the sea:
It spreads,—it rises,—now it seems a dome
Of burning gold! Higher and rounder now
It mounts, it swells; now, like a huge balloon
Of light and fire, it rests upon the rim
Of waters,—lingers there a moment, then—
Soars up!
                              Edwin Atherstone

ICEBERGS

They come again, those monsters of the sea,
    The north wind's brood, the children of the cold,
    Long lapped and cradled in white winter's fold,
  As worlds are cradled in eternity;
Lulled by the storm, the Arctic's euphony,
    Launched in hoarse thunder from a mountain mold
    Upon the sea the viking sailed of old,
  They come, the fleet of death, in spring set free.
Strange as the product of some other sphere,
    The huge imaginings the frost has wrought,
    Out of the land of the White Bear emerge;
Seeking the sunlight, from creation's verge
    Southward they wander, silent as a thought,
    And in the Gulf-stream drown and disappear.
                              William Prescott Foster

CALM AS THE CLOUDLESS HEAVEN

It is the midnight hour;—the beauteous sea,
  Calm as the cloudless heaven, the heaven discloses,
While many a sparkling star, in quiet glee,
  Far down within the watery sky reposes.
As if the ocean's heart were stirred
With inward life, a sound is heard,
  Like that of dreamer murmuring in his sleep;
'Tis partly the billow, and partly the air,
That lies like a garment floating fair
  Above the happy deep.
The sea, I ween, cannot be fann'd
By evening freshness from the land,
  For the land is far away;
But God hath will'd that the sky-born breeze
In the centre of the loneliest seas,
  Should ever sport and play.
    The mighty moon, she sits above,
    Encircled with a zone of love,
    A zone of dim and tender light,
    That makes her wakeful eye more bright:
    She seems to shine with a sunny ray,
    And the night looks like a mellow'd day!
    The gracious mistress of the main
    Hath now an undisturbed reign,
    And from her silent throne looks down,
    As upon children of her own,
  On the waves, that lend their gentle breast
  In gladness for her couch of rest!

John Wilson

6. "Roll on,
thou deep and dark
blue Ocean, Roll"

APOSTROPHE TO THE OCEAN

Roll on, thou deep and dark blue Ocean—roll!
Ten thousand fleets sweep over thee in vain;
Man marks the earth with ruin—his control
Stops with the shore;—upon the watery plain
The wrecks are all thy deed, nor doth remain
A shadow of man's ravage, save his own,
When, for a moment, like a drop of rain,
He sinks into thy depths with bubbling groan,
Without a grave, unknell'd, uncoffin'd, and unknown.

His steps are not upon thy paths,—thy fields
Are not a spoil for him,—thou dost arise
And shake him from thee; the vile strength he wields
For earth's destruction thou dost all despise,
Spurning him from thy bosom to the skies,
And send'st him, shivering in thy playful spray,
And howling, to his gods, where haply lies
His petty hope in some near port or bay,
And dashest him again to earth:—there let him lay.

The armaments which thunderstrike the walls
Of rock-built cities, bidding nations quake,
And monarchs tremble in their capitals,
The oak leviathans, whose huge ribs make
Their clay creator the vain title take

Of lord of thee, and arbiter of war;
These are thy toys, and, as the snowy flake,
They melt into thy yeast of waves, which mar
Alike the Armada's pride, or spoils of Trafalgar.

Thy shores are empires, changed in all save thee—
Assyria, Greece, Rome, Carthage, what are they?
Thy waters washed them power while they were
    free,
And many a tyrant since: their shores obey
The stranger, slave, or savage; their decay
Has dried up realms to deserts: not so thou;
Unchangeable save to thy wild waves' play—
Time writes no wrinkles on thine azure brow—
Such as creation's dawn beheld, thou rollest now.

Thou glorious mirror, where the Almighty's form
Glasses itself in tempests; in all time,
Calm, or convulsed—in breeze, or gale, or storm,
Icing the pole, or in the torrid clime
Dark-heaving; boundless, endless, and sublime—
The image of Eternity—the throne
Of the Invisible; even from out thy slime
The monsters of the deep are made; each zone
Obeys thee; thou goest forth, dread, fathomless, alone.

And I have loved thee, Ocean! and my joy
Of youthful sports was on thy breast to be
Borne like thy bubbles, onward: from a boy
I wanton'd with thy breakers—they to me
Were a delight; and if the freshening sea

Made them a terror—'twas a pleasing fear,
For I was as it were a child of thee,
And trusted to thy billows far and near,
And laid my hand upon thy mane—as I do here.
>>Lord Byron

THE LAST CHANTEY

"And there was no more sea"

Thus said the Lord in the Vault above the Cherubim,
Calling to the Angels and the Souls in their degree:
  "Lo! Earth has passed away
  On the smoke of Judgment Day,
That Our word may be established shall We gather up
    the sea?"

Loud sang the souls of the jolly, jolly mariners:
"Plague upon the hurricane that made us furl and flee!
  But the war is done between us,
  In the deep the Lord hath seen us—
Our bones we'll leave the barracout and God may sink
    the sea!"

Then said the soul of Judas that betrayèd Him:
"Lord hast Thou forgotten Thy covenant with me?
  How once a year I go
  To cool me on the floe?
And Ye take my day of mercy if Ye take away the
    sea!"

Then said the soul of the Angel of the Off-shore
    Wind:
(He that bits the thunder when the bull-mouthed
    breakers flee)
  "I have watch and ward to keep
  O'er Thy wonders on the deep,
And Ye take mine honour from me if Ye take away
    the sea!"

Loud sang the souls of the jolly, jolly mariners:
"Nay, but we were angry, and a hasty folk were we!
  If we worked the ship together
  Till she foundered in foul weather,
Are we babes that we should clamour for a vengeance
    on the sea?"

Then said the souls of the slaves that men threw over-
    board:
"Kennelled in the picaroon a weary band were we;
  But Thy arm was strong to save,
  And it touched us on the wave,
And we drowsed the long tides idle till Thy Trumpets
    tore the sea."

Then cried the soul of the stout Apostle Paul to God:
"Once we frapped a ship, and she laboured woundily.
  There were fourteen score of these,
  And they blessed Thee on their knees,
When they learned Thy Grace and Glory under
    Malta by the sea!"

Loud sang the souls of the jolly, jolly mariners:
Plucking at their harps, and they plucked unhandily:
  "Our thumbs are rough and tarred,
  And the tune is something hard—
May we lift a Deepsea Chantey such as seamen use at
    sea?"

Then said the souls of the gentlemen adventurers,
Fettered wrist to bar all for red iniquity:
  "Ho, we revel in our chains
  O'er the sorrow that was Spain's;
Heave or sink it, leave or drink it, we were masters of
    the sea!"

Up spake the soul of a grey Gothavn 'speckshioner—
(He that led the flinching in the fleets of fair Dundee)
  "Oh the ice-blink white and near,
  And the bowhead breaching clear!
Will Ye whelm them all for wantonness that wallow
    in the sea?"

Loud sang the souls of the jolly, jolly mariners,
Crying: "Under Heaven, here is neither lead nor lee;
  Must we sing for evermore
  On the windless, glassy floor?
Take back your golden fiddles and we'll beat to open
    sea!"

Then stooped the Lord, and He called the good sea up
    to Him,
And 'stablished its borders unto all Eternity,

That such as have no pleasure
  For to praise the Lord by measure,
They may enter into galleons and serve Him on the sea.

Sun, wind, and cloud shall fail not from the face of it,
Stinging, ringing spindrift, nor the fulmar flying free;
  And the ships shall go abroad
  To the Glory of the Lord
Who heard the silly sailor-folk and gave them back their sea!

Rudyard Kipling

SEA

Sea is wild marble waiting a stonecutter's hand, chaos crying for symmetry,
For recurrent shapes: the sea is less than mountains and birds
Whose heights and migrations follow laws, return precisely on wings.

Ships etch wild marble, hard prows cutting clear:
Thin veins are open, now deeper than foam; the pattern
Seems forever made. Then in salt curves... the blue annulment.

All other tracings pass, all faint designs depart:
Wind edge, the sun's point, moon fingers on the tide.
Life is averse to these still early waters: the sea
And the world of man are the last voids... pendulous, unborn.

Don Gordon

A HYMN TO THE SEA

I saunter by the shore and lose myself
In the blue waters, stretching on, and on,
Beyond the low-lying headland, dark with woods,
And on to the green waste of sea, content
To be alone—but I am not alone,
For solitude like this is populous,
And its abundant life of sky and sun,
High-floating clouds, low mists, and wheeling birds,
And waves that ripple shoreward all day long,
Whether the tide is setting in or out,
Forever rippling shoreward, dark and bright,
As lights and shadows and the shifting winds
Pursue each other in their endless play,
Is more than the companionship of man.

But thou, O Sea, whose majesty and might
Are mild and beautiful in this still bay,
But terrible in the mid-ocean deeps,
I never see thee but my soul goes out
To thee, and is sustained and comforted;
For she discovers in herself, or thee,
A stern necessity for stronger life,
And strength to live it: she surrenders all
She had, and was, and is possessed of more,
With more to come—endurance, patience, peace.

I love thee, Ocean, and delight in thee,
Thy colour, motion, vastness,—all the eye
Takes in from shore, and on the tossing waves;
Nothing escapes me, not the least of weeds

That shrivels and blackens on the barren sand.
I have been walking on the yellow sands,
Watching the long, white, ragged fringe of foam
The waves had washed up on the curves of beach,
The endless fluctuation of the waves,
The circuit of the seagulls, low, aloft,
Dipping their wings an instant in the brine,
And urging their swift flight to distant woods.
And round and over all the perfect sky,
Clear, cloudless, luminous in the summer noon.

Thou wert before the Continents, before
The hollow heavens, which like another sea
Encircles them, and thee; but whence thou wert,
And when thou wast created, is not known.
Antiquity was young when thou wast old.
There is no limit to thy strength, no end
To thy magnificence. Thou goest forth
On thy long journeys to remotest lands,
And comest back unwearied. Tropic isles,
Thick-set with pillared palms, delay thee not,
Nor arctic icebergs hasten thy return.
Summer and winter are alike to thee,
The settled sullen sorrow of the sky
Empty of light; the laughter of the sun;
The comfortable murmur of the wind
From peaceful countries, and the mad uproar
That storms let loose upon thee in the night
Which they create and quicken with sharp white fire,
And crash of thunders! Thou art terrible
In thy tempestuous moods, when the loud winds
Precipitate their strength against the waves;

They rave, and grapple and wrestle, until at last,
Baffled by their own violence, they fall back,
And thou art calm again, no vestige left
Of the commotion, save the long, slow roll
On summer days on beaches far away.

The heavens look down and see themselves in thee,
And splendors seen not elsewhere, that surround
The rising and the setting of the sun
Along thy vast and solitary realms.
The blue dominion of the air is thine,
And thine the pomps and pageants of the day,
The light, the glory, the magnificence,
The congregated masses of the clouds,
Islands, and mountains, and long promontories,
Floating at inaccessible heights whereto
Thy fathomless deeps are shallow—all are thine.
And thine the silent, happy, awful night,
When over thee and thy charmed waves the moon
Rides high, and when the last of stars is gone,
And darkness covers all things with its pall—
Darkness that was before the worlds were made,
And will be after they are dead.
Richard Henry Stoddard

THE TRACKLESS DEEPS

Those trackless deeps, where many a weary sail
Has seen, above the illimitable plain,
Morning and night, and night on morning rise;
Whilst still no land to greet the wanderer spread

>   Its shadowy mountains on the sun-bright sea,
>   Where the loud roaring of the tempest-waves
>   So long have mingled with the gusty wind
>   In melancholy loneliness, and swept
>   The desert of those ocean solitudes;
>   But, vocal to the sea-bird's harrowing shriek,
>   The bellowing monster and the rushing storm,
>   Now to the sweet and many-mingling sounds
>   Of kindliest human impulses respond.
>
>   *Percy Bysshe Shelley*

HYMN TO THE SEA

I.

Grant, O regal in bounty, a subtle and delicate largess;
    Grant an ethereal alms, out of the wealth of thy soul:
Suffer a tarrying minstrel, who finds, not fashions his numbers,—
    Who, from the commune of air, cages the volatile song,—
Here to capture and prison some fugitive breath of thy descant,
    Thine and his own as thy roar lisped on the lips of a shell,
Now while the vernal impulsion makes lyrical all that hath language,
    While, through the veins of the Earth, riots the ichor of Spring,
While, with throes, with raptures, with loosing of bonds, with unsealings,—

Arrowy pangs of delight, piercing the core of the
 world,—
Tremors and coy unfoldings, reluctances, sweet agita-
 tions,—
 Youth, irrepressibly fair, wakes like a wondering
 rose.

II.

Lover whose vehement kisses on lips irresponsive are
 squandered,
 Lover that wooest in vain Earth's imperturbable
 heart;
Athlete mightily frustrate, who pittest thy thews
 against legions,
 Locked with fantastical hosts, bodiless arms of the
 sky;
Sea that breakest for ever, that breakest and never art
 broken,
 Like unto thine, from of old, springeth the spirit of
 man,—
Nature's wooer and fighter, whose years are a suit and
 a wrestling,
 All their hours, from his birth, hot with desire and
 with fray;
Amorist agonist man, that, immortally pining and
 striving,
 Snatches the glory of life only from love and from
 war;
Man that, rejoicing in conflict, like thee when precipi-
 tate tempest,
 Charge after thundering charge, clangs on thy reso-
 nant mail,

Seemeth so easy to shatter, and proveth so hard to be cloven;
  Man whom the gods, in his pain, curse with a soul that endures;
Man whose deeds, to the doer, come back as thine own exhalations
  Into thy bosom return, weepings of mountain and vale;
Man with the cosmic fortunes and starry vicissitudes tangled,
  Chained to the wheel of the world, blind with the dust of its speed,
Even as thou, O giant, whom trailed in the wake of her conquests
  Night's sweet despot draws, bound to her ivory car;
Man with inviolate caverns, impregnable holds in his nature,
  Depths no storm can pierce, pierced with a shaft of the sun:
Man that is galled with his confines, and burdened yet more with his vastness,
  Born too great for his ends, never at peace with his goal;
Man whom Fate, his victor, magnanimous, clement in triumph,
  Holds as a captive king, mewed in a palace divine:
Wide its leagues of pleasance, and ample of purview its windows;
  Airily falls, in its courts, laughter of fountains at play;
Nought, when the harpers are harping, untimely reminds him of durance;

None, as he sits at the feast, whisper Captivity's
name;
But, would he parley with Silence, withdraw for awhile
unattended,
Forth to the beckoning world 'scape for an hour and
be free,
Lo, his adventurous fancy coercing at once and pro-
voking,
Rise the unscalable walls, built with a word at the
prime;
Lo, immobile as statues, with pitiless faces of iron,
Armed at each obstinate gate, stand the impassable
guards.

III.

Miser whose coffered recesses the spoils of eternity
cumber,
Spendthrift foaming thy soul wildly in fury away,—
We, self-amorous mortals, our own multitudinous
image
Seeking in all we behold, seek it and find it in thee:
Seek it and find it when o'er us the exquisite fabric of
Silence
Perilous-turreted hangs, trembles and dulcetly falls;
When the aërial armies engage amid orgies of music,
Braying of arrogant brass, whimper of querulous
reeds;
When, at his banquet, the Summer is purple and
drowsed with repletion;
When, to his anchorite board, taciturn Winter re-
pairs;
When by the tempest are scattered magnificent ashes
of Autumn;

When, upon orchard and lane, breaks the white
    foam of the Spring:
When, in extravagant revel, the Dawn, a bacchante up-
    leaping,
  Spills, on the tresses of Night, vintages golden and
    red;
When, as a token at parting, munificent Day, for re-
    membrance,
  Gives, unto men that forget, Ophirs of fabulous ore;
When, invincibly rushing, in luminous palpitant deluge,
  Hot from the summits of Life, poured is the lava of
    noon;
When, as yonder, thy mistress, at height of her mutable
    glories,
  Wise from the magical East, comes like a sorceress
    pale.
Ah, she comes, she arises,—impassive, emotionless,
    bloodless,
  Wasted and ashen of cheek, zoning her ruins with
    pearl.
Once she was warm, she was joyous, desire in her
    pulses abounding:
  Surely thou lovedst her well, then, in her conquering
    youth!
Surely not all unimpassioned, at sound of thy rough
    serenading,
  She, from the balconied night, unto her melodist
    leaned,—
Leaned unto thee, her bondsman, who keepest to-day
    her commandments,
  All for the sake of old love, dead at thy heart though
    it lie.

IV.

Yea, it is we, light perverts, that waver, and shift our
    allegiance;
  We, whom insurgence of blood dooms to be barren
      and waste;
We, unto Nature imputing our frailties, our fever and
    tumult;
  We, that with dust of our strife sully the hue of her
      peace.
Thou, with punctual service, fulfillest thy task, being
    constant;
  Thine but to ponder the Law, labour and greatly
      obey:
Wherefore, with leapings of spirit, thou chantest the
    chant of the faithful,
  Chantest aloud at thy toil, cleansing the Earth of her
      stain;
Leagued in antiphonal chorus with stars and the popu-
    lous Systems,
  Following these as their feet dance to the rhyme of
      the Suns;
Thou thyself but a billow, a ripple, a drop of that
    Ocean,
  Which, labyrinthine of arm, folding us meshed in
      its coil,
Shall, as now, with elations, august exultations and ar-
    dours,
  Pour, in unfaltering tide, all its unanimous waves,
When, from this threshold of being, these steps of the
    Presence, this precinct,
  Into the matrix of Life darkly divinely resumed,

Man and his littleness perish, erased like an error and cancelled,
 Man and his greatness survive, lost in the greatness of God.

Sir William Watson

UNFATHOMABLE SEA!

Unfathomable Sea! whose waves are years!
 Ocean of Time, whose waters of deep woe
Are brackish with the salt of human tears!
 Thou shoreless flood which in thy ebb and flow
Claspest the limits of mortality,
And, sick of prey, yet howling on for more,
Vomitest thy wrecks on its inhospitable shore!
Treacherous in calm, and terrible in storm,
 Who shall put forth on thee,
  Unfathomable Sea?

Percy Bysshe Shelley

THE BEATIFIC SEA

Old ocean was
Infinity of ages ere we breathed
Existence; and he will be beautiful
When all the living world that sees him now
Shall roll unconscious dust around the sun.
Quelling from age to age the vital throb
In human hearts, Death shall not subjugate
The pulse that dwells in his tremendous breast,

Or interdict his minstrelsy to sound
In thundering concert with the quiring winds.
But long as man to parent Nature owns
Instinctive homage, and in times beyond
The power of thought to reach, bard after bard
Shall sing thy glory, beatific Sea!
Thomas Campbell

THE OCEAN

How beautiful!—from his blue throne on high,
   The sun looks downward with a face of love
Upon the silent waters—and a sky,
   Lovelier than that which lifts its arch above,
Down the far depths of Ocean, like a sheet
   Of flame, is trembling!—the wild tempests cease
To wave their cloudy pinions!—Oh, 'tis sweet
   To gaze on Ocean in his hour of peace.

Years have gone by, since first my infant eyes
   Rested upon those waters. Once again,
As here I muse, the hours of childhood rise
   Faint o'er my memory, like some witching strain
Of half-forgotten music. Yon blue wave
   Still, still rolls on in beauty—but the tide
Of years rolls darkling o'er the lonely grave
   Of Hopes, that with my life's bright morning died!

Look! look!—the clouds' light shadows from above,
   Like fairy Islands, o'er the waters sweep!—
Oh I have dream'd my spirit thus could love
   To float for ever on the boundless deep,

Communing with the elements;—to hear,
    At midnight hour, the death-wing'd tempest rave,
Or gaze, admiring, on each starry sphere,
    Glassing its glories in the mirror wave;—

To dream—dream-mingling with the shades of eve—
    On Ocean's spirits, caves, and coral halls,
Where, cold and dark, the eternal billows heave,
    No zephyr breathes, nor struggling sunbeam falls;—
As round some far Isle of the burning zone,
    Where tropic groves perfume the breath of morn,
List to the Ocean's melancholy tone,
    Like a lone mourner's on the night-winds borne;—

To see the infant wave on yon blue verge,
    Like a young eagle, breast the sinking sun,
And twilight dying on the crimson surge,
    Till, down the deep dark zenith, one by one,
The lights of heaven were streaming;—or to weep,
    The lost, the beautiful, that calmly rest
Beneath the eternal wave—then sink to sleep,
    Hush'd by the beating of the Ocean's breast.

Oh it were joy to wander wild and free
    Where southern billows in the sunlight flash
Or Night sits brooding o'er the northern sea,
    And all is still, save the o'erwhelming dash
Of that dark world of waters; there to view
    The meteor hanging from its cloud on high,
Or see the northern fires, with blood-red hue,
    Shake their wild tresses o'er the startled sky!

"ROLL ON...."

'Tis sweet, 'tis sweet to gaze upon the deep,
   And muse upon its mysteries. There it roll'd
Ere yet that glorious sun had learn'd to sweep
   The blue profound, and bathe the heavens in gold;—
The morning stars, as up the skies they came,
   Heard their first music o'er the ocean rung,
And saw the first flash of their new-born flame
   Back from its depths in softer brightness flung!

And there it rolls!—Age after age has swept
   Down, down the eternal cataract of Time,
Men after men on earth's cold bosom slept,
   Still *there* it rolls, unfading and sublime!
As bright those waves their sunny sparkles fling,
   As sweetly now the bending heaven they kiss,
As when the Holy Spirit's boding wing
   Moved o'er the waters of the vast abyss!

There, *there* it rolls.—I've seen the clouds unfurl
   Their raven banner from the stormy west—
I've seen the wrathful Tempest Spirit hurl
   His blue fork'd lightnings at the Ocean's breast;
The storm-cloud pass'd—the sinking wave was hush'd—
   Those budding isles were glittering fresh and fair—
Serenely bright the peaceful waters blush'd,
   And heaven seem'd painting its own beauties there!

Ocean farewell!—Upon thy mighty shore,
   I loved in childhood's fairy hours to dwell!
But I am wasting—life will soon be o'er,
   And I shall cease to gaze on thee—farewell!—

Thou still wilt glow as fair as now—the sky
  Still arch as proudly o'er thee—Evening steal
Along thy bosom with as soft a dye—
  All be as now—but I shall cease to feel.

The evening mists are on their silent way,
  And thou art fading;—faint thy colors blend
With the last tinges of the dying day,
  And deeper shadows up the skies ascend;—
Farewell!—farewell!—the night is coming fast—
  In deeper tones thy wild notes seem to swell
Upon the cold wings of the rising blast—
  I go—I go—dear Ocean, fare thee well!

George D. Prentice

THE WAVE

Out of the darkness of time and the stress of an impulse unending,
  Out of the deep I arise, and shoreward unresting I roll;
Till the breaker resounds on the beach and it curls and it crashes descending,
  And rending the sands it subsides; and is scattered and swept from its goal.

I am the impact of light on your eyes, and the glow and the gleam of the vision.
  I am a second of sound and the echo that stirs in the brain;

And the past that awakes and regrets and aspires; and
  the hope of a harbor Elysian,
 Lost and recalled and disowned and restored,
  through a lifetime of passion and pain.

I am the march of events past the purpose that cradles
  creation;
 At the end of your millions of lives like the foam
  bells that whiten and fade;
And the roll of the drums down the ranks, and the
  charge of the steel crested wrath of a nation.
 I am the wailing of women that bury their dead in
  the shade.

I am the round of the seasons; the rose of the summer
  unfolding;
 Swelling of sap in the spring, and its shrinkage when
  winter turns white.
I am the song of your youth, and your autumn its
  bleakness beholding,
 I am the burden and the heat of the day, and the
  shadows and dreams of the night.

I am the beat of your heart, and the breath that you
  draw when the morning
 Rises in fire on the hills; and the setting of moon,
  and of sun.
I am the crest of today, and the fortune that fails
  without warning;
 And the triumph that fades; and the struggle with
  death; and the rest when the battle is done.

I am the spray that is scattered; the laughter and loves
 of the city.
 I am the darkness below and the lives that the weight
  of the world shall sustain.
I am the sorrow that sobs in the sea, and the tides of an
 infinite pity;
 And the whisper of winds, and the smile of a child,
  and the ripple and rush of the rain.

I am the passion whose strength is a snare, and the love
 whose redemption is friendless,
 I am your soul's resurrection from sin and from
  shame and the grave;
Growth of the grain, and the travail of life that toils
 through eternities endless.
 I am the pulse of the cosmos whose life is to God
  as a wave.

John Curtis Underwood

7. Nautica Mystica

PSALM CVII

Verses 23 ... 30

They that go down to the sea in ships, that do business
  in great waters;
These see the works of the Lord, and his wonders in
  the deep.
For he commandeth, and raiseth the stormy wind,
  which lifteth up the waves thereof.
They mount up to the heaven, they go down again to
  the depths: their soul is melted because of trouble.
They reel to and fro, and stagger like a drunken man,
  and are at their wit's end.
Then they cry unto the Lord in their trouble, and he
  bringeth them out of their distresses.
He maketh the storm a calm, so that the waves thereof
  are still.
Then are they glad because they be quiet; so he
  bringeth them unto their desired haven.

DAWN ON MID-OCEAN

Veiled are the heavens, veiled the throne,
  The sacred spaces of the vast
And virgin sea make sullen moan
  Into the Void whence God has passed.

With His right hand He wakened it,
  The sorrowing Deep, to sweet dismay,—
And sighed; with His left hand He lit
  The stars in heaven, and took His way,

Leaving this loveliness behind:
  The inconsolable Vacancy
Bears witness in the veiled night and blind
  To some departed Mystery.

Disconsolate for One withdrawn,
  Moan the vague mouths. One cold and clear
Star, like a lamp, in the pale dawn
  Trembles for passion: God was here!
John Hall Wheelock

THE SECRET OF THE DEEPS

We sailed by the old world's tideways, down through the long sea-lanes,
  Into the ends of the south, over horizons new;
Deeper the skies rose o'er us, and round us the ocean plains
  Were held in a lonelier silence and folded in softer blue.

There are no farther skies, no lonelier seas to seek,
  Never a bourne remoter for wandering sail to find.
But we hear no voice that is new,—the wind and the water speak
  As they spoke of old on the seas of the world we left behind.

The mystery eternal, that troubled the world of old,
  Here, in the midnight stillness, moves on the unknown deeps;
And here the ancient secret, that never to man was told,
  The rose of the morning treasures, the blue of the noonday keeps.

Haply, we think, the secret may be shown to us here and now,
  Far from the land's disquiet and the world's unresting crowds:
And near it seemed in the whisper of ripples beneath the bow;
  Half won, then lost, in the sighing of wind at night in the shrouds.

When the sea began to reveal it, when its azure almost gave
  The key, a wandering cloud stole it, bore it afar.
And again we had all but read it in the track of a star on the wave,
  And lo! it was gone, aloof in the silence beyond the star.

So passed we out of that ocean, as guests from a dim-lit hall
  When the night is late, and the sound of the music is heard no more,
And ghostly voices whisper, and soundless footsteps fall,
  Under the silent roof-tree, over the windy floor.

Sidney Royse Lysaght

THE CHAMBERED NAUTILUS

This is the ship of pearl, which, poets feign,
   Sails the unshadowed main,—
   The venturous bark that flings
On the sweet summer wind its purpled wings
In gulfs enchanted, where the Siren sings,
   And coral reefs lie bare,
Where the cold sea-maids rise to sun their streaming
      hair.

Its webs of living gauze no more unfurl;
   Wrecked is the ship of pearl!
   And every chambered cell,
Where its dim dreaming life was wont to dwell,
As the frail tenant shaped his growing shell,
   Before thee lies revealed,—
Its irised ceiling rent, its sunless crypt unsealed!

Year after year beheld the silent toil
   That spread his lustrous coil;
   Still, as the spiral grew,
He left the past year's dwelling for the new,
Stole with soft step its shining archway through,
   Built up its idle door,
Stretched in his last-found home, and knew the old no
      more.

Thanks for the heavenly message brought by thee,
   Child of the wandering sea,
   Cast from her lap, forlorn!
From thy dead lips a clearer note is born

Than ever Triton blew from wreathèd horn!
   While on mine ear it rings,
Through the deep caves of thought I hear a voice that
      sings:—

Build thee more stately mansions, O my soul,
   As the swift seasons roll!
   Leave thy low-vaulted past!
Let each new temple, nobler than the last,
Shut thee from heaven with a dome more vast,
   Till thou at length art free,
Leaving thine outgrown shell by life's unresting sea!
                 Oliver Wendell Holmes

THE SEA IS HIS

Almighty Wisdom made the land
Subject to man's disturbing hand,
And left it all for him to fill
With marks of his ambitious will,
But differently devised the sea
Unto an unlike destiny.

Urgent and masterful ashore,
Man dreams and plans,
And more and more,
As ages slip away, earth shows
How need by satisfaction grows,
And more and more its patient face
Mirrors the driving human race.

But he who ploughs the abiding deep
No furrow leaves, nor stays to reap.
Unmarred and unadorned, the sea
Rolls on as irresistibly
As when, at first, the shaping thought
Of God its separation wrought.

Down to its edge the lands-folk flock,
And in its salt embraces mock
Sirius, his whims. Forever cool,
Its depths defy the day-star's rule:
Serene it basks while children's hands
Its margin score and pit its sands.

And ever in it life abides,
And motion. To and fro its tides,
Borne down with waters, ever fare.
However listless hangs the air,
Still, like a dreamer, all at rest,
Rises and falls the ocean's breast.

Benign, or roused by savage gales;
Fog veiled, or flecked with gleaming sails;
A monster ravening for its prey,
Anon, the nations' fair highway—
In all its moods, in all its might,
'Tis the same sea that first saw light.

The sea the Tyrians dared explore;
The sea Odysseus wandered o'er;
The sea the cruising Northmen harried,
That Carthage wooed, and Venice married;
Across whose wastes, by faith led on,
Columbus tracked the westering sun.

NAUTICA MYSTICA

Great nurse of freedom, breeding men,
Who dare, and baffled, strive again!
A rampart round them in their youth,
A refuge in their straits and ruth,
And in their seasoned strength, a road
To carry liberty abroad.

When all about thy billows lie,
Sole answer to the questioning eye,
To where the firmament its bound
Stretches their heaving masses round,
With that above, and only thee,
Fixed in thine instability—

Then timely to the soul of man
Come musings on the eternal plan
Which man himself was made to fit,
And earth and waters under it;
Wherewith in harmony they move,
And only they, whose guide is love.

Who made the plan and made the sea
Denied not man a destiny
To match his thought. Though mists obscure
And storms retard, the event is sure.
Each surging wave cries evermore
"Death, also, has its further shore!"

Edward Sandford Martin

DOVER BEACH

The sea is calm tonight.
The tide is full, the moon lies fair
Upon the straits;—on the French coast the light
Gleams and is gone; the cliffs of England stand,
Glimmering and vast, out in the tranquil bay.
Come to the window, sweet is the night-air!
Only, from the long line of spray
Where the sea meets the moon-blanch'd sand,
Listen! you hear the grating roar
Of pebbles which the waves draw back, and fling,
At their return, up the high strand,
Begin, and cease, and then again begin,
With tremulous cadence slow, and bring
The eternal note of sadness in.

Sophocles long ago
Heard it on the Ægean, and it brought
Into his mind the turbid ebb and flow
Of human misery; we
Find also in the sound a thought,
Hearing it by this distant northern sea.

The sea of faith
Was once, too, at the full, and round earth's shore
Lay like the folds of a bright girdle furl'd.
But now I only hear
Its melancholy, long, withdrawing roar,
Retreating, to the breath
Of the night-winds, down the vast edges drear
And naked shingles of the world.

Ah, love, let us be true
To one another! for the world, which seems
To lie before us like a land of dreams,
So various, so beautiful, so new,
Hath really neither joy, nor love, nor light,
Nor certitude, nor peace, nor help for pain;
And we are here as on a darkling plain
Swept with confus'd alarms of struggle and flight,
Where ignorant armies clash by night.
Matthew Arnold

QUA CURSUM VENTUS

As ships becalmed at eve, that lay,
    With canvas drooping, side by side,
Two towers of sail at dawn of day
    Are scarce, long leagues apart, descried;

When fell the night, upsprung the breeze,
    And all the darkling hours they plied,
Nor dreamt but each the selfsame seas
    By each was cleaving, side by side:

E'en so—but why the tale reveal
    Of those whom, year by year unchanged,
Brief absence joined anew to feel,
    Astounded, soul from soul estranged?

At dead of night their sails were filled,
    And onward each, rejoicing, steered:
Ah! neither blame; for neither willed
    Or wist what first with dawn appeared.

To veer, how vain! On, onward strain,
  Brave barks! In light, in darkness too,
Through winds and tides, one compass guides:
  To that and your own selves be true.

But, O blithe breeze! and O great seas!
  Though ne'er, that earliest parting past,
On your wide plain they join again,
  Together lead them home at last!

One port, methought, alike they sought,
  One purpose hold, where'er they fare:
O bounding breeze! O rushing seas!
  At last, at last, unite them there!

Arthur Hugh Clough

GULF-WEED

A weary weed, tossed to and fro,
  Drearily drenched in the ocean brine,
Soaring high and sinking low,
  Lashed along without will of mine;
Sport of the spoom of the surging sea;
  Flung on the foam, afar and anear,
Mark my manifold mystery,—
  Growth and grace in their place appear.

I bear round berries, gray and red,
  Rootless and rover though I be;
My spangled leaves, when nicely spread,
  Arboresce as a trunkless tree;

Corals curious coat me o'er,
  White and hard in apt array;
Mid the wild waves' rude uproar,
  Gracefully grow I, night and day.

Hearts there are on the sounding shore,
  Something whispers soft to me,
Restless and roaming for evermore,
  Like this weary weed of the sea;
Bear they yet on each beating breast
  The eternal type of the wondrous whole—
Growth unfolding amidst unrest,
  Grace informing with silent soul.

Cornelius George Fenner

A CHRISTMAS DAWN AT SEA

The tireless flight of a pursuing gull,
The incessant, rhythmic motion of the sea,
The calm vouchsafed us by the morning lull,
Fill this glad Dawn with holy charity—
The Dawn we humbly dedicate on earth
To mark the Mystery of the Christ-Child's birth.

Somewhere beyond, His quiet eyes survey
This little ship upon this little sea;
Watch each soul set upon its little way
Forgetful of His Son's sublimity,
Forgetful, maybe, that upon this day
A Child stretched out His arms that we might pray!

Evan Morgan

IF I COULD GRASP A WAVE FROM THE GREAT SEA

If I could grasp a wave from the great sea,
Mold it a precious stone of faultless blue,
And with a lapidary's art could hew
Away each useless fragment skillfully,
The beauty its pellucid depths would hold
Of molten fire and agony of ice,
Of storm and calm, of love and sacrifice,
Would make a gem whose splendor none has told.

The sea has mirrored all known loveliness
Of sun and moon and stars, of day and night,
Of terror and the wind—the mystery
Of Aphrodite, born of the waves' caress;
And more than these, that flame holy and white,
The face of Him who walked on Galilee.

John Richard Moreland

O MARINERS!

"Death is a voyage," I heard it lightly told,
"Across an ocean conquered by the heart
Of faith, that finds beyond, the realms of gold."
But in this world death has no counterpart,
And abject is each poor analogy...
From mariners upon that mightier main
We have no tidings of discovery...
We only know that they come not again.

Da Gama, to what vaster Orient,—
Magellan, to what fabulous ports of morn,—
Came you on circling death's Dark Continent?
Came you on rounding death's stupendous Horn?
They for Eternity were outward bound:
Great as the quest should be the glory found.
Archibald Rutledge

THE OCEAN

Likeness of heaven!
Agent of power!
Man is thy victim,
Shipwrecks thy dower!
Spices and jewels
From valley and sea,
Armies and banners,
Are buried in thee!

What are the riches
Of Mexico's mines
To the wealth that far down
In the deep water shines?
The proud navies that cover
The conquering West—
Thou fling'st them to death
With one heave of thy breast.

From the high hills that vizor
Thy wreck-making shore,—
When the bride of the mariner
Shrieks at thy roar,

When, like lambs in the tempest
Or mews in the blast,
O'er thy ridge-broken billows
The canvas is cast,—

How humbling to one
With a heart and a soul,
To look on thy greatness,
And list to its roll;
To think how that heart
In cold ashes shall be,
While the voice of eternity
Rises from thee!

Yes! where are the cities
Of Thebes and of Tyre
Swept from the nations
Like sparks from the fire;
The glory of Athens,
The splendor of Rome,
Dissolved—and for ever—
Like dew in thy foam.

But thou art almighty—
Eternal—sublime—
Unweakened—unwasted—
Twin-brother of Time!
Fleets, tempests, nor nations
Thy glory can bow;
As the stars first beheld thee,
Still chainless art thou!

But hold! when thy surges
No longer shall roll,
And that firmament's length
Is drawn back like a scroll;
Then—then shall the spirit
That sighs by thee now,
Be more mighty, more lasting,
More chainless than thou!

John Augustus Shea

AT SEA

The night was made for cooling shade,
   For silence, and for sleep;
And when I was a child, I laid
My hands upon my breast, and pray'd,
   And sank to slumbers deep.
Childlike, as then, I lie tonight,
And watch my lonely cabin-light.

Each movement of the swaying lamp
   Shows how the vessel reels,
As o'er her deck the billows tramp,
And all her timbers strain and cramp
   With every shock she feels;
It starts and shudders, while it burns,
And in its hingèd socket turns.

Now swinging slow, and slanting low,
   It almost level lies:
And yet I know, while to and fro

I watch the seeming pendule go
  With restless fall and rise,
The steady shaft is still upright,
Poising its little globe of light.

O hand of God! O lamp of peace!
  O promise of my soul!
Though weak and toss'd, and ill at ease
Amid the roar of smiting seas,—
  The ship's convulsive roll,—
I own, with love and tender awe,
Yon perfect type of faith and law.

A heavenly trust my spirit calms,—
  My soul is fill'd with light;
The ocean sings his solemn psalms;
The wild winds chant; I cross my palms;
  Happy, as if tonight,
Under the cottage-roof again,
I heard the soothing summer rain.
John T. Trowbridge

A SONG OF THE WAVE

This is the song of the wave! The mighty one!
Child of the soul of silence, beating the air to sound.
White as a live terror, as a drawn sword,
                    This is the wave!

NAUTICA MYSTICA

This is the song of the wave, the white maned steed
   of the Tempest,
Whose veins are swollen with life,
In whose flanks abide the four winds,
                      This is the wave!

This is the song of the wave! The dawn leaped out of
   the sea
And the waters lay smooth as a silver shield,
And the sun-rays smote on the waters like a golden
   sword.
Then a wind blew out of the morning
               And the waters rustled
                             And the wave was born!

This is the song of the wave! The wind blew out of
   the noon,
And the white sea-birds like driven foam
Winged in from the ocean that lay beyond the sky;
And the face of the waters was barred with white,
              For the wave had many brothers,
And the wave leaped up in its strength
To the chant of the choral air:
                          This is the wave!

This is the song of the wave! The wind blew out of
   the sunset
And the west was lurid as Hell;
The black clouds closed like a tomb, for the sun was
   dead.
Then the wind smote full as the breath of God,
              And the wave called to its brothers,
                      "This is the crest of life!"

This is the song of the wave, that rises to fall,
Rises a sheer green wall like a barrier of glass
That has caught the soul of the moonlight,
Caught and prisoned the moonbeams.
And its edge is frittered with blossoms of foam—
                    This is the wave!

This is the song of the wave, of the wave that falls,
Wild as a burst of day-gold blown through the colors
    of morning;
It shivers in infinite jewels, in eddies of wind-driven
    foam
Up the rumbling steep of sand—
                    This is the wave!

This is the song of the wave, that died in the fulness
    of life.
The prodigal this, that lavished its largess of strength
            In the lust of attainment.
Aiming at things for Heaven too high,
Sure in the pride of life, in the richness of strength.
So tried it the impossible height, till the end was
    found:
When ends the soul that yearns for the fillet of morn-
    ing stars—
The soul in the toils of the journeying worlds,
Whose eye is filled with the Image of God—
                    And the end is death!
                George Cabot Lodge

OVER ALL THE FACE OF
EARTH MAIN OCEAN FLOWED

                    Over all the face of earth
Main ocean flow'd, not idle, but with warm
Prolific humor soft'ning all her globe
Fermented the great mother to conceive,
Satiate with genial moisture, when God said,
Be gather'd now, ye waters under heaven,
Into one place, and let dry land appear.
Immediately the mountains huge appear
Emergent, and their broad bare backs upheave
Into the clouds, their tops ascend the sky.
So high as heav'd the tumid hills, so low
Down sunk a hollow bottom broad and deep,
Capacious bed of waters: thither they
Hasted with glad precipitance, uproll'd
As drops on dust conglobing from the dry:
Part rise in crystal wall, or ridge direct,
For haste; such flight the great command imprest
On the swift floods: as armies at the call
Of trumpet, for of armies thou hast heard,
Troop to their standard, so the wat'ry throng,
Wave rolling after wave, where way they found;
If steep, with torrent rapture, if through plain,
Soft-ebbing; nor withstood them rock or hill,
But they, or under ground, or circuit wide
With serpent error wand'ring, found their way,
And on the washy ooze deep channels wore,
Easy, ere God had bid the ground be dry,

All but within those banks, where rivers now
Stream, and perpetual draw their humid train.
The dry land Earth, and the great receptacle
Of congregated waters He call'd Seas.

John Milton

DEEP SEA SOUNDINGS

Mariner, what of the deep?
                        This of the deep:
Twilight is there, and solemn changeless calm;
Beauty is there, and tender, healing balm—
Balm with no root in earth, or air, or sea,
Poised by the finger of God, it floateth free,
And, as it threads the waves, the sound doth rise,—
Hither shall come no further sacrifice;
Never again the anguished clutch at life,
Never again great Love and Death in strife;
He who hath suffered all need fear no more;
Quiet his portion now forevermore.

Mariner, what of the deep?
                        This of the deep:
Solitude dwells not there, though silence reign,
Mighty is the brotherhood of loss and pain;
There is communion past the need of speech,
There is love no words of love can reach;
Heavy the waves that superincumbent press,
But as we labor here with constant stress,

Hand doth hold out to hand not help alone,
But the deep bliss of being fully known.
There are no kindred like the kin of sorrow,
There is no hope like theirs who know no morrow.

Mariner, what of the deep?
                      This of the deep:
Though we have travelled past the line of day,
Glory of night doth light us on our way,
Radiance that comes not how nor whence,
Rainbows without rain, past duller sense,
Music of hidden reefs and waves long past,
Thunderous organ tones from far-off blast,
Harmony, victrix, throned in state sublime,
Couched on the wrecks be-gemmed with pearls of time;
Never a wreck but brings some beauty here;
Down where the waves are stilled the sun shines clear;
Deeper than life, the plan of life doth lie;
He who knows all, fears not. Great Death shall die.
Sarah Williams

THE MASTER SPIRIT

Give me a spirit that on life's rough sea
Loves to have his sails filled with a lusty wind,
Even till his sail-yards tremble, his masts crack,
And his rapt ship run on her side so low
That she drinks water, and her keel ploughs air.
There is no danger to a man who knows

What life and death is; there's not any law
Exceeds his knowledge; neither is it lawful
That he should stoop to any other law;
He goes before them and commands them all,
That to himself is a law rational.

George Chapman

SEA-VOYAGE

To what dark purpose was the will employed
  That fashioned, ere the dawn of time grew dim,
  The waste of ocean—from clear rim to rim
A crystal chamber, sorrowful and void?

For, surely, not without design He wrought
  These vast horizons on whose margins rest
  The extremes of heaven, nor from east to west
Widened the waters to the bounds of thought.

Half-hopeful, half-incredulous, I wait
  For some gigantic presence to assume
  His throne, in the large circle of the room.
The dreadful distances are desolate.

In vain! In vain! He is departed hence,
  Whose breath troubles the waters of the sea:
  Twilight and night are sworn to secrecy,
The heavens preserve their ancient innocence.

In the enormous throne-room of the sun
  No voice is audible. The waves are mute.
  Solitude, infinite and absolute,
Bears witness to the unreturning One.

NAUTICA MYSTICA

Evening, on the lorn reaches of the sea,
   Comes vast and patient; but the night is kind—
   Her hand is pity, scarfing up the blind
Sorrows and wastes of the immensity.

The wind is soft among the swaying spars.
   Heaven deepens; dusk reveals the glittering height
   And cloudless glory of the arch of night,
Bowed down from rim to rim with solemn stars.

When dawn across the broad and billowing plain
   Casts her pale fire, the monstrous solitude
   Of huddling waters—the old hope renewed—
Thrills with blind love, and yearns, but all in vain.

Sheer to the east, sheer to the west extend,
   Far as the wandering wings of thought may grope,
   The eternal vacancies. No hope, no hope—
Distance, distance forever, without end.

Hour by hour, and day on burning day,
   Our vessel plows the soft, reluctant foam;
   Hour by hour, and mile on mile, we roam
The lonely and the everlasting way.

Still fades before us the enormous round—
   Blue sea below, blue heaven overhead—
   The Void, eternal and untenanted,
A chamber for His splendor, without bound.

                        John Hall Wheelock

THE LOOKOUT

Low lies the land upon the sea.
Night speeds the sun into the west.
All's well, the course is set, our craft runs free.
The lookout's in his swaying nest.

Oh! humble man that you should stand
For magic hours at night, twixt sea and sky.
Alone with awe-struck gaze you scan
The blazing vaults where jewelled chariots fly.

Mark well Polaris, for its icy fire.
Take heart in their confiding leap
That beckoned men when Hiram sailed from Tyre.
Undimmed, they still a gleaming vigil keep.

You gaze, all enthroned atop the rugged spars.
Dim masthead lights, like jewelled fingers sway
In humble tribute to the flickering stars.
Sail on and watch, while day moves into day.

Now comes a sudden wind to break the spell.
A stir, like infants' voices calling from their sleep.
The stars invite, dream on, all's well.
'Twas but the hand of God upon the deep.

William Collins

OCEAN

Great Ocean! strongest of creation's sons,
Unconquerable, unreposed, untired,
That rolled the wild, profound, eternal bass
In nature's anthem, and made music such
As pleased the ear of God! original,
Unmarred, unfaded work of Deity!
And unburlesqued by mortal's puny skill;
From age to age enduring, and unchanged,
Majestical, inimitable, vast,
Loud uttering satire, day and night, on each
Succeeding race, and little pompous work
Of man; unfallen, religious, holy sea!
Thou bowedst thy glorious head to none, fearedst none,
Heardst none, to none didst honor, but to God
Thy Maker, only worthy to receive
Thy great obeisance.
Robert Pollok

THE PILOT

Man is a torch borne in the wind; a dream
But of a shadow, summ'd with all his substance;
And as great seamen, using all their wealth
And skill, in Neptune's deep invisible paths,
In tall ships richly ribb'd and built with brass,
To put a girdle round about the world;
When they have done it, (coming near their haven)

Are fain to give a warning piece, and call
A poor stay'd fisherman, that never past
His country's sight, to waft and guide them in;
So, when we wander farthest through the waves
Of glassy glory, and the gulphs of state,
Topt with all titles, spreading all our reaches,
As if each private arm would sphere the earth,
We must to Virtue for her guide resort,
Or we shall shipwreck in our safest port.

George Chapman

NIGHTS ON THE INDIAN OCEAN

Nights on the Indian Ocean,
   Long nights of moon and foam,
When silvery Venus low in the sky
   Follows the sun home.
Long nights when the mild monsoon
   Is breaking south-by-west,
And when soft clouds and the singing shrouds
   Make all that is seem best.

Nights on the Indian Ocean,
   Long nights of space and dream,
When silent Sirius round the Pole
   Swings on, with steady gleam;
When oft the pushing prow
   Seems pressing where before
No prow has ever pressed—or shall
   From hence for evermore.

Nights on the Indian Ocean,
  Long nights—with land at last,
Dim land, dissolving the long sea-spell
  Into a sudden past—
That seems as far away
  As this our life shall seem
When under the shadow of death's shore
  We drop its ended dream.

Cale Young Rice

FROM THE MARSHES OF GLYNN

Oh, what is abroad in the marsh and the terminal sea?
  Somehow my soul seems suddenly free
From the weighing of fate and the sad discussion of sin,
By the length and the breadth and the sweep of the marshes of Glynn.

. . . .

And the sea lends large, as the marsh: lo, out of his plenty the sea
Pours fast: full soon the time of the flood-tide must be:
Look how the grace of the sea doth go
About and about through the intricate channels that flow
  Here and there,
    Everywhere,
Till his waters have flooded the uttermost creeks and the low-lying lanes,
And the marsh is meshed with a million veins,

That like as with rosy and silvery essences flow
  In the rose-and-silver evening glow.
    Farewell, my lord Sun!
The creeks overflow: a thousand rivulets run
'Twixt the roots of the sod; the blades of the marsh-grass stir;
Passeth a hurrying sound of wings that westward whirr;
Passeth, and all is still; and the currents cease to run;
And the sea and the marsh are one.

How still the plains of the waters be!
The tide is in his ecstasy.
The tide is at his highest height:
    And it is night.
And now from the Vast of the Lord will the waters of sleep
Roll in on the souls of men,
But who will reveal to our waking ken
The forms that swim and the shapes that creep
    Under the waters of sleep?
And I would I could know what swimmeth below
  when the tide comes in
On the length and the breadth of the marvellous marshes of Glynn.

Sidney Lanier

8. "Love still has something of the Sea"

LOVE STILL HAS SOMETHING OF THE SEA

Love still has something of the Sea,
    From whence his Mother rose;
No time his Slaves from Doubt can free,
    Nor give their Thoughts repose:

They are becalm'd in clearest Days,
    And in rough Weather tost;
They wither under cold Delays,
    Or are in Tempests lost.

One while they seem to touch the Port,
    Then straight into the Main,
Some angry Wind in cruel sport
    The Vessel drives again.
Sir Charles Sedley

IS MY LOVER ON THE SEA?

Is my lover on the sea,
    Sailing east, or sailing west?
Mighty Ocean, gentle be,
    Rock him into rest!

Let no angry wind arise,
    Nor a wave with whitened crest;
All be gentle as his eyes
    When he is caressed!

Bear him (as the breeze above
    Bears the bird unto its nest)
Here—unto his home of love,
    And there bid him rest!

Barry Cornwall

THE SEA DANCETH

And lo! the sea that fleets about the land,
And like a girdle clips her solid waist,
Music and measure both doth understand;
For his great crystal eye is always cast
Up to the moon and on her fixèd fast;
    And as she danceth in her pallid sphere,
    So danceth he about his centre here.

Sometimes his proud green waves in order set,
One after other flow unto the shore,
Which, when they have with many kisses wet,
They ebb away in order as before;
And to make known his courtly love the more,
    He oft doth lay aside his three-forked mace,
    And with his arms the timorous earth embrace.

Only the earth doth stand for ever still:
Her rocks remove not, nor her mountains meet:
(Although some wits enriched with Learning's skill
Say heaven stands firm, and that the earth doth fleet,

And swiftly turneth underneath their feet)
  Yet tho' the earth is ever steadfast seen,
  On her broad breast hath dancing ever been.
Sir John Davies

SEA-CHANGE

You are no more, but sunken in a sea
Sheer into dream, ten thousand leagues, you fell;
And now you lie green-golden, while a bell
Swings with the tide, my heart; and all is well
Till I look down, and wavering, the spell—
Your loveliness—returns. There in the sea,
Where you lie amber-pale and coral-cool,
You are most loved, most lost, most beautiful.
Genevieve Taggard

BLACK-EYED SUSAN

All in the Downs the fleet was moored,
  The streamers waving in the wind,
When black-eyed Susan came on board:
  "Oh! where shall I my true love find?
Tell me, ye jovial sailors, tell me true,
If my sweet William sails among your crew?"

William, who, high upon the yard,
  Rock'd by the billows to and fro,
Soon as her well-known voice he heard,
  He sighed and cast his eyes below:

The cord glides swiftly through his glowing hands,
And quick as lightning on the deck he stands.

So the sweet lark, high-poised in air,
  Shuts close his pinions to his breast
If chance his mate's shrill call he hear,
  And drops at once into her nest:—
The noblest captain in the British fleet
Might envy William's lips those kisses sweet.

"O Susan, Susan, lovely dear,
  My vows shall ever true remain!
Let me kiss off that falling tear,—
  We only part to meet again:
Change as ye list, ye winds, my heart shall be
The faithful compass that still points to thee!

"Believe not what the landsmen say,
  Who tempt, with doubts, thy constant mind:
They'll tell thee, sailors, when away,
  In every port a mistress find.—
Yes, yes!—believe them when they tell thee so
For thou art present wheresoe'er I go!

"If to fair India's coast we sail,
  Thine eyes are seen in diamonds bright;
Thy breath is Afric's spicy gale,—
  Thy skin is ivory so white:
Thus every beauteous object that I view
Wakes in my soul some charm of lovely Sue.

"Though battle calls me from thy arms,
  Let not my pretty Susan mourn;
Though cannons roar, yet, free from harms,
  William shall to his dear return:
Love turns aside the balls that round me fly,
Lest precious tears should drop from Susan's eye."

The boatswain gives his dreadful word,—
  The sails their swelling bosoms spread;
No longer may she stay on board:
  They kiss: She sighs: He hangs his head.
Her lessening boat unwilling rows to land:
"Adieu!" she cries, and waves her lily hand.

John Gay

OF LITTLE FAITH

I said, when the word came, "She will break
Like a tall ship riven by the shore."
As a dream, I saw the white sails shake,
The masts fall, heard the smoking combers roar.
I saw the black reef shatter the broken hull,
I saw the dead ship drop from the shore's embrace
And over the empty waters only a screaming gull
Winging its endless way to mark the tragic place.
I felt the blown spume cut like driven snow—
"As a tall ship goes," I said, "so she will go."

I raised my head. I saw her stand
Like a tall ship won home from a gale.
Her eyes like the deep sea far from land,
Her white face calm as a sleeping sail.

The touch of her hand was cool as spray,
And her smile like the ripple at the prow
Of a tall ship going its silent way
Through an old swell, quietly breathing now,
After a storm. I said, "She has shown to me
The deathless glory of the ageless sea."

Harold T. Pulsifer

SONNET: LYKE AS A SHIP

Lyke as a ship, that through the Ocean wyde,
By conduct of some star, doth make her way;
Whenas a storme hath dimd her trusty guyde,
Out of her course doth wander far astray!
So I, whose star, that wont with her bright ray
Me to direct, with cloudes is over-cast,
Doe wander now, in darknesse and dismay,
Through hidden perils round about me plast;
Yet hope I well that, when this storme is past,
My Helice, the lodestar of my lyfe,
Will shine again, and looke on me at last,
With lovely light to cleare my cloudy grief,
   Till then I wander carefull, comfortlesse,
   In secret sorow, and sad pensivenesse.

Edmund Spenser

THE SEA'S SPELL

Beneath thy spell, O radiant summer sea,—
   Lulled by thy voice, rocked on thy shining breast,
   Fanned by thy soft breath, by thy touch caressed,—
Let all thy treacheries forgotten be.
Let me still dream the ships I gave to thee
   All golden-freighted in fair harbors rest;
   Let me believe each sparkling wave's white crest
Bears from thy depths my loved and lost to me.
   Let me not heed thy wrecks, nor count thy slain.
As o'er-fond lovers for love's sake forget
Their dearest wrongs, so I, with eyes still wet
   With thy salt tears, with heart still wrung with pain,
   Back to thy fierce, sweet beauty turn again,
And though thou wreck me, will I love thee yet!
                 Susan Marr Spalding

MIGHTY SEA! CAMELEON-LIKE THOU CHANGEST

               Mighty Sea!
Cameleon-like thou changest; but there's love
In all thy change, and constant sympathy
With yonder sky—thy mistress. From her brow
Thou tak'st thy moods, and wear'st her colors on
Thy faithful bosom—morning's milky white,
Noon's sapphire, or the saffron glow of eve;
And all thy balmier hours, fair Element,
Have such divine complexion, crispèd smiles,

Luxuriant heavings and sweet whisperings,
That little is the wonder Love's own Queen
Of old was fabled to have sprung from thee—
Creation's common!—which no human power
Can parcel or inclose. The lordliest floods
And cataracts, that the tiny hands of man
Can tame, conduct or bound, are drops of dew
To thee,—that could subdue the Earth itself,
And brook'st commandment from high Heaven alone
For marshalling thy waves.
Thomas Campbell

JACK'S FIDELITY

If ever a sailor was fond of good sport
   'Mongst the girls, why that sailor was I.
Of all sizes and sorts, I'd a wife at each port,
   But, when that I saw'd Polly Ply,
I hail'd her my lovely, and gov'd her a kiss,
   And swore to bring up once for all,
And from that time black Barnaby spliced us to this,
   I've been constant and true to my Poll,

And yet now all sorts of temptations I've stood,
   For I afterwards sail'd round the world,
And a queer set we saw of the devil's own brood,
   Wherever our sails were unfurl'd:
Some with faces like charcoal, and others like chalk,
   All ready one's heart to o'erhaul,
"Don't you go to love me, my good girl," said I—
     "walk;
   I've sworn to be constant to Poll."

"LOVE STILL HAS . . . ."

I met with a squaw out at India, beyond,
   All in glass and tobacco-pipes dress'd,
What a dear pretty monster! so kind and so fond,
   That I ne'er was a moment at rest.
With her bobs at her nose, and her quaw, quaw, quaw,
   All the world like a Bartlemy doll;
Says I, "You Miss Copperskin, just hold your jaw,—
   I've sworn to be constant to Poll."

Then one near Sumatra, just under the Line,
   As fond as a witch in a play;
"I loves you," says she, "and just only be mine,
   Or by poison I'll take you away."
"Curse your kindness," says I, "but you can't frighter me;
   You don't catch a gudgeon this haul;
If I do take your ratsbane, why then, do you see,
   I shall die true and constant to Poll."

But I 'scaped from them all, tawny, lily, and black,
   And merrily weathered each storm,
And, my neighbours to please, full of wonders came back,
   But, what's better, I'm grown pretty warm.
And so now to sea I shall venture no more.
   For you know, being rich, I've no call;
So I'll bring up young tars, do my duty ashore,
   And live and die constant to Poll.

Charles Dibdin

WATERS OF THE SEA

Lightest foam, straightest spray,
Waters of the sea,
Wearing out the sternest rocks
As love wears me.

Tides through time on glaciers,
Waters of the sea,
Wrecking mighty strength with scorn
As love wrecks me.

Time and tide, glaciers, rocks,
Waters of the sea,
Potent armies of the peace
Love takes from me.

Cecil Goldbeck

GULF STREAM

Lonely and cold and fierce I keep my way,
   Scourge of the lands, companioned by the storm,
Tossing to heaven my frontlet, wild and gray,
   Mateless, yet conscious ever of a warm
And brooding presence close to mine all day.

What is this alien thing, so near, so far,
   Close to my life always, but blending never,—
Hemmed in by walls whose crystal gates unbar
   Not at the instance of my strong endeavor
To pierce the stronghold where their secrets are?

"LOVE STILL HAS . . . ."

Buoyant, impalpable, relentless, thin,
  Rise the clear, mocking walls. I strive in vain
To reach the pulsing heart that beats within,
  Or, with persistence of a cold disdain,
To quell the gladness which I may not win.

Forever sundered and forever one,
  Linked by a bond whose spell I may not guess,
Our hostile yet embracing currents run;
  Such wedlock lonelier is than loneliness.
Baffled, withheld, I clasp the bride I shun.

Yet even in my wrath a wild regret
  Mingles; a bitterness of jealous strife
Tinges my fury as I foam and fret
  Against the borders of that calmer life,
Beside whose course my wrathful course is set.

But all my anger, all my pain and woe,
  Are vain to daunt her gladness; all the while
She goes rejoicing, and I do not know,
  Catching the soft irradiance of her smile
If I am most her lover or her foe.

Susan Coolidge

CHAMELEON

Who loves the sea has found its waters blue,
Blue as wild hyacinth when skies are clear;
Or sometimes furrowed green as Chinese jade
When Northern Lights enchant the atmosphere.

While often, black as ebony, its waves
Reflect the tempest howling through the night,
Until the dawn reveals its liquid floor
Like rare Carrara marble, wrinkled white.

The sea of love within my soul's embrace
Thus mirrors heaven's counterpart—your face.

Gordon LeClaire

FIGUREHEAD

I was not meant to stand in a sea-edge garden,
  Yearning across the wet brown sand for the rumor of ships,
Breasting the dusty surf of the upland daisies,
  Sick for the cry of the gulls and the salt on my lips.

Ours was the desolate way of the hovering petrel,
  Ours was the way of the reef and the perilous way of the fog.
If hearts must be stouter than yours for the keeping of sea faith,
  Shall a sea woman follow you home like a wife or a dog?

You who have piled white towers of thunder above us,
  You who have trysted afar in golden and fabulous lands,
Shall I watch you feeding the doves in a landsman's dooryard?
  Sweeping a landsman's hearth with a seaman's hands?

And what have you left to say to your inland woman?
   Will you speak to her of the white and dusty roads
      of our sea?
Safe in the candle shine—as the drowned are safe!—
   Will you speak of the bitter-bright peril you followed with me?

Ah, forget, if you can, the woman who rode at your
      bowsprit;
   Sit by the fire and forget, when the long tides cry
      to the moon;
Never remember our silver and vigiling cities,
   Never remember our star you've forsaken too soon!

And I shall go down once more to the sea and his
      mercy,
   Down to the desolate sea, alone, with the salt in
      my eyes—
I who have lived by the sword of his excellent beauty,
   Shall die, at the last, by his sword, as a sea woman
      dies.

Dorothy Paul

THE SEA-CAPTAIN

I am in love with the sea, but I do not trust her yet;
The tall ships she has slain are ill to forget;
Their sails were white in the morning, their masts
      were split by noon:
The sun has seen them perish, and the stars, and the
      moon.

As a man loves the woman, so I love the sea,
And even as my desire of her is her desire of me:
When we meet after parting, we put away regret,
Like lover joined with lover; but I do not trust her yet.
For fierce she is and strange, and her love is kin to hate;
She must slay whom she desires; she will draw me soon or late,
Down into darkness and silence, the place of drowned men,
Having her arms about me. And I shall trust her then.
Gerald Gould

LOOKE HOW THE PALE QUEENE

Looke how the pale Queene of the silent night,
Doth cause the Ocean to attend upon her,
And he as long as she is in his sight,
With his full tide is ready her to honour:
But when the siluer wagon of the Moone
Is mounted vp so high he cannot follow,
The sea cals home his crystall waues to mone,
And with low ebbe doth manifest his sorrow:
So you that are the soueraigne of my heart,
Haue all my joyes attending on your will,
My joyes low ebbing when you doe depart.
When you returne, their tide my heart doth fill.
  So as you come, and as you doe depart
    Joys ebbe and flow within my tender heart.
Charles Best

THE BIRTH OF VENUS

The ocean stood like crystal. The soft air
Stirred not the glassy waves, but sweetly there
Had rocked itself to slumber. The blue sky
Leaned silently above, and all its high
And azure-circled roof, beneath the wave
Was imaged back, and seemed the deep to pave
With its transparent beauty. While between
The waves and sky, a few white clouds were seen
Floating upon their wings of feathery gold,
As if they knew some charm the universe enrolled.

A holy stillness came, while in the ray
Of heaven's soft light, a delicate foam-wreath lay
Like silver on the sea. Look! look! why shine
Those floating bubbles with such light divine?
They break, and from their mist a lily form
Rises from out the wave, in beauty warm.
The wave is by the blue-veined feet scarce prest,
Her silky ringlets float about her breast,
Veiling its fairy loveliness; while her eye
Is soft and deep as the blue heaven is high.
The Beautiful is born, and sea and earth
May well revere the hour of that mysterious birth.
Anonymous

ANNABEL LEE

It was many and many a year ago,
   In a kingdom by the sea,
That a maiden there lived whom you may know
   By the name of Annabel Lee;
And this maiden she lived with no other thought
   Than to love and be loved by me.

I was a child and she was a child,
   In this kingdom by the sea,
But we loved with a love that was more than love,
   I and my Annabel Lee;
With a love that the wingèd seraphs of heaven
   Coveted her and me.

And this was the reason that, long ago,
   In this kingdom by the sea,
A wind blew out of a cloud, chilling
   My beautiful Annabel Lee;
So that her highborn kinsmen came
   And bore her away from me,
To shut her up in a sepulchre
   In this kingdom by the sea.

The angels, not half so happy in heaven,
   Went envying her and me;
Yes! that was the reason (as all men know,
   In this kingdom by the sea)
That the wind came out of the cloud by night,
   Chilling and killing my Annabel Lee.

But our love it was stronger by far than the love
  Of those who were older than we,
  Of many far wiser than we;
And neither the angels in heaven above,
  Nor the demons down under the sea,
Can ever dissever my soul from the soul
  Of the beautiful Anabel Lee:

For the moon never beams, without bringing me dreams
  Of the beautiful Annabel Lee;
And the stars never rise, but I feel the bright eyes
  Of the beautiful Annabel Lee;
And so, all the night-tide, I lie down by the side
Of my darling—my darling—my life and my bride,
  In her sepulchre there by the sea,
  In her tomb by the sounding sea.

Edgar Allan Poe

THE LOVER LIKE TO A SHIP TOSSED ON THE SEA

My galley chargèd with forgetfulness
Through sharp seas, in winter nights doth pass,
'Tween rock and rock; and eke my foe, alas,
That is my lord, steereth with cruelness;
And every hour, a thought in readiness,
As though that death were light in such a case.
An endless wind doth tear the sail apace

Of forced sighs, and trusty fearfulness.
A rain of tears, a cloud of dark disdain
Hath done the wearied cords great hinderance,
Wreathèd with error, and with ignorance.
The stars be hid that led me to this pain;
   Drownèd is reason that should be my comfort,
   And I remain, despairing of the port.
Sir Thomas Wyatt

AS HAPPY DWELLERS BY THE SEASIDE HEAR

As happy dwellers by the seaside hear
   In every pause the sea's mysterious sound,
   The infinite murmur, solemn and profound,
Incessant, filling all the atmosphere,
Even so I hear you, for you do surround
   My newly-waking life, and break for aye
About the viewless shores, till they resound
   With echoes of God's greatness night and day.
Refreshed and glad I feel the full flood-tide
   Fill every inlet of my waiting soul,
   Long-striving, eager hope, beyond control,
For help and strength at last is satisfied,
And you exalt me, like the sounding sea,
With ceaseless whispers of eternity.
Celia Thaxter

THE MARINER

Ye winds that sweep the grove's green tops
    And kiss the mountains hoar,
O softly stir the ocean-waves
    That sweep along the shore!
For my love sails the fairest ship
    That wantons on the sea;
O bend his masts with pleasant gales,
    And waft him hame to me.

O leave nae mair the bonny glen,
    Clear stream, and hawthorn grove,
Where first we walked in gloaming gray,
    And sighed and looked of love;
For faithless is the ocean wave,
    And faithless is the wind:
Then leave nae mair my heart to break
    'Mang Scotland's hills behind.
                      Allan Cunningham

THOUGHTS IN THE GULF STREAM

Who has described the wave
Crisping oblique from *Caronia's* bow
In clear summer midnight?
Brighter than snow the crumble, the running curling
    crumble
Flung from her wedgy stem:
Then a hollow, a lovely bending hollow,

Which swells up to a spread, an outward comb of
    breaker
Drawing veins and stripings
After it through the black:
And the little phosphor-sparkle,
The seethe along her side,
All this has never been properly described
Because no passenger ever sees it
With detached and watchful mind.
None of them
In clear summer midnight
Ever sees it alone.

Christopher Morley

9. Homeward Bound
—Making Port

HOMEWARD BOUND

There is no sorrow anywhere,
    Or care, or pain. The stinging hail
    Beats on our faces like a flail,
    Green water curls above the rail,
And all the storm's high trumpets blare,—
    Whistles the wind, and roars the sea,
    And canvas bellows to be free,
Spars whine, planks creak,—I only smile,
For home our keel creeps mile on mile.

I bend above the whirling wheel
    With hands benumbed, but happy face.
    Past us the wild sea-horses race,
    Leap up to seize each twanging brace,
Or slip beneath our lifting keel.
    Dreaming, I see the scudding clouds,
    And ice make in the forward shrouds,
And all the long waves topped with foam,—
Yet heed them not: I'm going home.

Nightly our Northern stars draw nigh,
    The Southern constellations sink.
    Soon we shall see along the brink
    Of these cold seas Fire Island blink
Its welcome in the frosty sky.

Beyond that light, beyond the glow
Of our great city spread below,
Thine eyes now wait to welcome me
Back where my heart has longed to be.

L. Frank Tooker

THE HOMEWARD BOUND
(Landfall)

There's the gals at the bar, there's the beer,
There's a hat goin' round:
There's a packet moored down at the pier,—
There's a ship homeward bound.

The gals is all laughin', an' "clink"
Goes glasses together.
"Breast the bar, now, me bullies, an' drink!
We'll wish her fair weather!"

There's the Missioner standin' outside,
Wi' a prayer, an' a hymn,—
There's a gal flings the swingin' door wide,—
"An' why don't ye come in?"

An' the Missioner's shakin' his head
At the gals an' the boys.
'Twas the words of a prayer that he said,
But 'twas drowned in our noise!

.   .   .   .   .

HOMEWARD BOUND—MAKING PORT

There's a packet at sea, runnin' home,
An' all dizzy her spars!
An' her topsails is drippin' wi' foam,
An' she's scrapin' the stars!

There's a laugh on the sea, a low wail
In the heart o' the blow;
There's the ghostly dim shape of her sail,
An' there's ice an' there's snow!

There's the lads wi' their faces all white,
But a laugh on their lips!
An' there's God, lookin' down on His night,
An' He's watchin' His ships.

There's a packet that never came home,
There's white birds that fly by,
All free feathered an' bright as the foam
\s the stars in the sky!

. . . . .

An' ashore there's the glasses go round,
While the Mission men pray
For the packet they watched, "homeward bound"
At the breakin' of day.

Bill Adams

THE COASTWISE LIGHTS

Our brows are wreathed with spindrift and the weed is on our knees;
Our loins are battered 'neath us by the swinging, smoking seas.
From reef and rock and skerry—over headland, ness and voe—
The Coastwise Lights of England watch the ships of England go!

Through the endless summer evenings, on the lineless, level floors;
Through the yelling Channel tempest when the syren hoots and roars—
By day the dipping house-flag and by night the rocket's trail—
As the sheep that graze behind us so we know them where they hail.

We bridge across the dark, and bid the helmsman have a care,
The flash that wheeling inland wakes his sleeping wife to prayer;
From our vexed eyries, head to gale, we bind in burning chains
The lover from the sea-rim drawn—his love in English lanes.

We greet the clippers wing-and-wing that race the Southern wool;
We warn the crawling cargo-tanks of Bremen, Leith and Hull;

HOMEWARD BOUND—MAKING PORT

To each and all our equal lamp at peril of the sea—
The white wall-sided warships or the whalers of Dundee!

Come up, come in from Eastward, from the guard-ports of the Morn!
Beat up, beat in from Southerly, O gipsies of the Horn!
Swift shuttles of an Empire's loom that weave us main to main,
The Coastwise Lights of England give you welcome back again!

Go, get you gone up-Channel with the sea-crust on your plates;
Go, get you into London with the burden of your freights!
Haste, for they talk of Empire there, and say, if any seek,
The Lights of England sent you and by silence shall ye speak.
Rudyard Kipling

PORT AFTER STORMIE SEAS

What if some little paine the passage have,
That makes fraile flesh to feare the bitter wave?
Is not short paine well borne, that brings long ease,
And layes the soule to sleepe in quiet grave?
Sleepe after toyle, port after stormie seas,
Ease after warre, death after life does greatly please.
Edmund Spenser

HEAVING THE LEAD

For England when with favoring gale
  Our gallant ship up channel steered,
And, scudding under easy sail,
  The high blue western land appeared;
To heave the lead the seaman sprung,
And to the pilot cheerly sung,
          "By the deep—*nine!*"

And bearing up to gain the port,
  Some well-known object kept in view,—
An abbey-tower, a harbor-fort,
  Or beacon to the vessel true;
While oft the lead the seaman flung,
And to the pilot cheerly sung,
          "By the mark—*seven!*"

And as the much-loved shore we near,
  With transport we behold the roof
Where dwelt a friend or partner dear,
  Of faith and love a matchless proof.
The lead once more the seaman flung,
And to the watchful pilot sung,
          "Quarter less *five!*"

Now to her berth the ship draws nigh:
  We shorten sail,—she feels the tide,—
"Stand clear the cable!" is the cry,—
  The anchor's gone; we safely ride.
The watch is set, and through the night
We hear the seaman with delight
          Proclaim,—"*All's well!*"

J. Pearce

From SAGA OF LEIF THE LUCKY

Leif was a man's name.
Over the great, white shoulder of the world he came,
Into a land as lonesome as a star
That God had set aside
For mortals not to mar—
Too huge for men—
Not till Leif's sons set foot upon the moon,
Will such a deed as this be done again.

Leif Erickson came rowing up the Charles
In the sea-battered dragon ships,
Stroked by the strong, blond carls
The rattle of whose oars
Had wakened sea lions on the glacial shores
Of Greenland, where the white Christ newly ruled.
Leif brought the old gods, too,
The grim, scarred northern crew;
Though Olaf had baptized Leif,
Grace irked him strangely
As conscience does a thief,
And he feared the hammer of Thor
And the voice of the Norns—
He was by sea winds schooled,
Mystery and fighting his trade,
And men had heard the braying of his horns
Above the boom and pother of the seas;
Thorgunna, the Sorceress, heard them at the Hebrides,
And Icelandic fjords, and dwellers
In the low eaved stone huts of Greenland villages,

Now roofless to the arctic sky
And the cold's malice
Five centuries staring up like a skull's eye
At the ghost dance of the borealis.
Leif steered southwest
Watching the stars slip
Over the carved hair of the dragon's crest,
Until he drove on foggy coasts,
With great flat rocks, porches to bleak plateaus,
Where crowding icebergs grind.
Next, a landfall of dark forests piled like thunderheads
Against long, frosty hills behind.
Then south,
Past inland twinkling mountains
And a vast river mouth,
While vague voices bellowed at them from the sea;
In calms they heard the breathing whales;
Strange fish leaped flapping on their decks;
Spears winked in starlight,
As they patched the ragged sails,
Or polished shields with ballast sand,
Staggering up quivering mountains to the stars;
Staggering down;
Leaving a spuming wake;
Till a great tongue of land
Turned them west again
Into a river and a lake.
So Leif came rowing up the Charles,
He and his golden bearded carls....

Hervey Allen

JUBILATE

Gray distance hid each shining sail,
  By ruthless breezes borne from me;
And, lessening, fading, faint, and pale,
  My ships went forth to sea.

Where misty breakers rose and fell
  I stood and sorrowed hopelessly;
For every wave had tales to tell
  Of wrecks far out at sea.

Today, a song is on my lips:
  Earth seems a paradise to me:
For God is good, and, lo, my ships
  Are coming home from sea!

George Arnold

A SAILOR'S SONG

As I sail home to Galveston
In oleander time,
I sing a chanty of the sea,
A swinging seaman's rhyme;
And tell the wind to wing my words
Across the churning foam
To let my own dear folk rejoice
That I am coming home.

Although I love the rolling keel,
The waves, and briny spray,
The Gulf is bluer far to me
Than Naples' cobalt bay;
And yearningly I face the west
Dyed orange, plum, and lime,
As I sail home to Galveston
In oleander time.

Salt cedars will be feathered pink,
And every humble street
Will flaunt the coral, rose, and white
Of oleanders sweet.
What joy my heart anticipates
In this sea-girdled clime
As I sail home to Galveston
In oleander time!

Hazel Harper Harri

HOMECOMING IN STORM

The ocean thunders in the caverned sky,
   And gulls fall straight against a crest of foam,
The black wind roars to bring the great storm by,
   And all my sails are full to bear me home!
Thus I come in with rain, and salty lips
   Crusted with spray, and eyes that see for miles
Over the harbor bar, to the huddled ships,
   And docks and roofs, and maple-darkened aisles.

The rain smells all of maple and of hay,
　And now I put the sea behind my back,
And cross the streets and fields in the old way,
　With all the clouds above me hanging black,
And stand here in the rain before your door,—
Moveless with joy, to know you near once more.

Bernice L. Kenyon

MAKING LAND

The fore-royal furled, I pause and I stand,
　Both feet on the yard, for a look around,
With eyes that ache for a sight of the land,
　For we are homeward bound.

Like a bowl of silver the ocean lies,
　Untouched by the fret of a single sail,
And over its edge the billows uprise
　And slide before the gale.

I see, close beneath me, the garn's'l bulge,
　And half of the tops'l swollen and round
Swells out above, where the bunts divulge
　The fores'l's snowy mound.

With a fill and a flap the jibs respond,
　As she rolls a-weather, then rolls a-lee,
And her bone as she leaps is thrown beyond
　The next o'ertaken sea.

And the hull beneath in its foamy ring
  Is narrowed in by the spread of sail,
And the waves as they wash her seem to fling
  Their heads above the rail.

And I hear the roar of the passing blast,
  And the hiss and gush of the parted sea
Is mixed with the groan of the straining mast,
  And the parrel's che, che, che.

Of the weather deck where the old man strides,
  From the break of the poop to the after-rail,
I can catch a glimpse, but all besides
  Is hid by swelling sail.

For the wake abaft is shut behind,
  Except when she yaws from her helm and throws;
Then like a green lane it seems to wind
  Aheap with drifted snows.

But lo! as I gaze the weather clew
  Of the topsail lifts to the watch's weight,
And the helmsman comes into perfect view,
  And at his side the mate.

As I swing my eyes ahead again
  For that one last look ere I drop below,
They catch as she lifts a grayish stain
  Athwart the orange glow.

My heart leaps up at the welcome sight,
  And I grasp the pole with a firmer hand,
And shading my eyes from the glancing light
  Make sure that it is land.

It seems to dance, but I catch it still
  As we lift to the sweep of a longer sea—
'T is the windy top of a far-off hill
  Whose shape is known to me.

Then I send a yell to the rolling deck,
  And start all hands from their work below;
As I point with a rigid arm at the speck—
  The cry comes back, "Land ho!"

And the mate looks up and gives a call,
  The old man stops in his clock-like walk,
The watch lets up on the top-sail fall
  And takes a spell of talk.

The skipper goes aft to the binnacle, where
  He shapes his hand on the compass card,
And takes with a glance the bearing there,
  Eying me on the yard.

And I stand with my right arm swinging out,
  With a finger true on the dancing speck,
Until on my ears falls the ringing shout:
  "All right! Lay down on deck!"

Thomas Fleming Day

HOMEWARD BOUND

She comes, majestic with her swelling sails,
  The gallant bark! along her watery way
Homeward she drives, before the favoring gales,
  Now flirting at their length the streamers play,

And now they ripple with the ruffling breeze.
  Hark to the sailors' shouts! the rocks rebound,
  Thundering in echoes to the joyful sound.
Long have they voyaged o'er the distant seas,
  And what a heart-delight they feel at last,
  So many toils, so many dangers past,
To view the port desired—he only knows
  Who on the stormy deep, for many a day,
  Hath tost, aweary of his ocean way,
And watched, all anxious, every wind that blows.
Robert Southey

OFF RIVIÈRE DU LOUP

O ship incoming from the sea
With all your cloudy tower of sail,
Dashing the water to the lee,
And leaning grandly to the gale,

The sunset pageant in the west
Has filled your canvas curves with rose,
And jewelled every toppling crest
That crashes into silver snows!

You know the joy of coming home,
After long leagues to France or Spain
You feel the clear Canadian foam
And the gulf water heave again.

Between these sombre purple hills
That cool the sunset's molten bars,
You will go on as the wind wills,
Beneath the river's roof of stars.

You will toss onward towards the lights
That spangle over the lonely pier,
By hamlets glimmering on the heights,
By level islands black and clear.

You will go on beyond the tide,
Through brimming plains of olive sedge,
Through paler shadows light and wide,
The rapids piled along the ledge.

At evening off some reedy bay
You will swing slowly on your chain,
And catch the scent of dewy hay,
Soft blowing from the pleasant plain.
Duncan Campbell Scott

THE SHIP

Over the shining pavement of the sea,
   Breathless, the white hind flees
Southward, with beating heart and fear-torn soul;
   Fast on her track she sees
Leap from their hidden caves the frantic wolves,
   Snarling, they race beside,
Dart at her unprotected throat and seek
   Hold on her foam-streaked side.

Lo! on her straining sight the harbor breaks,
  Panting, its shade she gains,
Hears but heeds not the baffled howls as now
  Down through its quiet lanes
Safely she takes her way and drops to rest,
  Peace-filled and unafraid.

Louise A. Doran

SHIPS AT SEA

I have ships that went to sea
  More than fifty years ago;
None have yet come home to me,
  But are sailing to and fro.
I have seen them in my sleep,
Plunging through the shoreless deep,
With tattered sails, and battered hulls,
While around them screamed the gulls,
  Flying low, flying low.

I have wondered why they strayed
  From me, sailing round the world;
And I've said, "I'm half afraid
  That their sails will ne'er be furled."
Great the treasures that they hold—
Silks, and plumes, and bars of gold;
While the spices that they bear
Fill with fragrance all the air,
  As they sail, as they sail.

Ah! each sailor in the port
  Knows that I have ships at sea,

Of the waves and winds the sport;
   And the sailors pity me.
Oft they come and with me walk,
Cheering me with hopeful talk,
Till I put my fears aside,
And, contented, watch the tide
     Rise and fall, rise and fall.

I have waited on the piers,
   Gazing for them down the bay,
Days and nights, for many years,
   Till I've turned, heart-sick, away.
But the pilots, when they land,
Stop and take me by the hand,
Saying, "You will live to see
Your proud ships come home from sea,
     One and all, one and all."

So I never quite despair,
   Nor let hope or courage fail;
And some day, when skies are fair,
   Up the bay my ships will sail.
I shall buy then all I need—
Prints to look at, books to read,
Horses, wines, and works of art,
Everything—except a heart
     That is lost, that is lost!

Once when I was pure and young,
   Richer, too, than I am now,
Ere a cloud was o'er me flung,
   Or a wrinkle creased my brow,

There was one whose heart was mine;
But she's something now divine,
And though come my ships from sea,
They can bring no heart to me
    Evermore, evermore.

Barry Gray

THE SHIPS

The bending sails shall whiten on the sea,
  Guided by hands and eyes made glad for home,
With graven gems and cedar and ebony
  From Babylon and Rome.

For here a lover cometh as to his bride,
  And there a merchant to his utmost price—
Oh, hearts will leap to see the good ships ride
  Safely to Paradise!

And this that cuts the waves with **brazen** prow
  Hath heard the blizzard groaning through her spars;
Battered with honour swings she nobly now
  Back from her bitter wars.

And that doth bring her silver work and spice,
  Peacocks and apes from Tarshish, and from Tyre
Great cloaks of velvet stiff with **gold** device,
  Coloured with sunset fire. . . .

And one, serenely through the golden gate,
  Shall sail and anchor by the ultimate shore,
Who, plundered of her gold by pirate Fate,
  Still keeps her richer store

Unrifled when her perilous journey ends
   And the strong cable holds her safe again:
Laughter and memories and the songs of friends
   And the sword edge of pain.

Theodore Maynard

THE *ARK* AND THE *DOVE*

When the *Ark* and *Dove* within the glassy wave
Beheld their sails,
After they'd crossed that more-than-tossing pave
Where walk the whales,
After they saw the emerald land, new-green,
Rise from the sea,
Scarfing them round like sunset clouds, serene,
With constancy,

"Angels we are," they said, "who with our wide,
Wide-spreading wings
Have brought to this new land, presanctified,
Its precious things.

"We've brought, clasped to our sunset-light-lit breasts,
The Chalice, the Host,
From England to this cloud-bank of the West's,
Our Mary's coast."

And as these ships swam river-ward still they sang,
Still with their bows,
This little song of foam which silver rang
Through worlds a-drowse.

Daniel Sargent

NORSE SAILOR'S JOY

Now, landsmen, list! There is no sight more fair
Than taut-strung cordage printed on pale air
When noon is high and bravely the ship's course
O'er-rides the riot of the reinless horse
That charge her bulwarks and go under, fleeing
Far in foiled wrath. There is no fairer seeing
Than tiny flags that flutter from the steep
Slim mastheads as they dance above the deep,
Crying aloud, "Good-by, good-by, you girls!"
And from the ship's side the last eddy whirls
Of land-locked water. There is nothing sweeter
To seamen's eyes than sight of the Blue Peter
Aloft and crying loudly to the land
"We leave you, now we leave you!"
                      Then each wand
Of corded wood becomes a violin
The wind's hand dallies with as out and in
His fingers wander, and the good ship goes
With ranked sea-horses plunging at her bows,
And in her sails the rumour of a drum
Struck by the Monster she shall overcome!
Yea, she shall overcome it and shall sing
Through all her topsails in her triumphing
When she rides down the level harbour fiord
Where lies one arm of ocean like a sword
All steely cold, and o'er the sheer crag shooting,
A sunbeam shows you all the gray gulls looting
Nigh the lank nets that late have drawn the shoals.
Then all the sailors sing with gladdened souls

To see the rockland after ocean-riding
Through long, loud nights and still fair peace abiding
That erst they knew ere that remembered day.
They left behind them their old Norroway;
For in their nostrils are the sweet pine-smells,
And in their ears the music of old bells,
And in their eyes the promise of delight
Round the warm ingle at the fall of night.
Wilfrid Thorley

MAKING PORT

All day long till the west was red,
    Over and under the white-flecked blue:
"Now lay her into the wind," he said;
    And south the harbor drew.

And tacking west and tacking east,
    Spray-showers upward going,
Her wake one zigzag trail of yeast'
    Her gunwale fairly flowing;

All flutterous clamor overhead,
    Lee scuppers white and spouting,
Upon the deck a stamping tread,
    And windy voices shouting;

Her weather shrouds as viol-strings,
    And leeward all a-clatter,–
The long, lithe schooner dips and springs;
    The waters cleave and scatter.

Shoulder to shoulder, breast to breast,
  Arms locked, hand over hand:
Bracing to leeward, lips compressed,
  Eyes forward to the land;

Driving the wheel to wind, to lee,
  The two men work as one;
Out of the southwest sweeps the sea;
  Low slants the summer sun.

The harbor opens wide and wide,
  Draws up on either quarter;
The Vineyard's low hills backward slide;
  The keel finds smoother water.

And tacking starboard, tacking port,
  Bows hissing, heeled to leeward,
Through craft of many a size and sort,
  She trails the long bay seaward.

Half-way, she jibes to come about,—
  The hurling wind drives at her;
The loud sails flap and flutter out,
  The sheet-blocks rasp and clatter.

A lumberman lies full abeam,—
  The flow sets squarely toward her;
We lose our headway in the stream
  And drift broadside aboard her.

A sudden flurry fore and aft,
  Shout, trample, strain, wind howling;
A ponderous jar of craft on craft,
  A boom that threatens fouling;

A jarring slide of hull on hull,—
  Her bowsprit sweeps our quarter;
Clang go the sheets; the jib draws full;
  Once more we cleave the water.

The anchor rattles from the bow,
  The jib comes wrapping downward;
And quiet rides the dripping prow,
  Wave-lapped and pointing townward.

O, gracious is the arching sky,
  The south wind blowing blandly;
The rippling white-caps fleck and fly;
  The sunset flushes grandly.

And all the grace of sea and land,
  And splendor of the painted skies,
And more I'd give to hold her hand,
  And look into her eyes!
                              J. T. McKay

CLEANING SHIP

Down on your knees, boys, holystone the decks,
Rub 'em down, scrub 'em down, stiffen out your necks,
For we're gettin' near t' home, lads, gettin' near t' home,
With a good stiff breeze and a wake o' shining foam.
Up on th' masts, boys, scrape 'em white an' clean,
Tar th' ropes an' paint th' rails an' stripe her sides with green,

For we're gettin' near t' home, lads, gettin' near t' home,
With a good stiff breeze an' a wake o' shining foam.
Charles Keeler

HOMEWARD BOUND

They will take us from the moorings, they will tow us down the Bay,
    They will pluck us up to windward when we sail.
We shall hear the keen wind whistle, we shall feel the sting of spray,
    When we've dropped the deep-sea pilot o'er the rail.
Then it's Johnnie heave an' start her, then it's Johnnie roll and go;
    When the mates have picked the watches, there is little rest for Jack.
But we'll raise the good old chanty that the Homeward Bounders know,
    For the girls have got the tow-rope, an' they're hauling in the slack.

In the dusty streets and dismal, through the noises of the town,
    We can hear the west wind humming through the shrouds;
We can see the lightning leaping when the tropic suns go down,
    And the dapple of the shadows of the clouds.
And the salt blood dances in us, to the tune of Homeward Bound,

To the call to weary watches, to the sheet and to
   the tack.
When they bid us man the capstan how the hands will
   walk her round!—
  For the girls have got the tow-rope, an' they're
     hauling in the slack.

Through the sunshine of the tropics, round the bleak
     and dreary Horn,
  Half across the little planet lies our way.
We shall leave the land behind us like a welcome that's
     outworn
  When we see the reeling mastheads swing and sway.
Through the weather fair or stormy, in the calm and
     in the gale,
We shall heave and haul to help her, we shall hold
     her on her track
And you'll hear the chorus rolling when the hands are
     making sail,
  For the girls have got the tow-rope, and they're
     hauling in the slack.

D. H. Rogers

NOW STRIKE YOUR SAILES YE JOLLY MARINERS!

I

Now strike your sailes ye jolly Mariners,
For we be come unto a quiet rode,
Where we must land some of our passengers,
And light this wearie vessell of her lode.

Here she a while may make her safe abode,
Till she repaired have her tackles spent,
And wants supplide. And then againe abroad
On the long voiage whereto she is bent:
Well may she speede and fairly finish her intent.

II

Who fares on sea, may not commaund his way,
Ne wind and weather at his pleasure call:
The sea is wide, and easie for to stray;
The wind unstable, and doth never stay.
But here a while ye may in safety rest,
Till season serve new passage to assay:
Better safe port, then be in seas distrest.

Edmund Spenser

10. Sailor Town

DOWN AMONG THE WHARVES

Down among the wharves—that's the place I like to wander!
   Smell of tar and salted fish and barrels soaked in brine!
Here and there a lobster-crate, and brown seines over yonder,
   And in among them, mending nets, an "old-salt" friend of mine.
That old-salt friend of mine—how we love to talk together!
   Breathless is the wonder of his tales about the sea!
His face is tanned and wrinkled by the roughest kind of weather,
   And he is like a hero in a story-book to me!

Down among the wharves when a stiff north wind is flying,
   Schooners rub and bump against the docks they lie beside;
Half-way up the masts, the billowed sails are pulled for drying;
   Hawsers all are straining at the turning of the tide.
The turning of the tide! Time of wonder and of dreaming!
   Fishing-sloops are slipping from their docks across the way;

How our wharf reechoes when their saucy tugs are screaming!
  How the green piles whiten with the tossing of their spray!

Down along the wharves among a wonderland of shipping—
  Rows of shining, slender masts that sway against the sky!
Every day at flood of tide we watch some schooner slipping
  Out among the circling gulls, my old-salt friend and I.
My old salt-friend and I—he will drop the nets he's mending,
  Watch with me each flapping jib, each straining yard and spar;
How we thrill together when the sails are full and bending—
  We who like to wander where the waiting vessels are!

Eleanore Myers Jewett

SEA TOWN

This is a salt steep-cobbled town
  where every morning the men go down
  to breathe the sun-wet sea;

where maples shadow the sloping street
  and the dawn-cool reek of fog is sweet
  in the dooryard chestnut tree.

SAILOR TOWN

This is the place where fishermen
   stride down to the silver wharves again,
   to the creak of the waiting hulls

where a lifting leeward wind comes through
   and a shaking sail with a patch or two
   is followed by flashing gulls.

This is a small brine-weathered town
   where the houses lean to winds gone down
   the other side of the world,

where chimney-smoke floats blue to gray,
   piling that creaks with ended day
   while the snagging ropes are hurled.

This is the place where fishermen
   stride up the cobbled hill again
   and scan the faint-starred skies,

where doors stand open to lilac-shine
   and supper-drift blows warm and fine
   and windows have seaward eyes.

Frances Frost

EVENING IN GLOUCESTER HARBOR

The very pulse of ocean now was still:
From the far-off profound, no throb, no swell!
Motionless on the coastwise ships the sails
Hung limp and white—their very shadows white!

The light-house windows drank the kindling red,
And flashed and gleamed as if the lamps were lit.
    And now 'tis sundown. All the light-houses—
Like the wise virgins, ready with their lamps—
Flash greeting to the night! There Eastern Point
Flames out! Lo, little Ten Pound Island follows!
See Baker's Island kindling! Marblehead
Ablaze! Egg Rock, too, off Nahant, on fire!
And Boston Light winking at Minot's Ledge!—

But when the moon shone crescent in the west,
And the faint outline of the part obscured
Thread-like curved visible from horn to horn,—
And Jupiter, supreme among the orbs,
And Mars, with rutilating beam, came forth,
And the great concave opened like a flower,
Unfolding firmaments and galaxies,
Sparkling with separate stars, or snowy white
With undistinguishable suns beyond,—
No cloud to dim the immeasurable arch—
They paused and rested on their oars again,
And looked around,—in adoration looked:
For, gazing on the inconceivable,
They felt God is, though inconceivable.

Epes Sargent

A SHIP COMES IN
Salem: 1825

From Java, Sumatra, and old Cathay,
Another ship is home today.

Now in the heat of the noonday sun
They are unloading cinnamon.

And even here in Town House Square
The pungent fragrance fills the air....

Oh, nothing is quite so exciting to me
As a ship just home from the China Sea.

So I will go down to the harbor soon
And stand around all afternoon.

Oliver Jenkins

THE SHIPMAN

A schipman was ther, wonyng fer by weste:
For ought I woot, he was of Dertemouthe.
He rood upon a rouncy, as he couthe,
In a gowne of faldyng to the kne.
A dagger hangyng on a laas hadde he
Aboute his nekke under his arm adoun.
The hoote somer had maad his hew al broun;
And certeinly he was a good felawe.
Ful many a draught of wyn had he drawe
From Burdeux-ward, whil that the chapman sleep.
Of nyce conscience took he no keep.
If that he foughte, and hadde the heigher hand,
By water he sente hem hoom to every land.
But of his craft to rikne wel the tydes,
His stremes and his dangers him besides,
His herbergh and his mone, his lodemenage,
Ther was non such from Hulle to Cartage.

Hardy he was, and wys to undertake;
With many a tempest hadde his berd ben schake.
He knew wel alle the havenes, as thei were,
From Scotlond to the cape of Fynestere,
And every cryk in Bretayne and in·Spayne;
His barge y-clepud was the *Magdelayne*.
                                            Geoffrey Chaucer

OUTWARD BOUND

I leave behind me the elm-shadowed square
And carven portals of the silent street,
And wander on with listless, vagrant feet
Through seaward-looking alleys, till the air
Smells of the sea, and straightway then the care
Slips from my heart, and life once more is sweet.
At the lane's ending lie the white-winged fleet.
O restless Fancy, whither wouldst thou fare?
Here are brave pinions that shall take thee far—
Gaunt hulks of Norway; ships of red Ceylon;
Slim-masted lovers of the blue Azores!
'Tis but an instant hence to Zanzibar,
Or to the regions of the Midnight Sun;
Ionian isles are thine, and all the fairy shores.
                                          Thomas Bailey Aldrich

PICTURES

"Some likes picturs o' women," said Bill, "an' some
  likes 'orses best,"
As he fitted a pair of fancy shackles on to his old sea
  chest,
"But I likes picturs o' ships," said he, "an' you can keep
  the rest.

"An' if I was a ruddy millionaire with dollars to burn
  that way,
Instead of a dead-broke sailorman as never saves his
  pay,
I'd go to some big paintin' guy, an' this is what I'd say:

" 'Paint me the *Cutty Sark*,' I'd say, 'or the old *Thermopylae*,
Or the *Star o' Peace* as I sailed in once in my young
  days at sea,
Shipshape and Blackwall fashion, too, as a clipper ought
  to be....

" 'An' you might do 'er outward bound, with a sky full
  o' clouds,
An' the tug just dropping astern, an' gulls flyin' in
  crowds,
An' the decks shiny-wet with rain, an' the wind
  shakin' the shrouds....

" 'Or else racin' up Channel with a sou'wester blowin',
Stuns'ls set aloft and alow, an' a hoist o' flags showin',
An' a white bone between her teeth so's you can see
  she's goin'....

" 'Or you might do 'er off Cape Stiff, in the high latitudes yonder,
With 'er main deck a smother of white, an' her lee-rail dippin' under,
An' the big greybeards racin' by an' breakin' aboard like thunder....

" 'Or I'd like old Tuskar somewheres abound ... or Sydney 'Eads maybe ...
Or a couple o' junks, if she's tradin' East, to show it's the China Sea ...
Or Bar Light ... or the Tail o' the Bank ... or a glimp o' Circular Quay.

" 'An' I don't want no dabs o' paint as you can't tell what they are,
Whether they're shadders, or fellers' faces, or blocks, or blobs o' tar,
But I want gear as looks like gear, an' a spar that's like a spar.

" 'An' I don't care if it's North or South, the Trades or the China Sea,
Shortened down or everything set—close-hauled or runnin' free—
You paint me a ship as is like a ship ... an' that'll do for me!' "

C. Fox Smith

SHIPS IN HARBOUR

I have not known a quieter thing than ships,
Nor any dreamers steeped in dreams as these;
For all that they have tracked disastrous seas,
And winds that left their sails in flagging strips;
Nothing disturbs them now, no stormy grips
That once had hurt their sides, no crash or swell;
Nor can the fretful harbour quite dispel
The quiet that they learned on lonely trips.

They have no part in all the noisy noons;
They are become as dreams of ships that go
Back to the secret waters that they know,
Each as she will, to unforgot lagoons,
Where nothing moves except her ghostly spars
That mark the patient watches on the stars.
David Morton

WAYFARERS

They were met in the Last Inn's tap-room, where the
    road strikes hands with the sea,
  And one was come from a weary ship that slept with
      folded sail,
And one was come from the brown highroad that spins
    across the lea,
  The third sat by the glowing hearth and sipped a
      mug of ale.

The sailor said: "It's good to be where warmth and safety are.
I'm weary of great waters and the never-broken sky;
I'm sick of hanging dizzy to the death-end of a spar;
I want another sort of life before I come to die.

"I want a bit of meadow, where the grass is to my knees,
And a little patch where I can kneel and watch the green things grow.
I want to look at flowers, cool my eyes with blooms and trees.
I am weary of great waters where the blind white vessels go."

The landsman said: "The sea is wide and ships are graceful things,
No man may say his life is done until he dares the deep.
When I was but a lad I dreamed of vessels with white wings,
And ghostly galleons made bold adventure of my sleep.

"I know a little meadow, like the hollow of God's hand,
And if you have a mind to trade I'll tell you where it lies,
And I will take your seaman's berth and you will take my land.
And you will look at blossoms for the cooling of your eyes.

"But I will look at naked things and find their utmost worth,
  Learn wisdom from the Book of Stars that guides me through the wave.
Your life for mine! Come, will you trade blue water for brown earth?"
  "Aye," said the sailor, "Life for life and grave for certain grave."

The drinker by the fire stirred and spake with curling lips.
  "What fools," he said, "what fools ye be!" and looked into their eyes.
"Let landsmen cleave unto the land and sailors keep their ships;
  For he who seeks to prove a dream shall lose his Paradise!"

The morning thrust a golden face in at the tavern door,
  The day wind blew upon the sea and rippled through the grass,
And one man sailed in a white-winged ship and one stayed on the shore,
  The third sat by the glowing hearth and smiled into his glass.

Dana Burnet

THE SHIPS OF SAINT JOHN

Where are the ships I used to know,
  That came to port on the Fundy tide
Half a century ago,
  In beauty and stately pride?

In they would come past the beacon light,
  With the sun on gleaming sail and spar,
Folding their wings like birds in flight
  From countries strange and far.

Schooner and brig and barkentine,
  I watched them slow as the sails were furled,
And wondered what cities they must have seen
  On the other side of the world.

Frenchman and Britisher and Dane,
  Yankee, Spaniard and Portugee,
And many a home ship back again
  With her stories of the sea.

Calm and victorious, at rest
  From the relentless rough sea-play,
The wild duck on the river's breast
  Was not more sure than they.

The creatures of a passing race,
  The dark spruce forests made them strong,
The sea's lore gave them magic grace,
  The great winds taught them song.

And God endowed them each with life—
  His blessing on the craftman's skill—
To meet the blind unreasoned strife
  And dare the risk of ill.

Not mere insensate wood and paint
  Obedient to the helm's command,
But often restive as a saint
  Beneath the Heavenly hand.

SAILOR TOWN

All the beauty and mystery
  Of life were there, adventure bold,
Youth, and the glamor of the sea
  And all its sorrows old.

And many a time I saw them go
  Out on the flood at morning brave,
As the little tugs had them in tow,
  And the sunlight danced on the wave.

There all day long you could hear the sound
  Of the caulking iron, the ship's bronze bell,
And the clank of the capstan going round
  As the great tides rose and fell.

The sailors' songs, the Captain's shout,
  The boatswain's whistle piping shrill,
And the roar as the anchor chain runs out,—
  I often hear them still.

I can see them still, the sun on their gear,
  The shining streak as the hulls careen,
And the flag at the peak unfurling,—clear
  As a picture on a screen.

The fog still hangs on the long tide-rips,
  The gulls go wavering to and fro,
But where are all the beautiful ships
  I knew so long ago?

Bliss Carman

MY LOST YOUTH

Often I think of the beautiful town
   That is seated by the sea;
Often in thought go up and down
The pleasant streets of that dear old town,
   And my youth comes back to me.
      And a verse of a Lapland song
      Is haunting my memory still:
"A boy's will is the wind's will,
And the thoughts of youth are long, long thoughts."

I can see the shadowy lines of its trees,
   And catch, in sudden gleams,
The sheen of the far-surrounding seas,
And islands that were the Hesperides
   Of all my boyish dreams.
      And the burden of that old song,
      It murmurs and whispers still:
"A boy's will is the wind's will,
And the thoughts of youth are long, long thoughts."

I remember the black wharves and the slips,
   And the sea-tides tossing free;
And Spanish sailors with bearded lips,
And the beauty and mystery of the ships,
   And the magic of the sea.
      And the voice of that wayward song
      Is singing and saying still:
"A boy's will is the wind's will,
And the thoughts of youth are long, long thoughts."

I remember the bulwarks by the shore,
  And the fort upon the hill;
The sunrise gun, with its hollow roar
The drum-beat repeated o'er and o'er,
  And the bugle wild and shrill.
    And the music of that old song
    Throbs in my memory still:
  "A boy's will is the wind's will,
And the thoughts of youth are long, long thoughts."

I remember the sea-fight far away,
  How it thundered o'er the tide!
And the dead captains, as they lay
In their graves, o'erlooking the tranquil bay,
  Where they in battle died.
    And the sound of that mournful song
    Goes through me with a thrill:
  "A boy's will is the wind's will,
And the thoughts of youth are long, long thoughts."
                    Henry Wadsworth Longfellow

SOUTH STREET

As I came down to the long street by the water, the
  sea-ships drooped their masts like ladies bowing,
Curtseying friendly in a manner olden,
Shrouds and sails in silken sunlight flowing,
Gleaming and shimmering from silverie into golden,
With the sea-winds through the sunlit spaces blowing.

As I came down to South Street by the glimmering,
    tossing water, the sweet wind blew, oh, softly,
    sweetly blew
O'er the lean, black docks piled high with curious
    bales,
Odorous casks, and bundles of foreign goods,
And all the long ships, with their fair, tall sails,
Lading the winey air with the spice of alien woods.

As I came down by the winding streets to the won-
    drous green sea-water, the sounds along the
    water-front were tuned to fine accord:
I heard the racket of the halliards slapping,
Along the bare poles stabbing up aloft;
I saw loose men, their garments ever flapping,
Lounging a-row along each wooden stair:
Their untamed faces in the golden sun were soft,
But their hard, bright eyes were wild, and in the sun's
    soft flare
Nothing they saw but sounding seas and the crush
    of the ravening wind;
Nothing but furious struggle with toil that never
    would end.
The call of mine ancient sea was clamoring through
    their blood;
Ah, they all felt that call, but nothing they under-
    stood,
As I came down by the winding streets to South Street
    by the water.

As I came down to South Street by the soft sea-water,
I saw long ships, their mast-heads ever bowing:

Sweet slender maids in clinging gowns of golden,
Curtseying stately in a fashion olden,
Bowing sweetly—each a king's fair daughter—
To me, their millionth, millionth lover,
I, the seventh son of the old sea-rover,
As I came down to South Street by the myriad moving water.

Francis E. Falkenbury

"ROUND CAPE HORN"

Ask any question in this town,
Of any one, by night or morn,
The answer will be always found
   "Round Cape Horn."

I ask the ladies where I call,
"Your husbands, are they here or gone?"
And get this answer from them all,—
   "Round Cape Horn."

I asked a child I chanced to meet,
"Where is your pa, my dear, this morn?"
She answered with a smile most sweet,—
   "Round Cape Horn."

I asked a boy as on he skipped,
"Where now, my lad, at early dawn?"
He answered (for he then had shipped),—
   "Round Cape Horn."

I asked an aged man one day,
How time had passed since he was born.
"My years," said he, "have passed away,
    'Round Cape Horn.'"

I asked a sailor bound away,
Where I should write when he was gone.
He said without the least delay,—
    "Round Cape Horn."

I asked a merchant for a fee.
He turned and answered me with scorn,—
"My property is all at sea,
    'Round Cape Horn.'"

I then to a mechanic went,
And he likewise bade me begone,
For all he had, and more, was sent
    "Round Cape Horn."

I asked a sister whom I saw,
Quite finely dressed in silks and lawn,
"Where's your brother?" She answered, "La!
    'Round Cape Horn.'"

I asked a maiden by my side,
Who sighed and looked to me forlorn,
"Where is your heart?" She quick replied,—
    "Round Cape Horn."

I asked a widow why she cried,
As she sat lonely taking on;
She said her husband lately died,
    "Round Cape Horn."

I asked a mother of the dead
From whom support she long had drawn,
"Where did he die?" She merely said,—
    "Round Cape Horn."

I said, "I'll let your fathers know,"
To boys in mischief on the lawn;
They all replied; "Then you must go
    'Round Cape Horn.'"

I asked a loafer idling round,
If he would work; when, with a yawn,
He answered, "No! till I am bound
    'Round Cape Horn.'"

In fact, I asked a little boy,
If he could tell where he was born;
He answered with a mark of joy,
    "Round Cape Horn."

There's scarce a thing I chance to see
Brought here, the Island to adorn,
But either was, or soon will be,
    "Round Cape Horn."

Thus merchants, sailors, women, men,
The old, or children lately born,
To all you ask, reply again,—
    "Round Cape Horn."

Now you who know, an answer give.
Do I stay here, or am I gone?
Tell me if I do surely live
    "Round Cape Horn."

Anonymous

AN OLD SEAPORT
(Evening Sketch)

Nooked underneath steep, sterile hills that rise
Tier upon tier, receding far away,
The quaint old port, wharf-flanked to seaward, lies,
A dingy crescent round the curving bay.
Small cruising craft about the harbor glide,
Mere chips of boats, each with its one bright wing—
Bright in the golden glow of eventide—
Wooing the faint land-wind. A wee white thing
Shows on the south sea-line, and grows and grows,
Slow shadowing ship-shape; while to westward far,
Outlined in the low-lying amber bar,
A sail sinks with the day. The sweet repose
Procured of peace prevails; and, folding all
In one wide zone of rest, glooms the gray evenfall.

Anonymous

II. Sea Wings

THE SEA BIRD
TO THE WAVE

On and on,
O white brother!
Thunder does not daunt thee!
How thou movest!
By thine impulse—
With no wing!
Fairest thing
The wild sea shows me!
On and on,
O white brother!
Art thou gone!

Padraic Colum

TO THE MAN-OF-WAR-BIRD

Thou who hast slept all night upon the storm,
Waking renew'd on thy prodigious pinions,
(Burst the wild storm? above it thou ascended'st,
And rested on the sky, thy slave that cradled thee,)
Now a blue point, far, far in heaven floating,
As to the light emerging here on deck I watch thee,
(Myself a speck, a point on the world's floating vast.)

Far, far at sea,
After the night's fierce drifts have strewn the shores
    with wrecks,
With re-appearing day as now so happy and serene,
The rosy and elastic dawn, the flashing sun,
The limpid spread of air cerulean,
Thou also re-appearest.

Thou born to match the gale, (thou art all wings,)
To cope with heaven and earth and sea and hurricane,
Thou ship of air that never furl'st thy sails,
Days, even weeks untired and onward, through spaces,
    realms gyrating,
At dusk that look'st on Senegal, at morn America,
That sport'st amid the lightning-flash and thunder-
    cloud,
In them, in thy experience, had'st thou my soul,
What joys! what joys were thine!
Walt Whitman

THE STORMY PETREL

A thousand miles from land are we,
Tossing about on the roaring sea—
From billow to bounding billow cast,
Like fleecy snow on the stormy blast.
The sails are scattered abroad like weeds;
The strong masts shake like quivering reeds;
The mighty cables and iron chains;
The hull, which all earthly strength disdains,—
They strain and they crack; and hearts like stone
Their natural, hard, proud strength disown.

SEA WINGS

Up and down!—up and down!
From the base of the wave to the billow's **crown**,
And amidst the flashing and feathery foam,
The stormy petrel finds a home;
A home, if such a place may be
For her who lives on the wide, wide sea,
On the craggy ice, in the frozen air,
And only seeketh her rocky lair
To warm her young, and to teach them to spring
At once o'er the waves on their stormy wing!

O'er the deep!—o'er the deep!
Where the whale, and the shark, and the swordfish sleep—
Outflying the blast and the driving rain,
The petrel telleth her tale—in vain;
For the mariner curseth the warning bird
Which bringeth him news of the storm unheard!
Ah! thus does the prophet of good or ill
Meet hate from the creatures he serveth still;
Yet he ne'er falters—so, petrel, spring
Once more o'er the waves on thy stormy wing!
Barry Cornwall

THE SAILOR TO HIS PARROT

Thou foul-mouthed wretch! Why dost thou choose
  To learn bad language, and no good;
Canst thou not say 'The Lord be praised'
  As easy as 'Hell's fire and blood'?

Why didst thou call the gentle priest
  A thief and a damned rogue; and tell
The deacon's wife, who came to pray,
  To hold her jaw and go to hell?

Thou art a foe, no friend of mine,
  For all my thoughts thou givest away;
Whate'er I say in confidence,
  Thou dost in evil hours betray.

Thy mind's for ever set on bad;
  I cannot mutter one small curse,
But thou dost make it endless song,
  And shout it to a neighbour's house.

Aye, swear to thy delight and ours,
  When here I welcome shipmates home,
And thou canst see abundant grog—
  But hold thy tongue when landsmen come.

Be dumb when widow Johnson's near,
  Be dumb until our wedding day;
And after that—but not before—
  She will enjoy the worst you say.

There is a time to speak and not;
  When we're together, all is well;
But damn thy soul—What! you damn *mine!*
  And you tell *me* to go to hell!

W. H. Davies

ALIEN

Here in this inland garden
   Unrumorous of surf,
Here where the willows warden
   Only the sunny turf,

Here in the windy weather,
   Here where the lake wind lulls,
Slowly on silver feather
   Drift overhead the gulls.

O heart estranged of grieving
   What is a sea-bird's wing?
What beauty past believing
   Are you remembering?
               Archibald MacLeish

SEA GULLS

For one carved instant as they flew,
The language had no simile—
Silver, crystal, ivory
Were tarnished. Etched upon the horizon blue,
The frieze must go unchallenged, for the lift
And carriage of the wings would stain the drift
Of stars against a tropic indigo
Or dull the parable of snow.
Now settling one by one
Within green hollows or where curled
Crests caught the spectrum from the sun,

A thousand wings are furled.
No clay-born lilies of the world
Could blow as free
As those wild orchids of the sea.

E. J. Pratt

TO A SEAMEW

When I had wings, my brother,
   Such wings were mine as thine:
Such life my heart remembers
In all as wild Septembers
As this when life seems other,
   Though sweet, than once was mine;
When I had wings, my brother,
   Such wings were mine as thine.

Such life as thrills and quickens
   The silence of thy flight,
Or fills thy note's elation
With lordlier exultation
Than man's, whose faint heart sickens
   With hopes and fears that blight
Such life as thrills and quickens
   The silence of thy flight.

Thy cry from windward clanging
   Makes all the cliffs rejoice;
Though storm clothe seas with sorrow,
Thy call salutes the morrow;

SEA WINGS

While shades of pain seem hanging
  Round earth's most rapturous voice,
Thy cry from windward clanging
  Makes all the cliffs rejoice.

We, sons and sires of seamen,
  Whose home is all the sea,
What place man may, we claim it;
But thine—whose thought may name it?
Free birds live higher than freemen,
  And gladlier ye than we—
We, sons and sires of seamen,
  Whose home is all the sea.

For you the storm sounds only
  More notes of more delight
Than earth's in sunniest weather:
When heaven and sea together
Join strength against the lonely
  Lost bark borne down by night,
For you the storm sounds only
  More notes of more delight.

Algernon Charles Swinburne

FLYING FISH

This cruising caballero of the deep
Knows lanes of pearl and amber carved in sleep...

His fins are sunbeams. On his spinning tail
The colors of the star of morning pale.

He is the lark of water on the wing,
Whose flight is song no land-locked bird can sing.

At home within the ebon halls of night,
He soars away when dawn-buds break to light.

Oh, herald of joy! Oh! flasher above sea-flowers!
Your wild heart beats with the rhythm of spray-flung
    hours!

J. Corson Miller

TO A SEA-BIRD

  Sauntering hither on listless wings,
    Careless vagabond of the sea,
  Little thou heedest the surf that sings,
  The bar that thunders, the shale that rings,—
    Give me to keep thy company.

  Little thou hast, old friend, that's new,
    Storms and wrecks are old things to thee:
  Sick am I of these changes, too;
  Little to care for, little to rue,—
    I on the shore and thou on the sea.

  All of thy wanderings, far and near,
    Bring thee at last to shore and me;
  All of my journeyings end them here,
  This our tether must be our cheer,—
    I on the shore and thou on the sea.

  Lazily rocking on ocean's breast,
    Something in common, old friend, have we;
  Thou on the shingle seek'st thy nest,
  I to the waters look for rest,—
    I on the shore and thou on the sea.

Bret Harte

WINGED MARINER

The seagull's narrow sails of feather lift
  Across the boundaries of the hemispheres;
Effortlessly, tirelessly they drift
  Along the ocean crest, the stars' frontiers,
Coasting the cloud, riding the winds of space,
  Winnowing the fog, each element their home—
Motion made music whose slow measured grace
  Beats to the long sonatas of the foam.

When the cold norther blows the ruddy west
  To ashen gray and seabirds landward flee,
Then watch the gull emerge and casually brave
  That steep descent from heaven to the sea,
Furling his wings at last to rock and rest
  In the green hollow of the stormy wave.
                    Grace Clementine Howes

THE FISH-HAWK

On the large highway of the awful air that flows
  Unbounded between sea and heaven, while twilight
    screened
The sorrowful distances, he moved and had repose;
  On the huge wind of the immensity he leaned
His steady body, in long lapse of flight—and rose

Gradual, through broad gyres of ever-climbing rest,
  Up the clear stair of the eternal sky, and stood
Throned on the summit! Slowly, with his widening breast,
  Widened around him the enormous solitude,
From the gray rim of ocean to the glowing west.

Headlands and capes forlorn, of the far coast, the land
  Rolling her barrens toward the south, he, from his throne
Upon the gigantic wind, beheld: he hung, he fanned
  The abyss, for mighty joy, to feel beneath him strown
Pale pastures of the sea, with heaven on either hand—

The world, with all her winds and waters, earth and air,
  Fields, folds, and moving clouds. The awful and adored
Arches and endless aisles of vacancy, the fair
  Void of sheer heights and hollows hailed him as her lord
And lover in the highest, to whom all heaven lay bare.

Till from that tower of ecstasy, that baffled height,
  Stooping, he sank; and slowly on the world's wide way
Walked, with great wing on wing, the merciless, proud Might,
  Hunting the huddled and lone reaches for his prey,
Down the dim shore—and faded in the crumbling light.

Slowly the dusk covered the land. Like a great hymn
  The sound of moving winds and waters was; the sea
Whispered a benediction, and the west grew dim
  Where evening lifted her clear candles quietly...
Heaven, crowded with stars, trembled from rim to rim.
John Hall Wheelock

ALBATROSS

Time cannot age thy sinews, nor the gale
Batter the network of thy feathered mail,
  Lone sentry of the deep!
Among the crashing caverns of the storm,
With wing unfettered, lo! thy frigid form
  Is whirled in dreamless sleep!

Where shall thy wing find rest for all its might?
Where shall thy lidless eye, that scours the night,
  Grow blank in utter death?
When shall thy thousand years have stripped thee bare,
Invulnerable spirit of the air,
  And sealed thy giant-breath?

Not till thy bosom hugs the icy wave,—
Not till thy palsied limbs sink in that grave,
  Caught by the shrieking blast,
And hurled upon the sea with broad wings locked,
On an eternity of waters rocked,
  Defiant to the last!
Charles Warren Stoddard

THE LITTLE BEACH-BIRD

Thou little bird, thou dweller by the sea,
  Why takest thou its melancholy voice,
    And with that boding cry
    Along the breakers fly?
O, rather, Bird, with me
  Through the fair land rejoice!

Thy flitting form comes ghostly dim and pale,
  As driven by a beating storm at sea;
    Thy cry is weak and scared,
    As if thy mates had shared
The doom of us: Thy wail,—
  What doth it bring to me?

Thou call'st along the sand, and haunt'st the surge,
  Restless and sad; as if, in strange accord
    With the motion and the roar
    Of waves that drive to shore,
One spirit did ye urge,—
  The Mystery,—the Word.

Of thousands, thou, both sepulchre and pall,
  Old Ocean! A requiem o'er the dead,
    From out thy gloomy cells,
    A tale of mourning tells,—
Tells of man's woe and fall,
  His sinless glory fled.

Then turn thee, little Bird, and take thy flight
   Where the complaining sea shall sadness bring
     Thy spirit never more;
       Come, quit with me the shore,
And on the meadows light,
   Where birds for gladness sing!
                    Richard Henry Dana

DEPRECATING PARROTS

Shu-lin was a parrot who sat on the shoulder
Of a merchant from Bankok in chestnut sarong,
He was traded at night to a Decoit for plunder
   And brought in a sampan up coast to Hongkong.

Then recklessly purchased and shipped on a liner
Where he stole from the galley cook, bunked with the crew
And learned all the words that weren't said in parlor,
   With a Siamese accent which turned the air blue.

Now he's owned by a captain who once was commander
Of a China tea packet and since lives ashore,
Who feeds him on curry cake, rum, corriander,
   While he swings on a temple bell filched from Lahore.
                    Beulah May

FAR AND WIDE SHE WENT

Far and wide she went, her own will she sought,
All around she flew, nowhere rest she found,
For the flood she might not with her flying feet
Perch upon the land....
   Then the wild bird went
For the ark a-seeking, in the even-tide,
Over the wan wave wearily to sink,
Hungry, to the hands of the holy man.
Caedmon

THALATTA

Far over the billows unresting forever
  She flits, my white bird of the sea,
Now skyward, now earthward, storm-drifted, but never
  A wing-beat nearer to me.

With eye soft as death or the mist-wreaths above her,
  She timidly gazes below;
O never had sea-bird a man for a lover,
  And little recks she of his woe.

One sweet, startled note of amazement she utters,
  One white plume floats downward to me—
Away in the darkness a snowy wing flutters—
  Night—darkness—alone with the sea.
Willis Boyd Allen

SEAGULLS ON THE SERPENTINE

Memory, out of the mist, in a long slow ripple
  Breaks, blindly, against the shore.
The mist has buried the town in its own oblivion.
  This, this is the sea once more.

Mist-mist-brown mist; but a sense in the air of snow-
      flakes!
  I stand where the ripples die,
Lift up an arm and wait, till my lost ones know me,
  Wheel overhead, and cry.

Salt in the eyes, and the seagulls, mewing and swoop-
      ing,
  Snatching the bread from my hand;
Brushing my hand with their breasts, in swift caresses
  To show that they understand.

Oh, why are you so afraid? We are all of us exiles!
  Wheel back in your clamorous rings!
We have all of us lost the sea, and we all remember.
  But you—have wings.

Alfred Noyes

FLYING FISH

  The flashing of an arc that bright and briefly
  Is bridging for a span where nothing is;
  Refulgent leap toward light but chiefly
  Illumined instant only that is his;

Intrepid instant only that impinges
Importunate on staring sentient eye,
Revealing just the merest foam that fringes
The coming wave. To know all is to die.
Yet, deep from out one deep immensity,
Into another deeper than the sea,
He grasps with pitiful intensity
A silver pause in some Eternity.

The God who kindly keeps the sparrow's toll
May He have mercy on a fish's soul.
Katherine Kelley Taylor

SEA-BIRDS

.... Where the Northern Ocean in vast whirls
Boils round the naked melancholy isles
Of farthest Thule, and the Atlantic surge
Pours in among the stormy Hebrides—
Who can recount what transmigrations there
Are annual made? what nations come and go?
And how the living clouds on clouds arise?
Infinite wings! till all the plume-dark air
And rude resounding shore are one wild cry.
James Thomson

12. Fishermen

THE THREE FISHERS

Three fishers went sailing away to the West,
   Away to the West as the sun went down;
Each thought on the woman who loved him best,
   And the children stood watching them out of the town;
   For men must work, and women must weep,
   And there's little to earn, and many to keep,
        Though the harbor bar be moaning.

Three wives sat up in the lighthouse tower,
   And they trimmed the lamps as the sun went down;
They looked at the squall, and they looked at the shower,
   And the night-rack came rolling up ragged and brown.
   But men must work, and women must weep,
   Though storms be sudden, and waters deep,
        And the harbor bar be moaning.

Three corpses lay out on the shining sands
   In the morning gleam as the tide went down,
And the women are weeping and wringing their hands
   For those who will never come home to the town;
   For men must work, and women must weep,
   And the sooner it's over, the sooner to sleep;
        And good-bye to the bar and its moaning.
Charles Kingsley

THE COD-FISHER

Where leap the long Atlantic swells
   In foam-streaked stretch of hill and dale,
Where shrill the north-wind demon yells,
   And flings the spindrift down the gale;
Where, beaten 'gainst the bending mast,
   The frozen raindrop clings and cleaves,
With stedfast front for calm or blast
   His battered schooner rocks and heaves.

   To some the gain, to some the loss,
      To each the chance, the risk, the fight:
   For men must die that men may live—
      Lord, may we steer our course aright.

The dripping deck beneath him reels,
   The flooded scuppers spout the brine;
He heeds them not, he only feels
   The tugging of a tightened line.
The grim white sea-fog o'er him throws
   Its clammy curtain, damp and cold;
He minds it not—his work he knows,
   'Tis but to fill an empty hold.

Oft, driven through the night's blind wrack,
   He feels the dread berg's ghastly breath,
Or hears draw nigh through walls of black
   A throbbing engine chanting death;
But with a calm, unwrinkled brow
   He fronts them, grim and undismayed,
For storm and ice and liner's bow—
   These are but chances of the trade.

Yet well he knows—where'er it be,
   On low Cape Cod or bluff Cape Ann—
With straining eyes that search the sea
   A watching woman waits her man:
He knows it, and his love is deep,
   But work is work, and bread is bread,
And though men drown and women weep
   The hungry thousands must be fed.

To some the gain, to some the loss,
   To each his chance, the game with Fate:
For men must die that men may live—
   Dear Lord, be kind to those who wait.
                     Joseph C. Lincoln

THE FISHERMAN

The fisherman goes out at dawn
   When everyone's abed,
And from the bottom of the sea
   Draws up his daily bread.

His life is strange; half on the shore
   And half upon the sea—
Not quite a fish, and yet not quite
   The same as you and me.

The fisherman has curious eyes,
   They make you feel so queer,
As if they had seen many things
   Of wonder and of fear.

They're like the wondrous tales he tells—
  Not gray, nor yet quite blue;
They're like the wondrous tales he tells—
  Not quite—yet maybe—true.

He knows so much of boats and tides,
  Of winds and clouds and sky!
But when I tell of city things,
  He sniffs and shuts one eye!

Abbie Farwell Brown

FISHERMAN'S LUCK

As I sunk the lobster-pots,
To myself I thought,
Luck's the cunning lobster
I have never caught.

Though I've fished for fifty year,
Man and boy, for me
Luck's the fish I've never
Drawn from the salt sea.

And good fortune, likely now,
Won't be mine to keep,
Till I go to seek it
Fifty fathom deep.

Wilfrid Wilson Gibson

THE LAST GLOUCESTERMAN

Hail and farewell! Lo, I am the last of a glorious fleet of sail.
Staunch of timber and sweet of line, I have spread my wings to the gale.
I have mothered my dories and fed my men, as my sisters of old have done.
"But times have changed," I hear men say, "and the age of sail has run."

I have trained my lads to be valiant men, as all Peter's sons must be;
I have faithfully answered the call of my sons, and delivered the fruits of the sea.
I have seen all my sisters cut down, like the reeds that the harvester ruthlessly mows,
With the skill and the pride and the glory of old that the veteran mariner knows.

My peerless booms will be cast aside, for I shall have done with them.
My shining topmasts be stripped away, my bowsprit shorn at the stem.
And I shall be given a Diesel heart to drive me where I must go,
A piteous, reeking relic, where the clean, sweet winds still blow.

Gordon Grant

ESCAPADE

For Demerara bound with cod she flies
Running a thousand miles with scarce a sail,
Mad for the Carib moon her rigging cries,
Her limbs half-naked in the chasing gale,
Makes port, disgorges, takes on, casts away.
Heavily laden she strikes a homeward tack,
Now tipsily sedate, demurely gay,
Down a long rolling rum-and-honey track.
Her mouth, cool-green in lift, foam-white in dip,
Sighs maudlin secrets for the sea to keep,
Withdraws, whispers, withdraws with lingering drip,
Forever thirsty, forever drinking deep.
This she'll remember, when off the foggy Banks
The clammy cod lie quivering on her planks.

Kenneth Leslie

THE HARVEST OF THE SEA

The earth grows white with harvest; all day long
    The sickles gleam, until the darkness weaves
Her web of silence o'er the thankful song
    Of reapers bringing home the golden sheaves.

The wave tops whiten on the sea fields drear,
    And men go forth at haggard dawn to reap;
But ever 'mid the gleaners' song we hear
    The half-hushed sobbing of the hearts that weep.

John McCrae

THE SKIPPER-HERMIT

For thirty year, come herrin'-time,
  Through many kind o' weather,
The "*Wren*" an' me have come an' gone,
  An' held our own together.
Do' know as she is good as new
  Do' know as I am, nuther;
But she is truer'n kit an' kin,
  Or any but a mother.

They're at me now to stay ashore,
  But while we've hand an' tiller,
She'll stick to me an' I to her,—
  To leave the "*Wren*" would kill her.
My feet have worn the deck; ye see
  How watches leave their traces,
An' write on oak an' pine as plain
  As winters on our faces!

But arter all is said an' done,
  There's somethin' sort o' human
About a boat that takes at last
  The place o' child and woman;
An' yet when I have seen some things—
  Their mothers let me toss 'em—
My boat, she seemed a barnacle
  'Longside a bran'-new blossom.

Sometimes to me the breeze off-shore
  Comes out upon the water,

As if it left the grave of her,—
  No wife to me nor daughter.
Lor! if I knowed where green or no
  The turf is sweet above her,
I'd buy a bit o' ground there,—wide
  As a gull's wings would cover.

We know the tricks of wind an' tide
  That mean an' make disaster,
An' balk 'em, too—the "*Wren*" an' me—
  Off on the Ol' Man's Pastur'.
Day out an' in the blackfish there
  Go wabblin' out an' under,
An' nights we watch the coasters creep
  From light to light in yonder.

An' then ag'in we lay an' lay
  Off Wonson's Cove or Oakses—
None go by our compass-light,
  Nor we by other folkses.
Ashore, the ball-room winders shine
  Till weary feet are warnin',
But here an' there's a sick-room light
  That winks away till mornin'.

An' Sundays we go nigher in',
  To hear the bells a-ringin'—
I aint no hand for sermons, you,
  But singin's allers singin'.
The weathercocks—no two agree—
  Like men they arg' an differ,
While in the cuddy-way I set
  An' take my pipe, an' whiff her.

My pipe—eh! p'ison? mighty s-l-o-w;
  It makes my dreamin' clearer,
Though what I fill it with now-days
  Is growin' dearer 'n' dearer
I takes my comfort when it comes,
  Then no lee-lurch can spill it,
An' if my net is empty, Lor'!
  Why, how can growlin' fill it?

An' so we jog the hours away,
  The gulls they coo an' tattle,
Till on the hill the sundown red
  Starts up the drowsin' cattle.
The seiners row their jiggers by;
  I pull the slide half over,
An' shet the shore out, an' the smell
  Of sea-weed sweeter'n clover.

Hiram Rich

SHIPS WITH YOUR SILVER NETS

Ships with your silver nets,
And white, sky-going spars,
What has the green sea yielded,
And the blue sea set with stars?
"Cod and haddock and mackerel;
These are the precious store
Our nets have dragged in the billowy dawn
From the shifting ocean floor."
"Haddock and cod and mackerel."

Stuff for the belly's need,
But what of the stuff of beauty
Frailer and rarer indeed?
What of the frail sea flowers
Your gleaming nets brought up?
What of the sea anemones
Fragile and fair as a cup?
What of the pulsing daphnids,
What of the shimmering sheen
Of the weedy forests your nets uproot,
Golden and brown and green?
And what of the red dawn's magic
Through which your white sails lift,
The high moon's silver reticence,
The high star's singing drift?
Fishermen out of all the world,
Netters of haddock and cod,
What has the green sea yielded,
And the blue sea starred of God?

Wade Oliver

THE BALLAD OF THE OYSTERMAN

It was a tall young oysterman lived by the harbor-side,
His shop was just upon the bank, his boat was on the tide;
The daughter of a fisherman, that was so straight and slim,
Lived over on the other bank, right opposite to him.

It was the pensive oysterman that saw a lovely maid,
Upon a moonlight evening, a-sitting in the shade;
He saw her wave her handkerchief, as much as if to say,
"I'm wide awake, young oysterman, and all the folks away."
Then up arose the oysterman, and to himself said he,
"I guess I'll leave the skiff at home, for fear that folks should see;
I read it in the story-book, that, for to kiss his dear,
Leander swam the Hellespont,—and I will swim this here."

And he has leaped into the waves, and crossed the shining stream,
And he has clambered up the bank, all in the moonlight gleam;
O there were kisses sweet as dew, and words as soft as rain,—
But they have heard her father's step, and in he leaps again!
Out spoke the ancient fisherman,—"O what was that, my daughter?"
"'T was nothing but a pebble, sir, I threw into the water."
"And what is that, pray tell me, love, that paddles off so fast?"
"It's nothing but a porpoise, sir, that's been a-swimming past."
Out spoke the ancient fisherman,—"Now bring me my harpoon!
I'll get into my fishing-boat, and fix the fellow soon."

Down fell that pretty innocent, as falls a snow-white
    lamb,
Her hair drooped round her pallid cheeks, like sea
    weed on a clam.
Alas for those two loving ones! she waked not from
    her swound,
And he was taken with the cramp, and in the waves
    was drowned;
But Fate has metamorphosed them, in pity of their
    woe,
And now they keep an oyster-shop for mermaids
    down below.

Oliver Wendell Holmes

THE FISHERMEN

Hurrah! the seaward breezes
    Sweep down the bay amain;
Heave up, my lads, the anchor!
    Run up the sail again!
Leave to the lubber landsmen
    The rail-car and the steed;
The stars of heaven shall guide us,
    The breath of heaven shall speed.

From the hill-top looks the steeple,
    And the lighthouse from the sand;
And the scattered pines are waving
    Their farewell from the land.

One glance, my lads, behind us,
   For the homes we leave one sigh,
Ere we take the change and chances
   Of the ocean and the sky.

Now, brothers, for the icebergs
   Of frozen Labrador,
Floating spectral in the moonshine,
   Along the low, black shore!
Where like snow the gannet's feathers
   On Brador's rocks are shed,
And the noisy murr are flying,
   Like black scuds overhead;

Where in mist the rock is hiding,
   And the sharp reef lurks below,
And the white squall smites in summer,
   And the autumn tempests blow;
Where, through gray and rolling vapor,
   From evening unto morn,
A thousand boats are hailing,
   Horn answering unto horn.

Hurrah! for the Red Island,
   With the white cross on its crown!
Hurrah! for Meccatina,
   And its mountains bare and brown!
Where the Caribou's tall antlers
   O'er the dwarf-wood freely toss,
And the footstep of the Mickmack
   Has no sound upon the moss.

There we'll drop our lines, and gather
   Old Ocean's treasures in,
Where'er the mottled mackerel
   Turns up a steel-dark fin.
The sea's our field of harvest,
   Its scaly tribes our grain;
We'll reap the teeming waters
   As at home they reap the plain!

Our wet hands spread the carpet,
   And light the hearth of home;
From our fish, as in the old time,
   The silver coin shall come.
As the demon fled the chamber
   Where the fish of Tobit lay,
So ours from all our dwellings
   Shall frighten Want away.

Though the mist upon our jackets
   In the bitter air congeals,
And our lines wind stiff and slowly
   From off the frozen reels;
Though the fog be dark around us,
   And the storm blow high and loud,
We will whistle down the wild wind,
   And laugh beneath the cloud!

In the darkness as in daylight,
   On the water as on land,
God's eye is looking on us,
   And beneath us is his hand!

Death will find us soon or later,
  On the deck or in the cot;
And we cannot meet him better
  Than in working out our lot.

Hurrah!—hurrah!—the west-wind
  Comes freshening down the bay,
The rising sails are filling,—
  Give way, my lads, give way!
Leave the lubber landsman clinging
  To the dull earth, like a weed,—
The stars of heaven shall guide us,
  The breath of heaven shall speed!
John Greenleaf Whittier

COROMANDEL FISHERS

Rise, brothers, rise; the wakening skies pray to the morning light,
The wind lies asleep in the arms of the dawn like a child that has cried all night.
Come, let us gather our nets from the shore, and set our *catamarans* free,
To capture the leaping wealth of the tide, for we are the kings of the sea!

No longer delay, let us hasten away in the track of the seagull's call,
The sea is our mother, the cloud is our brother, the waves are our comrades all.

What though we toss at the fall of the sun where the hand of the sea-god drives?
He who holds the storm by the hair, will hide in his breast our lives.

Sweet is the shade of the cocoanut glade, and the scent of the mango grove,
And sweet are the sands at the full o' the moon with the sound of the voices we love;
But sweeter, O brothers, the kiss of the spray and the dance of the wild foam's glee;
Row, brothers, row to the blue of the verge, where the low sky mates with the sea.

Sarojini Naidu

THE FISHERMAN'S HYMN

The osprey sails about the sound,
  The geese are gone, the gulls are flying;
The herring shoals swarm thick around,
  The nets are launched, the boats are plying;
    Yo ho, my hearts! let's seek the deep,
      Raise high the song, and cheerily wish her,
    Still as the bending net we sweep,
      "God bless the fish-hawk and the fisher!"

She brings us fish—she brings us spring,
  Good times, fair weather, warmth, and plenty,
Fine stores of shad, trout, herring, ling,
  Sheepshead and drum, and old-wives dainty.

FISHERMEN

Yo ho, my hearts! let's seek the deep,
   Ply every oar, and cheerily wish her,
Still as the bending net we sweep,
     "God bless the fish-hawk and the fisher!"

She rears her young on yonder tree,
   She leaves her faithful mate to mind 'em;
Like us, for fish, she sails to sea,
   And, plunging, shows us where to find 'em.
Yo ho, my hearts! let's seek the deep,
   Ply every oar, and cheerily wish her,
While the slow bending net we sweep,
     "God bless the fish-hawk and the fisher!"
Alexander Wilson

THRUSTARARORUM

What time I hear the storming sea,
Blood of my ancestor stirs in me;
The quiet stream awakes from sleep,
And I long to beard the tawny deep.

I meet the rushing wind's embrace,
I feel the sea-foam on my face,
I ride at will on the hissing wave,
And the wrath of bellowing ocean brave.

I wrestle alone with the terrible gale,
And in its teeth triumphant sail;
Or fly before the driving blast,
And laugh at the gulls, as I hurtle past.

Thrustararorum was his name,
The brave old fisher from whom I came!

From cold Newfoundland fogs he sailed
In his fishing boat, nor ever quailed
When fierce Atlantic's waking wrath
Piled mountain billows in his path.

The ghostly iceberg-wraith he cleared,
Though it crowded him close, like a phantom weird;
For a valiant sailorman was he,
And he scorned the dangers of the sea.

His sturdy arm ruled sure the helm;
No wild nor'east could his soul o'erwhelm;
He knew the pathways of the sea,
And loved his life of liberty.

For sun-kissed Manisses he steered,
Nor loud Point Judith's anger feared,
And he built him there an island home
Where the mackerel swarm and the sword-fish roam.

Thrustararorum was his name,
The brave old fisher from whom I came!

Afar the cliffs o'er the ocean loom,
Afar the thundering breakers boom;
The pastures lie in the golden light,
And the heart of the islander leaps at the sight.

There he taught the people fisher-lore—
Neptune afloat, Solon ashore,
Lived he and labored on Manisses fair,
Where the pond-lily breathes on the balmy air.

FISHERMEN

With brawny arm he hauled the net,
And I see in my hands the mark of it yet;
One of earth's toilers, strong and free,
He left me his love of liberty.

Thrustararorum was his name,
The brave old fisher from whom I came!

As I sing it now I seem to hear
The voice of ocean loud in my ear,
The rush and roll of the breaker's roar,
The lofty song of his island shore.

Thrustararorum was his name,
The brave old fisher from whom I came!

And when I tire of the tedious round,
I put out for the ancient fishing ground;
I and my ancestor fishing go,
Where the billows dance and the salt winds blow.

And the floods and the sky their welcome give,
And I feel what a joy it is to live,
And my soul escapes like a bird at the sound
Of our rippling bow—
As into the ocean's arms we bound!

Thrustararorum was his name,
The brave old fisher from whom I came!
       Henry Nehemiah Dodge

WE'LL GO TO SEA NO MORE

Oh blythely shines the bonnie sun
   Upon the isle of May,
And blythely comes the morning tide
   Into St. Andrew's Bay.
Then up, gude-man, the breeze is fair,
   And up, my braw bairns three;
There's gold in yonder bonnie boat
   That sails so well the sea!
      When life's last sun goes feebly down
      And death comes to our door,
      When all the world's a dream to us,
      We'll go to sea no more.

I've seen the waves as blue as air,
   I've seen them green as grass;
But I never feared their heaving yet,
   From Grangemouth to the Bass.
I've seen the sea as black as pitch,
   I've seen it white as snow:
But I never feared its foaming yet,
   Though the winds blew high or low.
      When life's last sun goes feebly down
      And death comes to our door,
      When all the world's a dream to us,
      We'll go to sea no more.

I never liked the landsman's life,
   The earth is aye the same;
Give me the ocean for my dower,
   My vessel for my hame.

Give me the fields that no man ploughs,
  The farm that pays no fee:
Give me the bonnie fish, that glance
  So gladly through the sea.
    When life's last sun goes feebly down
    And death comes to our door,
    When all the world's a dream to us,
    We'll go to sea no more.

The sun is up, and round Inchkeith
  The breezes softly blaw;
The gude-man has the lines aboard—
  Awa' my bairns, awa'
An' ye'll be back by gloaming grey,
  An' bright the fire will low,
An' in your tales and songs we'll tell
  How weel the boat ye row.
    When life's last sun goes feebly down
    And death comes to our door,
    When all the world's a dream to us,
    We'll go to sea no more.
                              Anonymous

THE FISHER'S LIFE

What joy attends the fisher's life!
            Blow, winds, blow!
The fisher and his faithful wife!
            Row, boys, row!

He drives no plough on stubborn land,
His fields are ready to his hand;
No nipping frosts his orchards fear,
He has his autumn all the year!

The husbandman has rent to pay,
   Blow, winds, blow!
And seed to purchase every day,
   Row, boys, row!
But he who farms the rolling deeps
Though never sowing, always reaps;
The ocean's fields are fair and free,
There are no rent days on the sea!

Anonymous

OUT FROM GLOUCESTER

Out where the white waves whisper;
 Out by the breaker's bell,
Boats bound south for Georges
 Surge on the scending swell.

Out on the sea line's lifting,
 In restless, rhythmic spell,
Boats bound south for Georges
 Sway in a slow farewell.

Harlan Trott

13. Naval Songs and Ballads

THE YANKEE MAN-OF-WAR

'Tis of a gallant Yankee ship that flew the stripes and stars,
And the whistling wind from the west-nor'-west blew through the pitch-pine spars;
With her starboard tacks aboard, my boys, she hung upon the gale;
On an autumn night we raised the light on the old Head of Kinsale.

It was a clear and cloudless night, and the wind blew steady and strong,
As gayly over the sparkling deep our good ship bowled along;
With the foaming seas beneath her bow the fiery waves she spread,
And bending low her bosom of snow, she buried her lee cat-head.

There was no talk of short'ning sail by him who walked the poop,
And under the press of her pond'ring jib, the boom bent like a hoop!
And the groaning water-ways told the strain that held her stout main-tack,
But he only laughed as he glanced aloft at a white and silvery track.

The mid-tide meets in the Channel waves that flow
 from shore to shore,
And the mist hung heavy upon the land from Feather-
 stone to Dunmore,
And that sterling light in Tusker Rock where the old
 bell tolls each hour,
And the beacon light that shone so bright was quench'd
 on Waterford Tower.

The nightly robes our good ship wore were her whole
 topsails three,
Her spanker and her standing jib—the courses being
 free,
"Now, lay aloft! my heroes bold, not a moment must
 be passed!"
And royals and top-gallant sails were quickly on each
 mast.

What looms upon our starboard bow? What hangs
 upon the breeze?
'Tis time our good ship hauled her wind abreast the
 old Saltees,
For by her ponderous press of sail and by her consorts
 four
We saw our morning visitor was a British man-of-war.

Up spake our noble Captain then, as a shot ahead of us
 past—
"Haul snug your flowing courses! lay your topsail to
 the mast!"

Those Englishmen gave three loud hurrahs from the deck of their covered ark,
And we answered back by a solid broadside from the decks of our patriot bark.

"Out booms! out booms!" our skipper cried, "out booms and give her sheet,"
And the swiftest keel that was ever launched shot ahead of the British fleet,
And amidst a thundering shower of shot, with stun'-sails hoisting away,
Down the North Channel Paul Jones did steer just at the break of day.

Anonymous

OLD IRONSIDES

Ay, tear her tattered ensign down!
   Long has it waved on high,
And many an eye has danced to see
   That banner in the sky;
Beneath it rung the battle shout,
   And burst the cannon's roar;—
The meteor of the ocean air
   Shall sweep the clouds no more.

Her deck, once red with heroes' blood,
   Where knelt the vanquished foe,
When winds were hurrying o'er the flood,
   And waves were white below,

No more shall feel the victor's tread,
    Or know the conquered knee;—
The harpies of the shore shall pluck
    The eagle of the sea!

Oh, better that her shattered hulk
    Should sink beneath the wave;
Her thunders shook the mighty deep,
    And there should be her grave;
Nail to the mast her holy flag,
    Set every threadbare sail,
And give her to the god of storms,
    The lightning and the gale!

Oliver Wendell Holmes

THE MEN BEHIND THE GUNS

A cheer and salute for the Admiral, and here's to the Captain bold,
And never forget the Commodore's debt when the deeds of might are told!
They stand to the deck through the battle's wreck when the great shells roar and screech—
And never they fear when the foe is near to practice what they preach:
But off with your hat and three times three for Columbia's true-blue sons,
The men below who batter the foe—the men behind the guns!

Oh, light and merry of heart are they when they swing
 into port once more,
When, with more than enough of the "green-backed
 stuff," they start for their leave-o'-shore;
And you'd think, perhaps, that the blue-bloused chaps
 who loll along the street
Are a tender bit, with salt on it, for some fierce
 "mustache" to eat—
Some warrior bold, with straps of gold, who dazzles
 and fairly stuns
The modest worth of the sailor boys—the lads who
 serve the guns!

But say not a word till the shot is heard that tells the
 fight is on,
Till the long, deep roar grows more and more from
 the ships of "Yank" and "Don,"
Till over the deep the tempests sweep of fire and burst-
 ing shell,
And the very air is a mad Despair in the throes of a
 living hell;
Then down, deep down, in the mighty ship, unseen by
 the midday suns,
You'll find the chaps who are giving the raps—the men
 behind the guns!

Oh, well they know how the cyclones blow that they
 loose from their cloud of death,
And they know is heard the thunder-word their fierce
 ten-incher saith!
The steel decks rock with the lightning shock, and
 shake with the great recoil,

And the sea grows red with the blood of the dead and reaches for his spoil—
But not till the foe has gone below or turns his prow and runs,
Shall the voice of peace bring sweet release to the men behind the guns!

John Jerome Rooney

FARRAGUT

Mobile Bay, August 5, 1864

Farragut, Farragut,
  Old Heart of Oak,
Daring Dave Farragut,
  Thunderbolt stroke,
Watches the hoary mist
  Lift from the bay,
Till his flag, glory-kissed,
  Greets the young day.

Far, by gray Morgan's walls,
  Looms the black fleet.
Hark, deck to rampart calls
  With the drums' beat!
Buoy your chains overboard,
  While the steam hums;
Men! to the battlement,
  Farragut comes.

See, as the hurricane
  Hurtles in wrath
Squadrons of clouds amain
  Back from its path!
Back to the parapet,
  To the guns' lips,
Thunderbolt Farragut
  Hurls the black ships.

Now through the battle's roar
  Clear the boy sings,
"By the mark fathoms four,"
  While his lead swings.
Steady the wheelmen five
  "Nor' by East keep her,"
"Steady," but two alive:
  How the shells sweep her!

Lashed to the mast that sways
  Over red decks,
Over the flame that plays
  Round the torn wrecks,
Over the dying lips
  Framed for a cheer,
Farragut leads his ships,
  Guides the line clear.

On by heights cannon-browed,
  While the spars quiver;
Onward still flames the cloud
  Where the hulks shiver.

See, yon fort's star is set,
  Storm and fire past.
Cheer him, lads—Farragut,
  Lashed to the mast!

Oh! while Atlantic's breast
  Bears a white sail,
While the Gulf's towering crest
  Tops a green vale,
Men thy bold deeds shall tell,
  Old Heart of Oak,
Daring Dave Farragut,
  Thunderbolt stroke!

William Tuckey Meredith

THE RIVER FIGHT

Would you hear of the River-Fight?
It was two of a soft spring night;—
  God's stars looked down on all,
And all was clear and bright
But the low fog's chilling breath—
Up the River of Death
  Sailed the Great Admiral.

On our high poop-deck he stood,
  And round him ranged the men
Who have made their birthright good
  Of manhood, once and again,—
Lords of helm and of sail,
Tried in tempest and gale,

Bronzed in battle and wreck:
Bell and Bailey grandly led
Each his Line of the Blue and Red,
Wainwright stood by our starboard rail,
   Thornton fought the deck.

And I mind me of more than they,
   Of the youthful, steadfast ones,
   That have shown them worthy sons
Of the Seamen passed away—
Tyson conned our helm that day,
   Watson stood by his guns.

What thought our Admiral then,
Looking down on his men?
   Since the terrible day,
     (Day of renown and tears!)
   When at anchor the Essex lay,
   Holding her foes at bay,
When, a boy, by Porter's side he stood
Till deck and plank-sheer were dyed with blood,
    'T is half a hundred years—
   Half a hundred years to-day!

Who could fail with him?
Who reckon of life or limb?
   Not a pulse but beat the higher!
There had you seen, by the starlight dim,
Five hundred faces strong and grim—
   The Flag is going under fire!
Right up by the fort, with her helm hard-a-port,
   The Hartford is going under fire:

The way to our work was plain,
Caldwell had broken the chain
(Two hulks swung down amain,
   Soon as 't was sundered).
Under the night's dark blue,
Steering steady and true,
Ship after ship went through,
Till, as we hove in view,
   Jackson out-thundered.

Back echoed Philip! ah, then
Could you have seen our men,
   How they sprung, in the dim night haze,
To their work of toil and of clamor!
How the loaders, with sponge and rammer,
And their captains, with cord and hammer,
   Kept every muscle ablaze!
How the guns, as with cheer and shout
Our tackle-men hurled them out,
   Brought up on the water-ways!

First, as we fired at their flash,
   'T was lightning and black eclipse,
With a bellowing roll and crash;
But soon, upon either bow,
   What with forts, and fire-rafts, and ships,
(The whole fleet was hard at it now,
All pounding away!) and Porter
Still thundering with shell and mortar,
   'T was the mighty sound and form
   Of an equatorial storm!

(Such you see in the Far South,
After long heat and drouth,
  As day draws nigh to even:
Arching from North to South,
    Blinding the tropic sun,
      The great black bow comes on.
Till the thunder-veil is riven,
When all is crash and levin,
And the cannonade of heaven
  Rolls down the Amazon!)

But, as we worked along higher,
  Just where the river enlarges,
Down came a pyramid of fire—
    It was one of your long coal barges
      (We had often had the like before).
'T was coming down on us to larboard,
  Well in with the eastern shore,
  And our pilot, to let it pass round,
    (You may guess we never stopped to sound)
Giving us a rank sheer to starboard,
  Ran the Flag hard and fast aground!

'T was nigh abreast of the Upper Fort,
  And straightway a rascal Ram
    (She was shaped like the devil's dam)
Puffed away for us with a snort,
  And shoved it with spiteful strength
Right alongside of us, to port.
    (It was all of our ship's length,

A huge crackling Cradle of the Pit,
  Pitch-pine knots to the brim,
  Belching flame red and grim)
What a roar came up from it!

Well, for a little it looked bad;
    But these things are, somehow, shorter
  In the acting than the telling.
  There was no singing-out nor yelling,
  Nor any fussing and fretting,
    No stampede, in short;
But there we were, my lad,
    All afire on our port quarter,
  Hammocks ablaze in the netting,
    Flames spouting in at every port,
  Our Fourth Cutter burning at the davit,
  No chance to lower away and save it.

In a twinkling the flames had risen
Halfway to maintop and mizzen,
  Darting up the shrouds like snakes.
  Ah, how we clanked at the brakes!
    And the deep steam-pumps throbbed under.
    Sending a ceaseless flow.
Our topmen, a dauntless crowd,
Swarmed in rigging and shroud—
  There, ('t was a wonder!)
The burning ratlines and strands
They quenched with their bare hard hands;
    But the great guns below
    Never silenced their thunder!

At last, by backing and sounding,
When we were clear of grounding,
   And under headway once more,
The whole rebel fleet came rounding
   The point. If we had it hot before,
   'T was now, from shore to shore,
   One long, loud thundering roar—
Such crashing, splintering, and pounding,
   And smashing as you never heard before!

But that we fought foul wrong to wreck,
   And to save the Land we loved so well,
You might have deemed our long gun deck
   Two hundred feet of hell!

For all above was battle,
Broadside, and blaze, and rattle,
   Smoke and thunder alone;
But, down in the sick-bay,
Where our wounded and dying lay,
   There was scarce a sob or a moan.

And at last, when the dim day broke,
And the sullen sun awoke,
   Drearily blinking
O'er the haze and the cannon-smoke,
That ever such morning dulls,
There were thirteen traitor hulls
   On fire and sinking!

Henry Howard Brownell

THE BALLAD OF
SIR PATRICK SPENS

The Sailing

The king sits in Dunfermline town,
   Drinking the blude-red wine:
"O where will I get a skeely skipper
   To sail this new ship of mine?"

O up and spake an eldern knight,
   Sat at the king's right knee:
"Sir Patrick Spens is the best sailor
   That ever sailed the sea."

Our king has written a braid letter,
   And sealed it with his hand,
And sent it to Sir Patrick Spens,
   Was walking on the strand.

"To Noroway, to Noroway,
   To Noroway, o'er the faem;
The king's daughter of Noroway,
   'T is thou maun bring her hame!"

The first word that Sir Patrick read,
   Sae loud loud laughed he;
The neist word that Sir Patrick read,
   The tear blindit his e'e.

"O wha is this has done this deed,
   And tauld the king o' me,
To send us out at this time o' the year,
   To sail upon the sea?

"Be it wind, be it weet, be it hail, be it sleet,
   Our ship must sail the faem;
The king's daughter of Noroway
   'T is we must fetch her hame."

They hoysed their sails on Monenday morn,
   Wi' a' the speed they may:
They hae landed in Noroway
   Upon a Wodensday....

The Return

"Make ready, make ready, my merrymen a'!
   Our gude ship sails the morn."—
"Now, ever alake! my master dear,
   I fear a deadly storm.

"I saw the new moon, late yestreen,
   Wi' the auld moon in her arms;
And if we gang to sea, master,
   I fear we'll come to harm."

They hadna sailed a league, a league,
   A league but barely three,
When the lift grew dark, and the wind blew loud,
   And gurly grew the sea.

The ankers brak, and the topmasts lap,
   It was sic a deadly storm;
And the waves came o'er the broken ship
   Till a' her sides were torn.

"O where will I get a gude sailor
   To take my helm in hand,
Till I get up to the tall topmast
   To see if I can spy land?"

"O here am I, a sailor gude,
   To take the helm in hand,
Till you go up to the tall topmast—
   But I fear you'll ne'er spy land."

He hadna gane a step, a step,
   A step, but barely ane,
When a boult flew out of our goodly ship,
   And the salt sea it came in.

"Gae fetch a web o' the silken claith,
   Another o' the twine,
And wap them into our ship's side,
   And letna the sea come in."

They fetched a web o' the silken claith,
   Another o' the twine,
And they wapped them roun' the gude ship's side;
   But still the sea came in.

O laith laith were our gude Scots lords
   To weet their cork-heeled shoon,
But lang or a' the play was played
   They wat their hats aboon!

And mony was the feather bed
   That floated on the faem;
And mony was the gude lords' son
   That never mair came hame!

The ladyes wrang their fingers white—
  The maidens tore their hair;
A' for the sake of their true loves—
  For them they'll see na mair.

O lang lang may the ladyes sit,
  Wi' their fans into their hand,
Before they see Sir Patrick Spens
  Come sailing to the strand!

And lang lang may the maidens sit,
  Wi' their gowd kaims in their hair,
A' waiting for their ain dear loves—
  For them they'll see na mair!

O forty miles off Aberdeen
  'T is fifty fathoms deep,
And there lies gude Sir Patrick Spens
  Wi' the Scots lords at his feet!

Anonymous

YE MARINERS OF ENGLAND

Ye Mariners of England
  That guard our native seas!
Whose flag has braved a thousand years
  The battle·and the breeze!
Your glorious standard launch again
  To match another foe;

And sweep through the deep,
  While the stormy winds do blow!
While the battle rages loud and long,
  And the stormy winds do blow.

The spirits of your fathers
  Shall start from every wave—
For the deck it was their field of fame,
  And Ocean was their grave:
Where Blake and mighty Nelson fell
  Your manly hearts shall glow,
As ye sweep through the deep
  While the stormy winds do blow!
While the battle rages loud and long,
  And the stormy winds do blow.

Britannia needs no bulwarks,
  No towers along the steep;
Her march is o'er the mountain-waves,
  Her home is on the deep.
With thunders from her native oak
  She quells the floods below,
As they roar on the shore,
  When the stormy winds do blow!
When the battle rages loud and long,
  And the stormy winds do blow.

The meteor flag of England
  Shall yet terrific burn;
Till danger's troubled night depart
  And the star of peace return.
Then, then, ye ocean-warriors!

Our song and feast shall flow
To the fame of your name,
  When the storm has ceased to blow!
When the fiery fight is heard no more,
  And the storm has ceased to blow.
Thomas Campbell

CASABIANCA

The boy stood on the burning deck,
  Whence all but him had fled;
The flame that lit the battle's wreck
  Shone round him o'er the dead.

Yet beautiful and bright he stood,
  As born to rule the storm;
A creature of heroic blood,
  A proud though childlike form.

The flames rolled on; he would not go
  Without his father's word;
That father, faint in death below,
  His voice no longer heard.

He called aloud, "Say, father, say,
  If yet my task be done?"
He knew not that the chieftain lay
  Unconscious of his son.

"Speak, father!" once again he cried,
  "If I may yet be gone!"
And but the booming shots replied,
  And fast the flames rolled on.

Upon his brow he felt their breath,
  And in his waving hair,
And looked from the lone post of death
  In still yet brave despair;

And shouted but once more aloud,
  "My father! must I stay?"
While o'er him fast, through sail and shroud,
  The wreathing fires made way.

They wrapt the ship in splendor wild,
  They caught the flag on high,
And streamed above the gallant child,
  Like banners in the sky.

There came a burst of thunder sound;
  The boy,—Oh! where was *he*?
Ask of the winds, that far around
  With fragments strewed the sea,—

With shroud and mast and pennon fair,
That well had borne their part,—
But the noblest thing that perished there
  Was that young, faithful heart.

Felicia Hemans

THE *CUMBERLAND*

At anchor in Hampton Roads we lay,
  On board of the *Cumberland*, sloop-of-war;
And at times from the fortress across the bay
    The alarum of drums swept past,
    Of a bugle blast
  From the camp on the shore.

Then far away to the south uprose
   A little feather of snow-white smoke,
And we knew that the iron ship of our foes
     Was steadily steering its course
       To try the force
   Of our ribs of oak.

Down upon us heavily runs,
   Silent and sullen, the floating fort;
Then comes a puff of smoke from her guns,
     And leaps the terrible death,
       With fiery breath,
   From each open port.

We are not idle, but send her straight
   Defiance back in a full broadside!
As hail rebounds from a roof of slate,
     Rebounds our heavier hail
       From each iron scale
   Of the monster's hide.

"Strike your flag!" the rebel cries,
   In his arrogant old plantation strain.
"Never!" our gallant Morris replies;
     "It is better to sink than to yield!"
       And the whole air pealed
   With the cheers of our men.

Then, like a kraken huge and black,
   She crushed our ribs in her iron grasp!
Down went the *Cumberland* all a wrack,
     With a sudden shudder of death,
       And the cannon's breath
   For her dying gasp.

Next morn, as the sun rose over the bay,
    Still floated our flag at the mainmast head.
Lord, how beautiful was Thy day!
        Every waft of the air
        Was a whisper of prayer,
    Or a dirge for the dead.

Ho! brave hearts that went down in the seas!
    Ye are at peace in the troubled stream;
Ho! brave land! with hearts like these,
        Thy flag, that is rent in twain,
        Shall be one again,
    And without a seam!

Henry Wadsworth Longfellow

DRAKE'S DRUM

Drake he's in his hammock an' a thousand mile away,
    (Capten, art tha sleepin' there below?)
Slung atween the round shot in Nombre Dios Bay,
    An' dreamin' arl the time o' Plymouth Hoe.
Yarnder lumes the Island, yarnder lie the ships,
    Wi' sailor lads a-dancin' heel-an'-toe,
An' the shore-lights flashin', an' the night-tide dashin',
    He sees et arl so plainly as he saw et long ago.

Drake he was a Devon man, an' ruled the Devon seas,
    (Capten, art tha sleepin' there below?)
Rovin' tho' his death fell, he went wi' heart at ease,
    An' dreamin' arl the time o' Plymouth Hoe.

"Take my drum to England, hang et by the shore,
  Strike et when your powder's runnin' low;
If the Dons sight Devon, I'll quit the port o' Heaven,
  An' drum them up the Channel as we drummed
    them long ago."

Drake he's in his hammock till the great Armadas
    come,
  (Capten, art tha sleepin' there below?)
Slung atween the round shot, listenin' for the drum,
  An' dreamin' arl the time o' Plymouth Hoe.
Call him on the deep sea, call him up the Sound,
  Call him when ye sail to meet the foe;
Where the old trade's plyin' an' the old flag's flyin',
  They shall find him ware an' wakin', as they found
    him long ago!

Sir Henry Newbolt

THE CAPTAIN STOOD ON THE CARRONADE

The captain stood on the carronade—"First lieuten-
    ant," says he,
"Send all my merry men aft here, for they must list
    to me:
I haven't the gift of the gab, my sons—because I'm
    bred to the sea;
That ship there is a Frenchman, who means to fight
    with we.
  Odds bobs, hammer and tongs, long as I've been to
    sea,
  I've fought 'gainst every odds—but I've gain'd the
    victory!

"That ship there is a Frenchman, and if we don't take
 she,
'Tis a thousand bullets to one, that she will capture
 we;
I haven't the gift of the gab, my boys; so each man to
 his gun;
If she's not mine in half an hour, I'll flog each mother's
 son.
  Odds bobs, hammer and tongs, long as I've been to
   sea,
  I've fought 'gainst every odds—and I've gain'd the
   victory!"

We fought for twenty minutes, when the Frenchman
 had enough;
"I little thought," said he, "that your men were of
 such stuff."
The captain took the Frenchman's sword, a low bow
 made to he;
"I haven't the gift of the gab, monsieur, but polite I
 wish to be.
  Odds bobs, hammer and tongs, long as I've been to
   sea,
  I've fought 'gainst every odds—and I've gain'd the
   victory!"

Our captain sent for all of us: "My merry men," said
 he,
"I haven't the gift of the gab, my lads, but yet I thank-
 ful be:
You've done your duty handsomely, each man stood
 to his gun;

If you hadn't, you villains, as sure as day, I'd have
　　flogg'd each mother's son.
Odds bobs, hammer and tongs, as long as I'm at sea,
I'll fight 'gainst every odds—and I'll gain the victory."
　　　　　　　　　　　　　　　Frederick Marryat

WHEN THE GREAT GRAY SHIPS COME IN

(New York Harbor, August 20, 1898)

To eastward ringing, to westward winging, o'er map-
　　less miles of sea,
On winds and tides the gospel rides that the further-
　　most isles are free,
And the furthermost isles make answer, harbor, and
　　height, and hill,
Breaker and beach cry each to each, " 'T is the Mother
　　who calls! Be still!"
Mother! new-found, beloved, and strong to hold from
　　harm,
Stretching to these across the seas the shield of her
　　sovereign arm,
Who summoned the guns of her sailor sons, who bade
　　her navies roam,
Who calls again to the leagues of main, and who calls
　　them this time home!

And the great gray ships are silent, and the weary
　　watchers rest,
The black cloud dies in the August skies, and deep in
　　the golden west

Invisible hands are limning a glory of crimson bars,
And far above is the wonder of a myriad wakened stars!
Peace! As the tidings silence the strenuous cannonade,
Peace at last! is the bugle blast the length of the long blockade,
And eyes of vigil weary are lit with the glad release,
From ship to ship and from lip to lip it is "Peace! Thank God for peace."

Ah, in the sweet hereafter Columbia still shall show
The sons of these who swept the seas how she bade them rise and go,—
How, when the stirring summons smote on her children's ear,
South and North at the call stood forth, and the whole land answered, "Here!"
For the soul of the soldier's story and the heart of the sailor's song
Are all of those who meet their foes as right should meet with wrong,
Who fight their guns till the foeman runs, and then, on the decks they trod,
Brave faces raise, and give the praise to the grace of their country's God!

Yes, it is good to battle, and good to be strong and free,
To carry the hearts of a people to the uttermost ends of sea,
To see the day steal up the bay where the enemy lies in wait,

To run your ship to the harbor's lip and sink her across
   the strait:—
But better the golden evening when the ships round
   heads for home,
And the long gray miles slip swiftly past in a swirl of
   seething foam,
And the people wait at the haven's gate to greet the
   men who win!
Thank God for peace! Thank God for peace, when
   the great gray ships come in!

Guy Wetmore Carryl

ON THE LOSS OF THE *ROYAL GEORGE*

Toll for the brave!
   The brave that are no more!
All sunk beneath the wave,
   Fast by their native shore!

Eight hundred of the brave,
   Whose courage well was tried,
Had made the vessel heel,
   And laid her on her side.

A land-breeze shook the shrouds,
   And she was overset;
Down went the *Royal George*
   With all her crew complete.

Toll for the brave!
　Brave Kempenfelt is gone;
His last sea-fight is fought,
　His work of glory done.

It was not in the battle;
　No tempest gave the shock;
She sprang no fatal leak;
　She ran upon no rock.

His sword was in its sheath,
　His fingers held the pen,
When Kempenfelt went down,
　With twice four hundred men.

Weigh the vessel up,
　Once dreaded by our foes!
And mingle with our cup,
　The tears that England owes.

Her timbers yet are sound,
　And she may float again,
Full charged with England's thunder,
　And plough the distant main.

But Kempenfelt is gone,
　His victories are o'er,
And he and his eight hundred
　Shall plough the wave no more.

William Cowper

THE CHEER OF THE *TRENTON*

(A Samoan Memory—1889)

Our anchors drag and our cables surge
  At every shock of the hurtling sea,
While the mist of breakers veils the verge
  Of the reef of coral under our lee.

From east by north to the north-northwest
  The wild typhoon veers sweep on sweep,
And from moment to moment the cross-wave's crest
  Buries our waist in its sidelong leap.

Under the blows of our plunging screw
  The whitening breakers foam and churn,
But for all that steam and steel can do
  We are drifting slowly, astern, astern.

On our starboard quarter, close aboard
  We can see the stanch *Calliope* loom,
While the black flood from her smoke-stack poured
  Covers the sea like a pall of doom.

Her topmasts struck and her yards braced sharp,
  She is headed out for the open main,
While the shrouds like the strings of a giant harp,
  Scream to the touch of the hurricane.

We, from our flag-ship *Trenton's* decks,
  Are watching her battle in hope and dread,
As she threads the throng of the tossing wrecks,
  Now beaten backward, now forging ahead.

She with the red-cross ensign aloft,
  And we, our starry banner below,
Lie beam to beam, as the frigates oft
  Ranged in old sea-fights long ago.

We watch the weight of the tempest fall
  On her flooded decks and her reeling bow,
And our hearts are beating one and all,
  For we both go down should she foul us now.

Through the darkest night there's a gleam to break;
  Fathom by fathom she forges past,
Till we know by the swirl of her eddying wake,
  That her seaward struggle is won at last.

The Admiral tosses his seacap high,
  And from station to station is passed the word,
And over the uproar of wave and sky
  The thunder roll of our cheer is heard.

And back from the Briton's taffrail came
  The gallant, grateful and proud reply,
That stirred our hearts like a pulse of flame—
  The seaman's and brother's last good-bye.

Oh, blood is thicker than water, and long
  Will England's memory hold it dear,
And the tale be told in fo'c's'le song
  Of the flagship *Trenton's* parting cheer.

Walter Mitchell

THE EARL O' QUARTERDECK

The wind it blew and the ship it flew;
   And it was "Hey for hame!
And ho for hame!" But the skipper cried,
   "Haud her oot o'er the saut sea faem."

Then up and spoke the king himsel':
   And he steered the ship sae free;
Wi' the wind astarn, he crowded sail,
   And stood right out to sea.

Quo' the king, "There's treason in this, I vow;
   This is something underhand!
'Bout ship!" Quo' the skipper, "Yer grace forgets
   Ye are king but o' the land!"

And still he held to the open sea;
   And the east wind sank behind;
And the west had a bitter word to say,
   Wi' a white-sea roarin' wind.

And he turned her head into the north.
   Said the king: "Gar fling him o'er."
Quo' the fearless skipper: "It's a' ye're worth:
   Ye'll ne'er see Scotland more."

The king crept down the cabin stair,
   To drink the gude French wine,
And up she came, his daughter fair,
   And luikit ower the brine.

She turned her face to the drivin' hail,
    To the hail but and the weet;
Her snood it brak; and, as lang's hersel',
    Her hair drave out in the sleet.

She turned her face frae the drivin' win'—
    "What's that ahead?" quo' she.
The skipper he threw himsel' frae the win',
    And he drove the helm a-lee.

"Put to yer hand, my lady fair!
    Put to yer hand," quoth he;
"Gin she dinna face the win' the mair,
    It the waur for you and me."

For the skipper kenned that strength is strength,
    Whether woman's or man's at last.
To the tiller the lady she laid her han',
    And the ship laid her cheek to the blast.

For that slender body was full o' soul,
    And the will is mair than shape;
As the skipper saw when they cleared the berg,
    And he heard her quarter scrape.

Quo' the skipper: "Ye are a lady fair,
    And a princess grand to see;
But ye are a woman, and a man wad sail
    To hell in yer company."

She lifted a pale and queenly face;
    Her een flashed, and syne they swam.
"And what for no to heaven?" she says,
    And she turned awa' frae him.

But she took na her han' frae the good ship's helm,
    Until the day did daw';
And the skipper he spak', but what he said
    It was said atween them twa.

And then the good ship, she lay to,
    With the land far on the lee;
And up came the king upo' the deck;
    Wi' wan face and bluidshot ee.

The skipper he louted to the king;
    "Gae wa', gae wa'," said the king.
Said the king, like a prince, "I was a'wrang,
    Put on this ruby ring."

And the wind blew lowne, and the stars came oot,
    And the ship turned to the shore;
And, afore the sun was up again,
    They saw Scotland ance more.

That day the ship hung at the pierheid,
    And the king he stept on the land.
"Skipper, kneel down," the king he said.
    "Hoo daur ye afore me stand?"

"But wi' what ye will I redeem my ring;
    For ance I am at your beck.
And first, as ye loutit, skipper o' Doon,
    Rise up Yerl o' Quarterdeck."

The skipper he rose and looked at the king
    In his een for all his croon;
Said the skipper, "Here is yer grace's ring,
    And yer daughter is my boon."

The skipper he louted on his knee,
  The king his blade he drew:
Said the king, "How daured ye contre me?
  I'm aboard my ain ship noo.

"I canna mak' ye a king," said he.
  "For the Lord alone can do that,
And beside ye took it intil yer ain han',
  And crooned yersel' sae pat!"

The reid blude sprang into the king's face,—
  A wrathful man to see:
"The rascal loon abuses our grace;
  Gae hang him upon yon tree."

But the skipper he sprang aboard his ship,
  And he drew his biting blade;
And he struck the chain that held her fast,
  But the iron was ower weel made.

And the king he blew a whistle loud;
  And tramp, tramp, down the pier,
Cam' twenty riders on twenty steeds
  Clankin' wi' spur and spear.

"He saved your life!" cried the lady fair;
  "His life ye daurna spill!"
"Will ye come atween me and my hate?"
  Quo' the lady, "And that I will."

And on cam' the knights wi' spur and spear,
  For they heard the iron ring.
"Gin ye care na for yer father's grace?
  Mind ye that I am the king?"

"I kneel to my father for his grace,
   Right lowly on my knee;
But I stand and look the king in the face,
   For the skipper is king o' me."

She turned and she sprang upo' the deck;
   And the cable splashed in the sea.
The good ship spread her wings sae white,
   And away with the skipper goes she.

Now was not this a king's daughter?
   And a brave lady beside?
And a woman with whom a man might sail
   Into high heaven wi' pride?

George MacDonald

THE FLAG OF THE *CONSTELLATION*

   The stars of the morn
   On our banner borne,
With the Iris of Heaven are blended;
   The hand of our sires
   First mingled those fires
And by us they shall be defended.
   Then hail the true
   Red, White and Blue,
The flag of the *Constellation*,
   It sails as it sailed,
   By our forefathers hailed,
O'er battles that made us a nation.

What hand so bold
As strike from its fold
One star or one stripe of its bright'ning,
For him be those stars
Each a fiery Mars,
And each stripe be as terrible lightning.

Its meteor form
Shall ride the storm
Till the fiercest of foes surrender;
The storm gone by
It shall gild the sky,
A rainbow of peace and of splendor.

Peace, peace to the world,
Is our motto unfurled,
Though we shun not the field that is gory;
At home or abroad,
Fearing none but our God
We will carve our own pathway to glory.
Then hail the true
Red, White and Blue,
The flag of the *Constellation*,
It sails as it sailed,
By our forefathers hailed,
O'er battles that made us a nation.

Thomas Buchanan Read

14. "Ah blows!"

THE COAST OF PERU

Come all ye bold sailors
  Who sail round Cape Horn,
Come all ye bold whalers
  Who cruise round for sperm:
The captain has told us,
  An' I hope 'twill prove true,
That there's plenty of sperm whales
  Off the coast of Peru.

The first whale we saw
  Near the close of the day.
Our captain came on deck,
  And thus did he say:
"Now, all my good sailors,
  Pray be of good glee,
For we'll see him in the mornin',
  P'raps under our lee."

It was early next morning,
  Just as the sun rose,
The man at the masthead
  Cried out, " 'Ere she blows!"
"Where away?" cried the captain,
  As he sprang up aloft.
"Three points off our lee bow,
  And scarce two miles off!"

"Now brace up your yard, boys,
  We'll fasten anear,
Get your lines in your boats,
  See your box lines all clear;

Haul back the mainyard, boys,
  Stand by, each boat's crew,
Lower away, lower away,
  My brave fellows, do!

"Now bend to your oars, boys,
  Just make the boat fly,
But whatever you do, boys,
  Keep clear from his eye!"
The first mate soon struck,
  And the whale he went down,
While the old man pulled up,
  And stood by to bend on.

But the whale soon arose,
  To the windward he lay.
We hauled up 'longside
  And he showed us fair play.
We caused him to vomit,
  Thick blood for to spout,
And in less than ten minutes
  We rolled him fin out.

We towed him alongside
  With many a shout,
That day cut him in
  And began to boil out.
Oh, now he's all boiled out
  And stowed down below,
And we're waiting to hear 'em
  Sing out " 'Ere she blows!"

Anonymous

NANTUCKET WHALERS

This is the breed that followed the tails
Of clumsy, crowding, challenging whales,
Choosing infinite toil instead
Of the indolent lives the Blackbeards led,
Spurning such foul wealth as might be
In opium or "black ivory,"
Seeking instead of Pieces of Eight,
Or ropes of pearl or Portugal plate,
Blubber for their Golden Fleece—
Barrels sloshing with whales' grease.

These were the circumnavigators
Who thought themselves but mere harpooners
Nor dreamed that the malodorous schooners
Were the galleons of creators
Who, seeking whales with single heart,
Starred with names the rude sea chart.

These are the men sagacious whales
Lured away from wives and daughters
Down to brassy, palm-fringed waters,
Spouting beyond their clouding sails,
Lifting a frolicking fluke or nose
To the masthead's roar of "There she blows!"
Playing a perilous hide-and-seek
From Newfoundland to Mozambique,
These were the whales of enmity—
Plotting with typhoons, ice-choked seas,
Bladed reefs, insidious shoal,
To cheat a skipper of his goal.

II

This is the isle of the new Ulysses
Who dropped his sails in coral rings,
Fearless of blow-guns, war-clubs, krisses,
Who wandered home from the world's abysses
And made no boast of his voyagings,
Leaving laconic logs to tell
That his ship was saved by a miracle
From the bull sperm carrying in his hide—
As token of triumphant wars—
A dozen irons, a score of scars
From hounding whalemen long defied;
How he drew them into a milling school
And drenched them in a blood whirlpool;
How he crushed mate Obed in his jaws
And drowned Saul, clawing at his back,
And turning, took the ship for mark
And hurled his bulk against the bark,
Making the stalwart timbers shake
Like red froth in the creature's wake—
How yet the master, as he swayed,
Hurled unerringly his blade
And saw his rallying sailors drag
The Killer, spouting a crimson flag.

III

This is the isle where the women mated
And gave their men to the deep and waited,
Bearing their babies alone
And by the lone hearthstone
Battling the awful dread

Interminable absence bred:
This is the isle whose roofs are towers
Where women watched eternal hours
For the lovely and incredible sight
Of a yearned-for ship in its homing flight.

IV

Such were the old Nantucketers
And men of Bedford and Vineyard Haven—
Would that their spirits were our spurs,
Whose decks were never trod by craven:
Who dared the unknown, took the chance
And rose the kings of circumstance—
Yet reverent beneath the span
Of heaven's infinite caravan,
Or as they brooded on the scroll
Jehovah spread from pole to pole:
Who lived supremely and who went
Leaving their moorland eloquent
Of men who found in their sea goal
Riches propitious for the soul—
Such fortitude and grace
As grudging ocean yields a conquering race.
Daniel Henderson

THERE SHE BLOWS!

Lo, as the sun from his ocean bed rising
   Wide o'er the water his glitt'ring beam throws,
Hark! from the masthead a voice cheer'ly crying,
   "Hard on our lee-beam, a whale there she blows!"

*Call up your sleepers then, larboard and starboard
    men,*
  Main yard aback and your boats lower away,
  Broad on our lee-beam, see the white water gleam,
    Wreathing its foam in a garland of spray!

Lo, the leviathan in vastness is lying,
  Making the ocean his voluptuous bed;
While o'er and around him the sea birds are flying,
  Dark, foaming billows dash over his head.
    *Now each man watch with care, there goes his
      flukes in air;*
      Slowly but stately he sinks in the main:
    *Now peak your oars a while, rest from your weary
      toil,*
      Waiting and watching his rising again.

Now row, hearties, row as you love your salvation;
  Row, hearties, row, let your reeking sweat flow!
Give to your blood a free circulation,
  Bend to your oars, lads, give way all you know.
    *Now see each boat advance, eager to gain first
      chance,*
      Fleeting like shadows o'er the blue main.
    *Stand up an' give him some, send both your irons
      home;*
      *Cheerily stern all, trim the boat, give him the
        line!*

Gallied and sore, fins and flukes in commotion,
  Blackskin and boats are cleaving the spray,
While long, loud, and shrill winds his pipe o'er the
  ocean,

Frightened, bewildered, he brings to in dismay.
Now haul line, every man, gather in all you can,
  As lances and spades from your thwarts clear away:
Now take your oars again, each and every man
As safely and surely we hold him in play.

The power of man o'er the king of the ocean
  Is shown by the end when we gain our desire;
For a lance in his life creates a commotion.
  Slowly he sinks with his chimney on fire.
    Hear now the glad shout, from each and every seaman out,
    Matching the billow's most turbulent roar.
    From his spouthole on high, see the red signal fly
    Slowly he dies and the battle is o'er!
                                    Anonymous

JONAH AND THE WHALE

  He sported round the watery world.
His rich oil was a gloomy waveless lake
Within the waves. Affrighted seamen hurled
  Their weapons in his foaming wake.

  One old corroding iron he bore
Which journeyed through his flesh but yet had not
Found out his life. Another lance he wore
  Outside him pricking in a tender spot.

So distant were his parts that they
Sent but a dull faint message to his brain.
He knew not his own flesh, as great kings may
   Not know the farther places where they reign.

His play made storm in a calm sea;
His very kindness slew what he might touch;
And wrecks lay scattered on his anger's lee.
   The Moon rocked to and fro his watery couch.

His hunger cleared the sea. And where
He passed, the ocean's edge lifted its brim.
He skimmed the dim sea-floor to find if there
   Some garden had its harvest ripe for him.

But in his sluggish brain no thought
Ever arose. His law was instinct blind.
No thought or gleam or vision ever brought
   Light to the dark of his old dreamless mind.

Until, one day, sudden and strange
Half-hints of knowledge burst upon his sight.
Glimpses he had of Time, and Space, and Change,
   And something greater than his might;

And terror's leap to imagine sin;
And blinding Truth half-bare unto his seeing.
It was the living man who had come in,—
   Jonah's thoughts flying through his being.

Viola Meynell

THE WHALE

" 'Tis a hundred years," said the bosun bold,
   "Since I was a boy at sea;
'Tis a hundred years, so I've been told,
   And that's the truth," said he.
"We sailed one day from Milford Bay,
   The North Pole for to see;
And we found it too, without much a-do,
   And that's the truth," said he.

"We sailed and sailed, and one fair noon
   A great whale we espied,
So we took a rope and a long harpoon,
   And stuck him in the starboard side.
Then away and away went the great big whale,
   And away and away went we:
Tied fast to his tail to the North we did sail,
   And that's the truth," said he.

"And when we came to the great North Star
   An iceberg we did see.
Said the captain: 'Now we have come thus far,
   I am not going back,' said he.
So we tickled the tail of that great big whale
   With a tenpenny nail did we,
And we sailed right through that iceberg blue,
   And that's the truth," said he.

"And then the North Pole we did see,
   And we anchored the whale astern,
But he gave us a whack, that sent us back,
   Or I shouldn't have been spinning this yarn.

So messmates all" said the bosun bold,
  "If the North Pole you would see,
You've only got to sail at the tail of a whale,
  And that's the truth," said he.

Anonymous

FATHER MAPPLE'S HYMN
From *Moby Dick*

The ribs and terrors in the whale,
  Arched over me a dismal gloom,
While all God's sun-lit waves rolled by,
  And lift me deepening down to doom.

I saw the opening maw of hell,
  With endless pains and sorrows there;
Which none but they that feel can tell—
  Oh, I was plunging to despair.

In black distress, I called my God,
  When I could scarce believe him mine,
He bowed his ear to my complaints—
  No more the whale did me confine.

With speed he flew to my relief,
  As on a radiant dolphin borne;
Awful, yet bright, as lightning shone
  The face of my Deliverer God.

My song for ever shall record
   That terrible, that joyful hour;
I give the glory to my God,
   His all the mercy and the power.
Herman Melville

THE STONE FLEET

(An Old Sailor's Lament)
December 1861

I have a feeling for those ships,
   Each worn and ancient one,
With great bluff bows, and broad in the beam:
   Aye, it was unkindly done.
     But so they serve the Obsolete—
     Even so, Stone Fleet!

You'll say I'm doting; do but think
   I scudded round the Horn in one—
The *Tenedos*, a glorious
   Good old craft as ever run—
     Sunk (how all unmeet!)
     With the Old Stone Fleet.

An India ship of fame was she,
   Spices and shawls and fans she bore;
A whaler when her wrinkles came—
   Turned off! till, spent and poor,
     Her bones were sold (escheat)!
     Ah! Stone Fleet.

Four were erst patrician keels
  (Names attest what families be),
The *Kensington*, and *Richmond* too,
  Leonidas, and *Lee:*
    But now they have their seat
    With the Old Stone Fleet.

To scuttle them—a pirate deed—
  Sack them, and dismast;
They sunk so slow, they died so hard,
  But gurgling dropped at last.
    Their ghosts in gales repeat
    Woe's us, Stone Fleet!

And all for naught. The waters pass—
  Currents will have their way;
Nature is nobody's ally; 'tis well;
  The harbor is bettered—will stay.
    A failure, and complete,
    Was your Old Stone Fleet.

Herman Melville

BRAND FIRE NEW WHALING SONG RIGHT FROM THE PACIFIC OCEAN

'Pull, men, for, lo, see there they blow!
  They're going slow as night, too.
Pull, pull, you dogs! they lie like logs,—
  Thank Heaven they're headed right, too.'

"AH BLO-O-OWS!"

'The chance is ours!' the mate now roars.
  Spring, spring, nor have it said, men,
That we could miss a chance like this
  To take them head and head, men.
There's that old *sog*, he's like a log.
  Spring, lads, and show your mettle;
Strain every oar; let's strike before
  He's *gallied*, *mill*, or *settle!*

And so it is the chance is his.
  The others peak their oars now.
From his strained eyes the lightning flies,
  And lion-like he roars now.
'Pull, pull, my lads! why don't you pull?
  For God's sake, pull away, men!
Hell's blazes! pull but three strokes more,
  And we have won the day, men!

'Stand up there, foreward—pull the rest—
  Hold water—give it to her!
Stern all, stern all—now heave it, heave
  Your other iron through her!
We're fast, we're fast—stern out her way!
  Here, let me come ahead, men.
There, peak your oars—wet—line—wet—line—
  Why bloody zounds, you're dead men!'

Till from the deep, with mighty leap,
  Full length the monster breaches,—
So strongly sped, his scarred gray head
  High as our topmast reaches;

And, like a rock, with startling shock,
   From mountain height descending,
Down thunders he upon the sea,
   Ocean with ether blending.

And, hark! once more that lengthened roar,
   As from his spout-hole gushing,
His breath, long spent, now finds a vent,
   Like steam from boiler gushing.

Anonymous

THE DOLPHINS

As threads spilling dew-drops
   On rose-trees where the spider spins,
So weave through the wave-tops
   Dolphins, dolphins.

Strike bubbles in the blue glass,
   Wind out invisible balls;
No ship ever shall pass
   Your silver trawls.

Spin into the red west,
   Slip through the crystal floes,
For how should you ever rest,
   Sea-spinners of woes?

Ebony half-moons that soar
   From pools where the half-light begins,
To set when on what far shore,
   Dolphins, dolphins?

Hamish Maclaren

AND GOD CREATED THE GREAT WHALES

And God created the great whales, and each
Soul living, each that crept, which plenteously
The waters generated by their kinds,
And every bird of wing after his kind;
And saw that it was good, and bless'd them, saying,
Be fruitful, multiply, and in the seas,
And lakes, and running streams, the waters fill;
And let the fowl be multiply'd on the earth.
Forthwith the sounds and seas, each creek and bay,
With fry innumerable swarm, and shoals
Of fish, that with their fins and shining scales
Glide under the green wave, in sculls that oft
Bank the mid sea: part single, or with mate,
Graze the sea weed their pasture, and through groves
Of coral stray, or sporting with quick glance
Show to the sun their wav'd coats dropt with gold;
Or in their pearly shells at ease attend
Moist nutriment, or under rocks their food
In jointed armor watch: on smooth the seal
And bended dolphins play; part huge of bulk,
Wallowing unwieldy, enormous in their gait,
Tempest the ocean; there Leviathan,
Hugest of living creatures, on the deep
Stretch'd like a promontory sleeps, or swims
And seems a moving land, and at his gills
Draws in, and at his trunk spouts out a sea.

John Milton

THE WHALEMAN'S SONG

Has a love of adventure, a promise of gold,
   Or an ardent desire to roam,
Ever tempted you far o'er the watery world
   Away from your kindred and home
With a storm beaten Captain, free hearted and bold,
   And a score of brave fellows or two,
Inured to the hardship of hunger and cold,
   A fearless and jolly good crew?

Have you ever stood watch, where Diego's bold shores
   Loom up from the Antarctic wave;
Where the snowy plumed albatross merrily soars
   O'er many a poor mariner's grave;
Have you heard the masthead man sing out, *"There she blows!"*
   Seen the boats gaily leave the ship's side,
Or the giant fish writhe 'neath the harpoon's blow,
   While the blue sea with crimson was dyed.

Have you seen the foam fly, when the mighty Right Whale,
   Thus boldly attacked in his lair;
With a terrible blow of his ponderous tail,
   Sent the boat spinning up in the air,
Or where the fair Isles of the evergreen glades
   Are teeming with dainties so rare,
Have you ever made love 'neath the cocoa's green shade
   To the sweet, sunny maids that dwell there?

And have you e'er joined in the boisterous cheer,
　　Ringing far through the heaven's blue dome,
When rich in the spoils you have purchased so dear,
　　You hoisted your topsails for home;
Or when the dark hills of Columbia arose
　　From out the blue waves of the main,
Have you e'er realized the unspeakable joys
　　Of meeting with loved ones again?

Let those who delight in the comforts of home
　　And the joys of a warm fireside,
Who deem it a peril the Ocean to roam,
　　In the cots of their fathers abide;
But not a day nearer we reckon our death,
　　Though we daily sport over our grave;
Nor sweeter they'll slumber the green sod beneath,
　　Than we in the boisterous wave!

Anonymous

A SONG OF THE HATTERAS WHALE

To an ebbing tide, all sail apeak,
And a blustery freshening wind,
The good ship ploughs her way to the deep,
Land fading in haze behind.

Four moons rise to a south'ard course,
And the lair of the game is sought,
The eye is keen and the arm is strong
For the battle which must be fought.

A cry of "Blow" from the mainmast head,
A splash of boats in the sea,
Then the rhythmic swing of swaying backs
For the prey lies far to the lee.

A silent dash to the monster's side,
A form at the cutter's prow,
A deadly lunge from cruel harpoon
And the combat waits us now.

A swirl and plunge to old ocean's depths,
A tug on the singing line,
Then thrust on thrust from the lancer's hand
While the blood flows warm like wine.

A bellow and rush of the mighty hulk,
A crimson spout to'rd the sky,
A cauldron of foam in the water's blue
As the king rolls o'er to die.

A joyous pull to the distant craft,
A draught of burning gin,
A word of praise from the master's lips
For the lay we helped to win.

Sing ho! for the tang of the salt sea air,
Sing ho! for the whistling gale,
Sing ho! for the ones we left at home,
Sing ho! for the Hatteras whale!

Anonymous

WHALE

Rain, with a silver flail;
  Sun, with a golden ball;
Ocean, wherein the whale
  Swims minnow-small;

I heard the whale rejoice
  And cynic sharks attend;
He cried with a purple voice,
  "The Lord is my friend!"

" 'With flanged and battering tail,
  With huge and dark baleen,'
He said, 'Let there be Whale
  In the Cold and Green!'

"He gave me a water spout,
  A side like a harbor wall;
The Lord from cloud looked out
  And planned it all.

"With glittering crown atilt
  He leaned on a glittering rail;
He said, 'Where sky is spilt,
  Let there be Whale.'

"Tier upon tier of wings
  Blushed and blanched and bowed;
Phalanxed fiery things
  Cried in the cloud;

"Million-eyed was the mirk
  At the plan not understood;
But the Lord looked on His work
  And saw it was good.

"He gave me marvelous girth
  For the curve of back and breast,
And a tiny eye of mirth
  To hide His jest.

"He made me a floating hill,
  A plunging deep-sea mine.
This was the Lord's will;
  The Lord is Divine.

"I magnify His name
  In earthquake and eclipse,
In weltering molten flame
  And wrecks of ships,

"In waves that lick the moon;
  I, the plough of the sea!
I am the Lord's boon
  The Lord made me!"

The sharks barked from beneath,
  As the great whale rollicked and roared,
"Yes, and our grinning teeth,
  Was it not the Lord?"

Then question pattered like hail
  From fishes large and small.
"The Lord is mighty," said Whale,
  "The Lord made all!

"His is a mammoth jest
  Life never may betray;
He has laid it up in His breast
  Till Judgment Day;

"But high when combers foam
  And tower their last of all,
My power shall haul you home
  Through Heaven wall.

"A trumpet then in the gates,
  To the ramps a thundering drum,
I shall lead you where He waits
  For His Whale to come.

"Where His cloudy seat is placed
  On high in an empty dome,
I shall trail the Ocean abased
  In chains of foam.

"Unwieldy, squattering dread;
  Where the blazing cohorts stand
At last I shall lift my head
  As it feels His hand.

"Then wings with a million eyes
  Before mine eyes shall quail:
'Look you, all Paradise,
  I was His Whale!' "

*I heard the Whale rejoice,
  As he splayed the waves to a fan;*
"And the Lord shall say with His Voice,
  'Leviathan!'

"The Lord shall say with His Tongue,
  'Now let all Heaven give hail
To my Jest when I was young,
  To my very Whale.'"

Then the Whale careered in the Sea,
  He floundered with flailing tail;
Flourished and rollicked he,
  "Aha! Mine Empery!
For the Lord said, 'Let Whale Be!'
  And there was Whale!"

William Rose Benét

THE WHALE AND THE *ESSEX*

When storms go growling off to lonely places,
Breathless for all their bluster on the path
Of oak and steel, there comes the aftermath
When winds grow playful and the zephyr chases

A rainbow tail in circles through the cool
White silence of the Tasman Sea. Here whalers
Out of Nantucket challenged Hobart sailors
To follow the dolphin toward the blowing school

Of sperm whale in the emptiness of water
Below MacQuarrie Isle, where once the breath
Of the Antarctic made a frosty wreath
Over the blubber pots and smell of slaughter.

"AH BLO-O-OWS!"

Sperm candles lit the world, if not too bright,
And sperm oil lit the dancing eyes of greed;
Sea butchers killed beyond all wisdom's need
Till Hobart and Nantucket felt the blight.

In the blue void of the sea, a thousand miles
Sou'west of Hobart, the *Essex* sighted plumes
Brushing against the sky like gentle brooms;
The boats were launched, and three men traded wiles

With sportive cachalot, but one bull whale
Turned headlong on the *Essex* in huge anger
And stove her sides before men saw the danger,
Her timbers breaking beneath the giant flail.

The *Essex* heaved and foundered in slow pain,
Held buoyant by the barrels' hissing air,
Young Captain Pollard lost a battle there,
The strangest ever fought upon the main.

His crews rowed on, the hungry and the sick,
Whales spouting everywhere as if to taunt
Nantucket with its failure, while the gaunt
Men ate each other. The whale was Moby Dick...

A. M. Sullivan

A PERILOUS LIFE

A perilous life, and hard as life may be,
Hath the brave whaleman on the lonely sea;
On the wide water laboring, far from home,
For a bleak pittance still compelled to roam;
Few friends to cheer him through his dangerous life,
Or strong to aid him in the stormy strife;
Companion of the Sea and silent air,
The hardy whaleman has no envied fare.
Anonymous

TRIUMPH OF THE WHALE

Io! Paean! Io! sing,
To the finny people's king:
Not a mightier whale than this
In the vast Atlantic is;
Not a fatter fish than he,
Flounders round the Polar Sea.
Charles Lamb

15. Pirates and Buccaneers

THE BALLAD OF O'BRUADIR

When Captain O'Bruadir shook a sword across the sea,
>*Rolling glory on the water,*

I had a mind O'Bruadir would make an earl of me,
>*Rolling glory on the water;*

So I shut my eyes on women, forgot their sturdy hips,
And yet I stuffed my 'kerchief by playing on their lips,
While skirting by the brambles, I quickly took to ships,
>*Rolling glory on the water!*

Then out went knife and cutlass, blunderbuss and gun,
>*Rolling glory on the water;*

With boarding and with broadside we made the Dutchmen run,
>*Rolling glory on the water;*

And down among the captains in their green skin shoes,
I sought for Hugh O'Bruadir and got but little news
Till I shook him by the hand in the bay of Santa Cruz,
>*Rolling glory on the water.*

O'Bruadir said kindly, "You're a fresh blade from Mayo,
>*Rolling glory on the water,*

But come among my captains, to Achill back we go,
>*Rolling glory on the water.*

Although those Spanish beauties are dark and not so dear,

I'd rather taste in Mayo, with April on the year,
One bracing virgin female; so swing your canvas here,
　　Rolling glory on the water!"

He gripped hands with a stranger, who said, "I'd rather grip
　　O'Bruadir in glory on the water."
"Well I'm your man," said Bruadir, "and you're aboard my ship
　　Rolling glory on the water."
They drank to wilder friendship in ocean roguery;
They went ashore together, and between you and me
We found O'Bruadir dangling within an airy tree,
　　Ghosting glory from the water!
　　　　　　　　　　　　　　F. R. Higgins

DERELICT

A Reminiscence of R.L.S.'s "Treasure Island" and Cap'n Billy Bones, his Song.

"Fifteen men on the dead man's chest—
Yo-ho-ho and a bottle of rum!
Drink and the devil had done for the rest—
Yo-ho-ho and a bottle of rum!"
　The mate was fixed by the bo's'n's pike,
　The bo's'n brained with a marlinspike,
　And Cookey's throat was marked belike
　　It had been gripped
　　　By fingers ten;
　　And there they lay,
　　　All good, dead men,
Like break-o'-day in a boozing ken—
　Yo-ho-ho and a bottle of rum!

Fifteen men of a whole ship's list—
Yo-ho-ho and a bottle of rum!
Dead and be-damned and the rest gone whist!—
Yo-ho-ho and a bottle of rum!
  The skipper lay with his nob in gore
  Where the scullion's axe his cheek had shore—
  And the scullion he was stabbed times four.
    And there they lay,
      And the soggy skies
    Dripped all day long
      In up-staring eyes—
At murk sunset and at foul sunrise—
  Yo-ho-ho and a bottle of rum!

Fifteen men of 'em stiff and stark—
Yo-ho-ho and a bottle of rum!
Ten of the crew had the murder mark—
Yo-ho-ho and a bottle of rum!
  'T was a cutlass swipe, or an ounce of lead,
  Or a yawing hole in a battered head,—
  And the scuppers glut with a rotting red.
    And there they lay—
      Aye, damn my eyes!—
    All lookouts clapped
      On paradise—
All souls bound just contrariwise—
  Yo-ho-ho and a bottle of rum!

Fifteen men of 'em good and true—
Yo-ho-ho and a bottle of rum!
Every man-jack could ha' sailed with **Old Pew**—
Yo-ho-ho and a bottle of rum!

There was chest on chest full of Spanish gold,
With a ton of plate in the middle hold,
And the cabins, riot of loot untold.
    And they lay there
      That had took the plum,
    With sightless glare
      And their lips struck dumb,
While we shared all by the rule of thumb—
  Yo-ho-ho and a bottle of rum!

More was seen through the sternlight screen—
Yo-ho-ho and a bottle of rum!
Chartings ondoubt where a woman had been—
Yo-ho-ho and a bottle of rum!
  A flimsy shift on a bunker cot,
  With a thin dirk slot through the bosom-spot,
  And the lace stiff-dry in a purplish blot...
    Or was she wench,
      Or some shuddering maid
    That dared the knife
      And took the blade?
By God! She was stuff for a plucky jade;
  Yo-ho-ho and a bottle of rum!

Fifteen men on the dead man's chest—
Yo-ho-ho and a bottle of rum!
Drink and the devil had done for the rest—
Yo-ho-ho and a bottle of rum!
  We wrapped 'em all in a mains'l tight,
  With twice ten turns of a hawser's bight,
  And we heaved 'em over and out of sight—

With a yo-heave-ho!
  And a fare-you-well!
 And a sullen plunge
  In the sullen swell,
Ten fathoms deep on the road to hell!
 Yo-ho-ho and a bottle of rum!

Young E. Allison

SONG OF THE CORSAIRS

O'er the glad waters of the dark-blue sea,
Our thoughts as boundless, and our souls as free,
Far as the breeze can bear, the billows foam,
Survey our empire, and behold our home!
These are our realms, no limits to their sway;
Our flag the sceptre all who meet obey.
Ours the wild life in tumult still to range
From toil to rest, and joy in every change.
Oh! who can tell? not thou, luxurious slave!
Whose soul would sicken o'er the heaving wave;
Not thou, vain lord of wantonness and ease!
Whom slumber soothes not, pleasure cannot please,—
Oh! who can tell, save he whose heart hath tried,
And danced in triumph o'er the waters wide,
The exulting sense, the pulse's maddening play,
That thrills the wanderer of that trackless way?

Lord Byron

THE LAST BUCCANEER

Oh England is a pleasant place for them that's rich and high,
But England is a cruel place for such poor folks as I;
And such a port for mariners I ne'er shall see again
As the pleasant Isle of Avès, beside the Spanish main.

There were forty craft in Avès that were both swift and stout,
All furnished well with small arms and cannons round about;
And a thousand men in Avès made laws so fair and free
To choose their valiant captains and obey them loyally.

Thence we sailed against the Spaniard with his hoards of plate and gold,
Which he wrung with cruel tortures from Indian folk of old;
Likewise the merchant captains, with hearts as hard as stone,
Who flog men and keel-haul them, and starve them to the bone.

Oh the palms grew high in Avès, and fruits that shone like gold,
And the colibris and parrots they were gorgeous to behold;
And the negro maids to Avès from bondage fast did flee,
To welcome gallant sailors, a-sweeping in from sea.

Oh sweet it was in Avès to hear the landward breeze,
A-swing with good tobacco in a net between the trees,
With a negro lass to fan you, while you listened to the roar
Of the breakers on the reef outside, that never touched the shore.

But Scripture saith, an ending to all fine things must be;
So the King's ships sailed on Avès, and quite put down were we.
All day we fought like bulldogs, but they burst the booms at night;
And I fled in a piragua, sore wounded, from the fight.

Nine days I floated starving, and a negro lass beside,
Till for all I tried to cheer her, the poor young thing she died;
But as I lay a-gasping, a Bristol sail came by,
And brought me home to England here, to beg until I die.

And now I'm old and going—I'm sure I can't tell where;
One comfort is, this world's so hard, I can't be worse off there:
If I might but be a sea-dove, I'd fly across the main,
To the pleasant Isle of Avès, to look at it once again.

Charles Kingsley

THE SEA-KING

From out his castle on the sand
He led his tawny-bearded band
In stormy bark from land to land.

The red dawn was his goodly sign:
He set his face to sleet and brine,
And quaffed the blast like ruddy wine.

And often felt the swirling gale
Beat, like some giant thresher's flail,
Upon his battered coat of mail.

Or sacked, at times, some windy town,
And from the pastures, parched and brown,
He drove the scurrying cattle down;

And kissed the maids, and stole the bell
From off the church below the fell,
And drowned the priest within the well.

And he had seen, on frosty nights,
Strange, whirling forms and elfin sights,
In twilight land, by Northern Lights.

Or, sailing on by windless shoal,
Had heard, by night, the song of troll
Within some cavern-haunted knoll.

Off Iceland, too, the sudden rush
Of waters falling, in a hush
He heard the ice-fields grind and crush.

His prow the shining south seas clove;
Warm, spicèd winds from lemon-grove
And heated thicket round him drove.

The storm-blast was his deity;
His lover was the fitful sea;
The wailing winds his melody.

By rocky scaur and beachy head
He followed where his fancy led,
And down the rainy waters fled;

And left the peopled towns behind,
And gave his days and nights to find
What lay beyond the western wind.
L. Frank Tooker

THE LAST BUCCANEER

The winds were yelling, the waves were swelling,
  The sky was black and drear,
When the crew with eyes of flame brought the ship
    without a name
  Alongside the last Buccaneer.

"Whence flies your sloop full sail before so fierce a gale,
 When all others drive bare on the seas?
Say, come ye from the shore of the holy Salvador,
 Or the gulf of the rich Caribbees?"

"From a shore no search hath found, from a gulf no line can sound,
 Without rudder or needle we steer;
Above, below our bark, dies the sea-fowl and the shark,
 As we fly by the last Buccaneer.

"Tonight there shall be heard on the rocks of Cape de Verde
 A loud crash and a louder roar;
And tomorrow shall the deep, with a heavy moaning, sweep
 The corpses and wreck to the shore."

The stately ship of Clyde securely now may ride,
 In the breath of the citron shades;
And Severn's towering mast securely now hies fast,
 Through the sea of the balmy Trades.

From St. Jago's wealthy port, from Havannah's royal fort,
 The seaman goes forth without fear;
For since that stormy night not a mortal hath had sight
 Of the flag of the last Buccaneer.

Lord Macaulay

COLUMBUS

The wild and plunging seas have smote our sides;
The wild and trampling winds have rent our sails:
Yet if God means the gulfing waves to whelm
My galleons under, let God's will be done!
I can rest content,
In the sea's ooze, or drifting to and fro,
A lifeless corpse made animate by the tides.
My sightless eyes shall see when great ships pass;
And my dead ears shall hear their deck-bells ring;
And I shall know brave seamen guide their helm,
And still shall guide, till all my Quest is won.
Beyond the beckoning sunset, and beyond
All ultimate far seas, the alluring gold
Of India waits.
What words are these! No gleaming mines of gold,
Or flashings of great pearls, or odorous trees,
Or mounds of whitest ivory, or the sheen
Of opalescent silks, allure my keels.
I would the shore of India bleaker were
Than all the storm-wracked Hebrides! the womb
Of all her mountains barren! her great pearls
Swart as black lava, so all fools should learn
I seek not wealth, I only seek to know.
I urged the gold of India as the bait
For those who find no profit but in gold.
Mayhap my wrist shall feel the bite of chains,
And on my head the curse of fools may break
For that I prove them fools—yet what to me?
Mine are rewards that they can never give:
And in my soul a peace they cannot know.

I saw the hand of God blaze through the sky;
I heard the voice of God in all the winds:
The hand wrote, Follow! and the voice rang, Go!
And I obeyed the vision and the dream.
Seeing no visions, ye call visions lies;
Dreaming no dreams, ye held mine own untrue—
Knowing no truth but that of touch, taste, smell,
Seeing and hearing. Beasts of little mold,
My bait of pearls and gold was well devised!
                                    Percy Hutchison

A DUTCH PICTURE

Simon Danz has come home again,
    From cruising about with his buccaneers;
He has singed the beard of the King of Spain,
And carried away the Dean of Jaen
    And sold him in Algiers.

In his house by the Maese, with its roof of tiles,
    And weathercocks flying aloft in air,
There are silver tankards of antique styles,
Plunder of convent and castle, and piles
    Of carpets rich and rare.

In his tulip-garden there by the town,
    Overlooking the sluggish stream,
With his Moorish cap and dressing-gown,
The old sea-captain, hale and brown,
    Walks in a waking dream.

A smile in his gray mustachio lurks
    Whenever he thinks of the King of Spain;
And the listed tulips look like Turks,
And the silent gardener as he works
    Is changed to the Dean of Jaen.

The windmills on the outermost
    Verge of the landscape in the haze,
To him are towers on the Spanish coast,
With whiskered sentinels at their post,
    Though this is the river Maese.

But when the winter rains begin,
    He sits and smokes by the blazing brands,
And old seafaring men come in,
Goat-bearded, gray, and with double chin,
    And rings upon their hands.

They sit there in the shadow and shine
    Of the flickering fire of the winter night;
Figures in color and design
Like those by Rembrandt of the Rhine,
    Half darkness and half light.

And they talk of ventures lost or won,
    And their talk is ever and ever the same,
While they drink the red wine of Tarragon,
From the cellars of some Spanish Don,
    Or convent set on flame.

Restless at times with heavy strides
    He paces his parlor to and fro;

He is like a ship that at anchor rides,
And swings with the rising and falling tides
   And tugs at her anchor-tow.

Voices mysterious far and near,
   Sound of the wind and sound of the sea,
Are calling and whispering in his ear,
"Simon Danz! Why stayest thou here?
   Come forth and follow me!"

So he thinks he shall take to the sea again
   For one more cruise with his buccaneers,
To singe the beard of the King of Spain,
And capture another Dean of Jaen
   And sell him in Algiers.
                   Henry Wadsworth Longfellow

PIRATE TREASURE

A lady loved a swaggering rover;
The seven salt seas he voyaged over,
Bragged of a hoard none could discover,
   Hey! Jolly Roger, O.

She bloomed in a mansion dull and stately,
And as to Meeting she walked sedately,
From the tail of her eye she liked him greatly,
   Hey! Jolly Roger, O.

Rings in his ears and a red sash wore he,
He sang her a song and he told her a story;
"I'll make ye Queen of the Ocean!" swore he,
    Hey! Jolly Roger, O.

She crept from bed by her sleeping sister;
By the old gray mill he met and kissed her.
Blue day dawned before they missed her,
    Hey! Jolly Roger, O.

And while they prayed her out of Meeting,
Her wild little heart with bliss was beating,
As seaward went the lugger fleeting,
    Hey! Jolly Roger, O.

Choose in haste and repent at leisure;
A buccaneer life is not all pleasure,
He set her ashore with a little treasure,
    Hey! Jolly Roger, O.

Off he sailed where waves were dashing,
Knives were gleaming, cutlasses clashing,
And a ship on jagged rocks went crashing,
    Hey! Jolly Roger, O.

Over his bones the tides are sweeping;
The only trace of the rover sleeping
Is what he left in the lady's keeping,
    Hey! Jolly Roger, O.

Two hundred years is his name unspoken,
The secret of his hoard unbroken;
But a black-browed race wears the pirate's token,
    Hey! Jolly Roger, O.

Sea-blue eyes that gleam and glisten,
Lips that sing—and you like to listen—
A swaggering song. It might be this one:
  "Hey! Jolly Roger, O."

Abbie Farwell Brown

PIRATES

Pirates, after all, were usually
Such young men!
At yard-arms or docks they hanged them,
Or on beaches now and then.
So between the prayers of parsons
At the gallows-tree
In their ears came softly lisping
The whisper of the sea.

Their own sea of sails and fighting,
Of storm and wound,
Scattered with uncharted beaches
For the men that they marooned;
Spanish towns with plate and treasure;
Jungle; fever; heat;
And the clicking of the glasses
In some safe retreat.

In that school a man grew crafty,
Limber in his hates.
Their white scars were often left them
By their bosom mates.

What extraordinary stories
That no one now can know
Died upon those wind-blown gallows
At twenty-one or so!

Elizabeth Coatsworth

THE PIRATE OF HIGH BARBARY

A lofty ship from Salcombe came,
  Blow high, blow low, and so sailed we;
Her golden trucks they shone like flame,
  Sailing down the coast of High Barbary.

"Masthead, masthead!" is the captain's hail,
  Blow high, blow low, and so sailed we;
"Look out and about! D'ye see a sail?"
  Sailing down the coast of High Barbary.

"A ship's a-looming straight ahead,"
  Blow high, blow low, and so sailed we;
"Her color's aloft and blows out red,"
  Sailing down the coast of High Barbary.

"O ship ahoy, and where do you steer?"
  Blow high, blow low, and so sailed we;
"Are you man-o'-war, or are you privateer?"
  Sailing down the coast of High Barbary.

"I'm neither one of the two," said he,
  Blow high, blow low, and so sailed we;
"I'm a pirate an' a-lookin' for my fee,"
  Sailing down the coast of High Barbary.

"I'm a jolly pirate, an' I'm out for gold,"
  Blow high, blow low, and so sailed we;
"I'll come aboard and rummage through your after
    hold!"
  Sailing down the coast of High Barbary.

The grumbling guns they flashed and roared,
  Blow high, blow low, and so sailed we;
Till the pirate's mast went overboard,
  Sailing down the coast of High Barbary.

"Oh quarter, oh quarter!" the jolly pirate cried,
  Blow high, blow low, and so sailed we;
The quarter they gave soon sank 'em in the tide,
  Sailing down the coast of High Barbary.

They fired shots till the pirate's deck,
  Blow high, blow low, and so sailed we;
Was blood and spars and broken wreck,
  Sailing down the coast of High Barbary.

"I'll never haul my red flag down!"
  Blow high, blow low, and so sailed we;
"I'll hold all fast until we drown!"
  Sailing down the coast of High Barbary.

They called for kegs of wine and drank,
  Blow high, blow low, and so sailed we;
And sang their songs until she sank,
  Sailing down the coast of High Barbary.

So now we'll brew long cans of flip,
  Blow high, blow low, and so sailed we;
And drain them down to that Salcombe ship,
  Sailing down the coast of High Barbary.

Anonymous

16. Neptune's Kingdom

A HYMNE IN PRAYSE OF NEPTUNE

Of Neptunes Empyre let us sing,
At whose command the waves obay:
To whom the Rivers tribute pay,
Downe the high mountaines sliding.

To whom the skaly Nation yeelds
Homage for the Cristall fields
      Wherein they dwell;
And every Sea-god paies a Iem,
Yeerely out of his watry Cell,
To decke great *Neptunes* Diadem.

The *Trytons* dauncing in a ring,
Before his Pallace gates, doo make
The water with their Ecchoes quake,
Like the great Thunder sounding:
The Sea-Nymphes chaunt their Accents shrill,
And the *Syrens* taught to kill
      With their sweet voyce;
Make ev'ry ecchoing Rocke reply,
Unto their gentle murmuring noyse,
The prayse of *Neptunes* Empery.
                    Thomas Campion

THE FORSAKEN MERMAN

Come, dear children, let us away;
Down and away below.
Now my brothers call from the bay;
Now the great winds shorewards blow;
Now the salt tides seawards flow;
Now the wild white horses play,
Champ and chafe and toss in the spray.
Children dear, let us away.
This way, this way.

Call her once before you go.
Call once yet.
In a voice that she will know:
"Margaret! Margaret!"
Children's voices should be dear
(Call once more) to a mother's ear:
Children's voices, wild with pain
Surely she will come again.
Call her once and come away.
This way, this way.
"Mother dear, we cannot stay."
The wild white horses foam and fret
Margaret! Margaret!

Come, dear children, come away down.
Call no more.
One last look at the white-wall'd town,
And the little grey church on the windy shore.
Then come down.

NEPTUNE'S KINGDOM

She will not come though you call all day.
Come away, come away.

Children dear, was it yesterday
We heard the sweet bells over the bay?
In the caverns where we lay,
Through the surf and through the swell
The far-off sound of a silver bell?
Sand-strewn caverns, cool and deep,
Where the winds are all asleep;
Where the spent lights quiver and gleam;
Where the salt weed sways in the stream;
Where the sea-beasts ranged all round
Feed in the ooze of their pasture-ground;
Where the sea-snakes coil and twine,
Dry their mail and bask in the brine;
Where great whales come sailing by,
Sail and sail, with unshut eye,
Round the world for ever and aye?
When did music come this way?
Children dear, was it yesterday?

Children dear, was it yesterday
(Call yet once) that she went away?
Once she sate with you and me,
On a red gold throne in the heart of the sea,
And the youngest sate on her knee.
She comb'd its bright hair, and she tended it well,
When down swung the sound of the far-off bell.
She sigh'd, she look'd up through the clear green sea.
She said; "I must go, for my kinsfolk pray
In the little grey church on the shore today.

'Twill be Easter-time in the world—ah me!
And I lose my poor soul, Merman, here with thee."
I said; "Go up, dear heart, through the waves.
Say thy prayer, and come back to the kind sea-caves."
She smiled, she went up through the surf in the bay.
Children dear, was it yesterday?

Children dear, were we long alone?
"The sea grows stormy, the little ones moan.
Long prayers," I said, "in the world they say.
Come," I said, and we rose through the surf in the bay.
We went up the beach, by the sandy down
Where the sea-stocks bloom, to the white-wall'd town.
Through the narrow paved streets, where all was still,
To the little grey church on the windy hill.
From the church came a murmur of folk at their prayers,
But we stood without in the cold blowing airs.
We climb'd on the graves, on the stones, worn with rains,
And we gazed up the aisle through the small leaded panes.
She sate by the pillar; we saw her clear:
"Margaret, hist! come quick, we are here.
Dear heart," I said, "we are long alone.
The sea grows stormy, the little ones moan."
But, ah, she gave me never a look,
For her eyes were seal'd to the holy book.
Loud prays the priest; shut stands the door.
Come away, children, call no more.
Come away, come down, call no more.

NEPTUNE'S KINGDOM

Down, down, down.
Down to the depths of the sea.
She sits at her wheel in the humming town,
Singing most joyfully.
Hark, what she sings; "O joy, O joy,
For the humming street, and the child with its toy.
For the priest, and the bell, and the holy well.
For the wheel where I spun,
And the blessed light of the sun."
And so she sings her fill,
Singing most joyfully,
Till the shuttle falls from her hand,
And the whizzing wheel stands still.
She steals to the window, and looks at the sand;
And over the sand at the sea;
And her eyes are set in a stare;
And anon there breaks a sigh,
And anon there drops a tear,
From a sorrow-clouded eye,
And a heart sorrow-laden,
A long, long sigh.
For the cold strange eyes of a little Mermaiden,
And the gleam of her golden hair.

Come away, away children.
Come children, come down.
The salt tide rolls seaward.
Lights shine in the town.
She will start from her slumber
When gusts shake the door;
She will hear the winds howling,
Will hear the waves roar.

THE ETERNAL SEA

We shall see, while above us
The waves roar and whirl,
A ceiling of amber,
A pavement of pearl.
Singing, "Here came a mortal,
But faithless was she.
And alone dwell for ever
The kings of the sea."

But, children, at midnight,
When soft the winds blow;
When clear falls the moonlight;
When spring-tides are low:
When sweet airs come seaward
From heaths starr'd with broom;
And high rocks throw mildly
On the blanch'd sands a gloom:
Up the still, glistening beaches,
Up the creeks we will hie;
Over banks of bright seaweed
The ebb-tide leaves dry.
We will gaze, from the sand-hills,
At the white, sleeping town;
At the church on the hill-side—
And then come back down.
Singing, "There dwells a loved one,
But cruel is she.
She left lonely for ever
The kings of the sea."

Matthew Arnold

THE DEEP

   There's beauty in the deep;
The wave is bluer than the sky;
And though the lights shine bright on high,
More softly do the sea-gems glow
That sparkle in the depths below;
The rainbow's tints are only made
When on the waters they are laid,
And Sun and Moon most sweetly shine
Upon the ocean's level brine.
   There's beauty in the deep.

   There's music in the deep:—
It is not in the surf's rough roar,
Nor in the whispering, shelly shore—
They are but earthly sounds, that tell
How little of the sea nymph's shell,
That sends its loud, clear note abroad,
Or winds its softness through the flood,
Echoes through groves with coral gay,
And dies, on spongy banks, away.
   There's music in the deep.

   There's quiet in the deep:—
Above, let tides and tempests rave,
And earth-born whirlwinds wake the wave;
Above, let care and fear contend,
With sin and sorrow to the end;
Here, far beneath the tainted foam,
That frets above our peaceful home,

>   We dream in joy, and wake in love,
> Nor know the rage that yells above.
>   There's quiet in the deep.
>
> John G. C. Brainard

THE SIRENS' SONG

> Steer hither, steer your wingéd pines,
>   All beaten mariners:
> Here lie undiscovered mines,
>   A prey to passengers:
> Perfumes far sweeter than the best
> That make the phoenix urn and nest:
>   Fear not your ships,
> Nor any to oppose you save our lips:
>   But come on shore,
> Where no joy dies till love has gotten more.
>
> For swelling waves our panting breasts,
>   Where never storms arise,
> Exchange; and be awhile our guests:
>   For stars, gaze on our eyes.
> The compass, love shall hourly sing,
> And, as he goes about the ring,
>   We will not miss
>   To tell each point he nameth with a kiss.

William Browne

THE SEA-MAIDEN

There was a lily and rose sea-maiden
   In marvellous depths of far-away seas,
Whose eyes were blue, and whose head was laden
   With luminous curls like the honey of bees.

Half-hidden by corals, and swaying rushes,
   And vines of the ocean, she sat arrayed
In a tremulous veil of delicate blushes
   And robes of quivering light and shade.

The sun-fish came to worship her graces;
   The dog-fish lingered, and marvelled beside;
And she gayly smiled in their whimsical faces,
   And sang them songs till they laughed or cried.

A poet of earth looked down upon her,
   And loved and beckoned, and told his love;
But her soul was coy with a sea-maiden's honor,
   And she would not go to the world above.

So there he staid by the crystalline water;
   He leaned and gazed, with his heart on fire,
And died at last for the ocean's daughter,—
   Died of sorrow and long desire.

And still she sits in the peace of ocean,
   The peace of the mouth of the ocean-caves,—
A damsel without an earthly emotion,
   Who cares not for men, their loves, or their graves.

Thus, deep in calms of woman's life, covers
  Herself some maiden on aureate sands
Of duty and innocence, far from lovers,
  From beatings of hearts, and reachings of hands.

J. W. de Forest

THE CORAL GROVE

Deep in the wave is a coral grove,
Where the purple mullet and gold-fish rove,
Where the sea-flower spreads its leaves of blue,
That never are wet with falling dew,
But in bright and changeful beauty shine,
Far down in the green and glassy brine.
The floor is of sand like the mountain drift
And the pearl-shells spangle the flinty snow;
From coral rocks the sea-plants lift
Their boughs, where the tides and billows flow;
The water is calm and still below,
For the winds and waves are absent there,
And the sands are bright as the stars that glow
In the motionless fields of upper air:
There with its waving blade of green,
The sea-flag streams through the silent water,
And the crimson leaf of the dulse is seen
To blush, like a banner bathed in slaughter:
There with a light and easy motion,
The fan-coral sweeps through the clear, deep sea:
And the yellow and scarlet tufts of ocean
Are bending like corn on the upland lea:

And life, in rare and beautiful forms,
Is sporting amid those bowers of stone,
And is safe, when the wrathful spirit of storms
Has made the top of the wave his own:
And when the ship from his fury flies,
Where the myriad voices of ocean roar,
When the wind-god frowns in the murky skies,
And demons are waiting the wreck on shore;
Then far below, in the peaceful sea,
The purple mullet and gold-fish rove,
Where the waters murmur tranquilly,
Through the bending twigs of the coral grove.
James Gates Percival

NEXT UNTO HIM WAS NEPTUNE PICTURED

Next unto him was Neptune pictured,
In his divine resemblance wondrous lyke:
His face was rugged, and his hoarie hed
Dropped with brackish deaw: his threeforkt Pyke
He stearnly shooke, and therewith fierce did stryke
The raging billowes, that on every syde
They trembling stood, and made a long broad dyke,
That his swift charet might have passage wyde
Which foure great Hippodames did draw in temewise
    tyde.
His seahorses did seeme to snort amayne,
And from their nosethrilles blow the brynie streame,
That made the sparckling waves to smoke agayne,

And flame with gold; but the white fomy creame
Did shine with silver, and shoot forth his beame.
Edmund Spenser

LEGEND

When the wounded seaman heard the ocean daughters
   With their dreamy call
Lull the stormy demon of the waters,
   He remembered all.

He remembered knowing of an island charted,
   "Past a flying fire,"
Where a fruit was growing, winey-hearted,
   Called "the mind's desire."

Near him broke the stealing rollers into jewels
   Round a tree, and there
Sorrow's end and healing, renewals
   Ripened in the air.

So he knew he'd found it and he watched the glory
   Burning on the tree
With the dancers round it—like the story—
   In the swinging sea.

Lovely round the honey-colored fruit, the motion
   Made a leafy stir.
Songs were in that sunny tree of ocean
   Where the apples were.

NEPTUNE'S KINGDOM

First the ocean sung them, then the daughters after,
   Dancing to the word.
Beauty danced among them with low laughter
   And the harp was heard.

In that sea's immeasurable music sounded
   Songs of peace, and still
From the bough the treasure hung down rounded
   To the seaman's will.

Redder than the jewel-seeded beach and sharper
   Were the wounds he bore,
Hearing, past the cruel dark, a harper
   Lulling on the shore.

Long he watched the wonders, ringed with lovely
     perils,
   Watched the apples gleam
In the sleepy thunders on the beryls,
   Then he breathed his dream:

"Bloody lands and flaming seas and cloudy slaughter,
   Hateful fogs unfurled,
Steely horror, shaming sky and water,
   These have wreathed the world.

"Give me fruit for freighting, till my anchor grapples
   Home, in harbor cast:
Earth shall end her hating through the apples
   And be healed at last."

Then the sea-girls, lifting up their lovely voices
  With the secret word,
Sang it through the drifting ocean noises
  And the sailor heard:

Ocean-old the answers reached his failing sinew,
  Touched, unveiled his eyes:
"Beach and bough and dancers are within you,
  There the island lies.

"Though the heavens harden, though the thunders hover,
  Though our songs be mute,
Burning in our garden for the lover,
  Still unfolds the fruit."

Outward from that shore the happy sailor, turning,
  Passed the fleets of sleep,
Passed his pain and bore the secret, burning,
  Homeward to the deep.

Ridgely Torrence

HOMERIC HYMN TO NEPTUNE

Neptune, the mighty Marine God, I sing:
Earths mover; & the fruitless Oceans king.
That Helicon, and th' Aegean Deepes dost hold.
O thou Earth-shaker; Thy Command, two-fold
The Gods have sorted; making thee, of Horses
The awfull Tamer; and of Navall Forces

The sure Preserver. Haile (O Saturns Birth)
Whose gracefull greene hayre, circkles all the Earth.
Beare a benigne minde; and thy helpfull hand,
Lend All, submitted, to thy drad Command.
George Chapman

SUNKEN GOLD

In dim green depths rot ingot-laden ships;
    And gold doubloons, that from the drowned hand fell,
  Lie nestled in the ocean-flower's bell
With love's old gifts, once kissed by long-drowned lips;

And round some wrought gold cup the sea-grass whips;
    And hides lost pearls, near pearls still in their shell,
  Where sea-weed forests fill each ocean dell
And seek dim sunlight with their restless tips.

So lie the wasted gifts, the long-lost hopes
  Beneath the now hushed surface of myself,
In lonelier depths than where the diver gropes;

They lie deep, deep; but I at times behold
  In doubtful glimpses, on some reefy shelf,
The gleam of irrecoverable gold.
Eugene Lee-Hamilton

SONNET TO THE SEA SERPENT

Welter upon the waters, mighty one—
And stretch thee in the ocean's trough of brine;
　Turn thy wet scales up to the wind and sun,
And toss the billows from thy flashing fin;
Heave thy deep breathings to the ocean's din,
　And bound upon its ridges in thy pride:
　Or dive down to its lowest depths, and in
The caverns where its unknown monsters hide,
Measure thy length beneath the gulf-stream's tide—
　Or rest thee on that naval of the sea
Where, floating on the Maelstrom, abide
　The krakens sheltering under Norway's lee;
But go not to Nahant, lest men should swear,
You are a great deal bigger than you are.
　　　　　　　　　　　　John G. C. Brainard

METHOUGHT I SAW A THOUSAND FEARFUL WRECKS

Methought I saw a thousand fearful wrecks,
A thousand men that fishes gnawed upon,
Wedges of gold, great anchors, heaps of pearl,
Inestimable stones, unvalued jewels,
All scattered in the bottom of the sea.
Some lay in dead men's skulls; and in those holes,
Where eyes did once inhabit, there were crept,
As 'twere in scorn of eyes, reflecting gems

That woo'd the slimy bottom of the deep,
And mocked the dead bones that lay scattered by.
William Shakespeare

HE SAW FAR IN THE CONCAVE GREEN OF THE SEA

He saw far in the concave green of the sea
An old man sitting calm and peacefully.
Upon a weeded rock this old man sat,
And his white hair was awful, and a mat
Of weeds were cold beneath his cold thin feet;
And, ample as the largest winding-sheet,
A cloak of blue wrapp'd up his aged bones,
O'erwrought with symbols by the deepest groans
Of ambitious magic: every ocean-form
Was woven in with black distinctness; storm
And calm, and whispering, and hideous roar,
Quicksand, and whirlpool, and deserted shore,
Were emblem'd in the woof; with every shape
That skims, or dives, or sleeps, 'twixt cape and cape.
The gulphing whale was like a dot in the spell,
Yet look upon it, and 'twould size and swell
To its huge self; and the minutest fish
Would pass the very hardest gazer's wish,
And show his little eye's anatomy.
Then there was pictur'd the regality
Of Neptune; and the sea nymphs round his state,
In beauteous vassalage, look up and wait.
Beside this old man lay a pearly wand,

And in his lap a book, the which he conn'd
So stedfastly, that the new denizen
Had time to keep him in amazed ken,
To mark these shadowings, and stand in awe.

(The old man speaks)
Now shall I lay my head
In peace upon my watery pillow: now
Sleep will come smoothly to my weary brow.
O Jove! I shall be young again, be young!
O shell-borne Neptune, I am pierc'd and stung
With new-born life! What shall I do? Where go,
When I have cast this serpent-skin of woe?—
I'll swim to the syrens, and one moment listen
Their melodies, and see their long hair glisten;
Anon upon that giant's arm I'll be,
That writhes about the roots of Sicily:
To northern seas I'll in a twinkling sail,
And mount upon the snortings of a whale
To some black cloud; thence down I'll madly sweep
On forkèd lightning, to the deepest deep,
Where through some sucking pool I will be hurl'd
With rapture to the other side of the world!

John Keats

MERMAIDS AND MERMEN

Mermaids
Fathoms deep beneath the wave,
   Stringing beads of glistening pearl;
Singing the achievements brave
   Of many an old Norwegian earl;

Dwelling where the tempest's raving
  Falls as light upon our ear
As the sigh of lover, craving
  Pity from his lady dear,—
Children of Thule, we,
From the deep caves of the sea,
As the lark springs from the lea,
Hither come to share your glee.

Mermen

From reining of the water-horse,
  That bounded till the waves were foaming,
Watching the infant tempest's course,
  Chasing the sea-snake in its roaming;
From winding charge-notes on the shell,
  When the huge whale and swordfish duel;
Or tolling shroudless seamen's knell,
  When the winds and waves are cruel,—
Children of wild Thule, we
Have ploughed such furrows on the sea,
As the steer draws on the lea,—
And hither we come to share your glee.

Mermaids and Mermen

We heard you in our twilight caves,
  A hundred fathoms deep below;
For notes of joy can pierce the waves
  That drown each sound of war and woe.
Those who dwell beneath the sea
  Love the sons of Thule so well;
Thus, to aid your mirth, bring we
  Dance and song and sounding shell.

Children of dark Thule, know
Those who dwell by haaf and voe,
Where your daring shallops row,
Come to share the festal show.

Sir Walter Scott

THE GARDENS OF THE SEA

Beneath the ocean's sapphire lid
   We gazed far down, and who had dreamed,
   Till pure and cold its treasures gleamed,
What lucent jewels there lay hid?—

Red sparks that give the dolphin pause,
   Lamps of the ocean-elf, and gems
   Long lost from crystal diadems,
And veiled in shrouds of glowing gauze.

Splendid and chill those gardens shone,
   Where sound is not, and tides are winds—
   Where, fugitive, the naiad finds
Eternal autumn, hushed and lone;

Till one had said that in her bow'rs
   Were mixt the nacres of the dawn,
   That thence the sunset's dyes were drawn,
And there the rainbow sank its tow'rs.

Where gorgeous flowers of chrysoprase
   In songless meadows bared their blooms,
   The deep's unweariable looms
With shifting splendors lured the gaze—

Undulant bronze and glossy toils
  That shuddered in the lustrous tide,
  And forms in restless crimson dyed
That caught the light in stealthy coils.

And in those royal halls lay lost
  The oriflammes and golden oars
  Of argosies from lyric shores—
'Mid glimmering crowns and croziers tost.

Far down we gazed, nor dared to dream
  What final sorceries would be
  When in those gardens of the sea
The lilies of the moon should gleam.
George Sterling

THE COURT OF NEPTUNE

O Muse! by thee conducted down, I dare
The secrets of the watery world declare;
For nothing 'scapes thy view; to thee 'tis given,
To range the space of earth, and seas, and heaven,
Descry a thousand forms, conceal'd from sight,
And in immortal verse to give the visions light.
  A rock there lies, in depth of sea profound,
About its clefts, rich beds of pearl abound,
Where sportful Nature, covering her retreat
With flowing waters, holds her secret seat
In woods of coral, intricate she strays,
And wreathes the shells of fish a thousand ways,
And animates the spawn of all her finny race.

Th' unnumber'd species of the fertile tide,
In shoals, around their mighty mother, glide.
From out the rock's wide caverns deep below,
The rushing ocean rises to its flow;
And, ebbing, here retires; within its sides,
In roomy caves the god of sea resides.
Pillars unhewn, of living stone, bear high
His vaulted courts; in storms the billows fly
O'er th' echoing roof, like thunder through the skies,
And warn the ruler of the floods to rise,
And check the raving winds, and the swoln waves chastise.
Rich spoils, by plundering tempests hither borne,
An universe of wealth, the palace-rooms adorn.
Before its entrance, broken wrecks are seen
In heaps deform'd a melancholy scene.
But far within, upon a mossy throne,
With washy ooze and samphire overgrown,
The sea-green king his forky sceptre rears;
Awful his aspect, numerous are his years.
A pearly crown circles his brows divine;
His beard and dewy hair shed trickling drops of brine.
John Hughes

SUBMARINE MOUNTAINS

Under the sea, which is their sky, they rise
   To watery altitudes as vast as those
    Of far Himalayan peaks impent in snows
   And veils of cloud and sacred deep repose.

NEPTUNE'S KINGDOM

Under the sea, their flowing firmament,
  More dark than any ray of sun can pierce,
  The earthquake thrust them up with mighty tierce,
And left them to be seen but by the eyes
Of awed imagination inward bent.

Their vegetation is the viscid ooze,
  Whose mysteries are past belief or thought.
  Creation seems around them devil-wrought,
  Or by some cosmic urgence gone distraught.
A-down their precipices, chill and dense
  With the dank midnight, creep or crawl or climb
  Such tentacled and eyeless things of slime,
Such monster shapes as tempt us to accuse
Life of a miscreative impotence.

About their peaks the shark, their eagle, floats
  In the thick azure far beneath the air,
  Or downward sweeps upon what prey may dare
  Set forth from any silent, weedy lair.

But one desire on all their slopes is found,
  Desire of food, the awful hunger strife;
  Yet here, it may be, was begun our life,
Here all the dreams on which our vision dotes
In unevolved obscurity were bound.

Too strange it is, too terrible! And yet
  It matters not how we were wrought, or whence
  Life came to us with all its throb intense,
  If in it is a Godly Immanence.

It matters not,—if haply we are more
   Than creatures half-conceived by a blind force
   That sweeps the universe in a chance course:
For only in Unmeaning Might is met
The intolerable thought none can ignore.
Cale Young Rice

THE SEA-DEEPS

Deeper than the narwhal sinketh,
Deeper than the sea-horse drinketh,
There are miles and miles of sea,
Where darkness reigns eternally.
Nor length of line, nor sounding lead,
Have ever reached the deep sea-bed;
Nor aught again beheld the light,
Which touched that land of endless night.
Above, a ship might strike and ground,
Below, no bottom could be found,
Though, o'er the rocks the white waves hiss,
Unfathomed lay the dark abyss.
Depths measureless—rocks that were hurled
From the foundations of the world.
Deeper than plummet e'er can go
Lie those grim endless depths below,
Which neither wind nor wave come near,
For all is dark and silent there.
Perchance, huge monsters feed and sleep
Below that black and soundless deep;
Monsters of such weight and size,
That they have no power to rise:

The mighty kraken, which they say,
Will heave upon that awful day,
When the last trumpet's startling sound
Shall pierce the inmost depths profound;
And many a league of ocean part,
While his huge bulk he doth uprear,
And like an island vast appear.
Such monstrous things, they say, now sleep
Within the caverns of the deep.

Thomas Miller

ELEGY
(*On a Dead Mermaid Washed Ashore at Plymouth Rock*)

Pallidly sleeping, the Ocean's mysterious daughter
Lies in the lee of the boulder that shattered her charms.
Dawn rushes over the level horizon of water
And touches to flickering crimson her face and her arms,
While every scale in that marvelous tail
Quivers with colour like sun on a Mediterranean sail.

Could you not keep to the ocean that lulls the equator,
Soulless, immortal, and fatally fair to the gaze?
Or were you called to the north by an ecstasy greater
Than any you knew in those ancient and terrible days
When all your delight was to flash on the sight
Of the wondering sailor and lure him to death in the watery night?

Was there, perhaps, on the deck of some far-away vessel
A lad from New England whose fancy you failed to ensnare?
Who, born of this virtuous rock, and accustomed to wrestle
With beauty in all of its forms, became your despair,
And awoke in your breast a mortal unrest
That dragged you away from the south to your death in the cold northwest?

Pallidly sleeping, your body is shorn of its magic,
But death gives a soul to whatever is lovely and dies.
Now Ocean reclaims you again, lest a marvel so tragic
Remain to be mocked by our earthly and virtuous eyes,
And reason redeems already what seems
Only a fable like all our strange and beautiful dreams.

Robert Hillyer

17. Ghost Ships and Phantoms

LAST CARGO

> *"Drive renewed to move hulks out of harbor. Old square riggers still feel call of sea.... When ice forms in the harbor tributaries, the vessels have been known to break away as a rising tide pushed ice against the old hulls, leading police boats, fireboats and tugs a merry chase to return them to proper moorings."—News Item.*

What are the voices that harass their dreaming?
What are the sirens that sing to their wood?
Water-logged derelicts, stripped to their beaming,
Riding at moorings, as derelicts should.

Velvety nights on the tropical ocean
(Silk under hatches and stars in the shrouds).
Flashing black arc of the porpoise's motion,
Mountains of water, and temples of clouds.

Fog-haunted seas, and the buoy's warning clamor.
Rounding the Horn to the tune of its gales.
Hail-beaten decks, and the wind like a hammer
Booming aloft in the shuddering sails.

Here comes the ice from the winter-bound river,
Crowding the hulks as they passively ride.
How the black, rotting sides tremble and shiver,
Straining to move with the outgoing tide!

Up with each ghostly mast—fore, main and mizzen!
Break out the shadow-sails! Race with the clouds!
Out to the sea, where a light wind has risen—
Silk under hatches, and stars in the shrouds!

Silence Buck Bellows

THE SHIPS OF ARCADY

Through the faintest filigree
Over the dim waters go
Little ships of Arcady
When the morning moon is low.

I can hear the sailors' song
From the blue edge of the sea,
Passing like the lights along
Thro' the dusky filigree.

Then where moon and waters meet
Sail by sail they pass away,
With little friendly winds replete
Blowing from the breaking day.

And when the little ships have flown,
Dreaming still of Arcady
I look across the waves, alone
In the misty filigree.

Francis Ledwidge

THE OLD SHIPS

I have seen old ships sail like swans asleep
Beyond the village which men still call Tyre,
With leaden age o'ercargoed, dipping deep
For Famagusta and the hidden sun
That rings black Cyprus with a lake of fire;
And all those ships were certainly so old
Who knows how oft with squat and noisy gun,
Questing brown slaves or Syrian oranges,
The pirate Genoese
Hell-raked them till they rolled
Blood, water, fruit and corpses up the hold.
But now through friendly seas they softly run,
Painted the mid-sea blue or shore-sea green,
Still patterned with the vine and grapes in gold.

But I have seen,
Pointing her shapely shadows from the dawn
And image tumbled on a rose-swept bay,
A drowsy ship of some yet older day;
And, wonder's breath indrawn,
Thought I—who knows—who knows—but in that same
(Fished up beyond Æaea, patched up new
—Stern painted brighter blue—)
That talkative, bald-headed seaman came
(Twelve patient comrades sweating at the oar)
From Troy's doom-crimson shore,
And with great lies about his wooden horse
Set the crew laughing, and forgot his course.

It was so old a ship—who knows, who knows?
—And yet so beautiful, I watched in vain
To see the mast burst open with a rose,
And the whole deck put on its leaves again.
                              James Elroy Flecker

WATERFRONT
(Salem)

*Nereid, Grand Turk, Good Intent,
Friendship, Light Horse, Astrea*—
from the far gulfs of the Indies,
creaking alongside the dark wharves...

Who has come upon them,
glimpsing their ghostly hulls
rising and dipping
with the slow moving of water?
Who has come upon them,
prowling along the desolate wharves
in the dead of night?
                              Oliver Jenkins

THE SONG OF THE DERELICT

Ye have sung me your songs, ye have chanted your
    rimes.
  (I scorn your beguiling, O sea!)
Ye fondle me now, but to strike me betimes.
  (A treacherous lover, the sea!)

Once I saw as I lay, half a-wash in the night
A hull in the gloom—a quick hail—and a light
And I lurched o'er to leeward and saved her for spite
   From the doom that ye meted to me.

I was sister to *Terrible*, seventy-four,
   (Yo ho! for the swing of the sea!)
And ye sank her in fathoms a thousand or more.
   (Alas! for the might of the sea!)
Ye taunt me and sing me her fate for a sign!
What harm can ye wreak more on me or on mine?
Ho braggart! I care not for boasting of thine—
   A fig for the wrath of the sea!

Some night to the lee of the land I shall steal,
   (Heigh-ho to be home from the sea!)
No pilot but Death at the rudderless wheel,
   (None knoweth the harbor as he!)
To lie where the slow tides creep hither and fro
And the shifting sand laps me around, for I know
That my gallant old crew are in Port long ago—
   For ever at peace with the sea!

                     John McCrae

CLOUDS

When I have lain an hour watching the skies,
With oaken boughs above my grassy bed,
An ocean seems to open on my eyes,
With ships becalmed that linger overhead
As if their motion was a kind of rest;

And argosies I see and navies brave
With flame of flags and pomp of pennons dressed,
Trailing their splendors through the colored wave.
Triumphant galleons freighted to the rail,
Lean toward their harbors with extended sail.

Whither, ah, whither all that wealth and worth,
That sky-borne booty floating toward a bourne
Beyond all ken, beyond all touch of earth?
And we,—that steer and tack, struggle and mourn
To win a point or round a promontory,
Nursing the shore and angling with the wind,
To gain a tinsel, quaint, ephemeral glory,
And leave a fortune or a name behind,—
Are drifting toward some goal insensibly,
Like those slow-moving treasures of the sky.
John Jay Chapman

THE DEAD SHIP
OF HARPSWELL

What flecks the outer gray beyond
    The sundown's golden trail?
The white flash of a sea-bird's wing,
    Or gleam of slanting sail?
Let young eyes watch from Neck and Point,
    And sea-worn elders pray,—
The ghost of what was once a ship
    Is sailing up the bay!

From gray sea-fog, from icy drift,
  From peril and from pain,
The home-bound fisher greets thy lights,
  O hundred-harbored Maine!
But many a keel shall seaward turn,
  And many a sail outstand,
When, tall and white, the Dead Ship looms
  Against the dusk of land.

She rounds the headland's bristling pines;
  She threads the isle-set bay;
No spur of breeze can speed her on,
  Nor ebb of tide delay.
Old men still walk the Isle of Orr
  Who tell her date and name,
Old shipwrights sit in Freeport yards
  Who hewed her oaken frame.

What weary doom of baffled quest,
  Thou sad sea-ghost, is thine?
What makes thee in the haunts of home
  A wonder and a sign?
No foot is on thy silent deck,
  Upon the helm no hand;
No ripple hath the soundless wind
  That smites thee from the land!

For never comes the ship to port,
  Howe'er the breeze may be;
Just when she nears the waiting shore
  She drifts again to sea.

No tack of sail, nor turn of helm,
  Nor sheer of veering side;
Stern-fore she drives to sea and night,
  Against the wind and tide.

In vain o'er Harpswell Neck the star
  Of evening guides her in;
In vain for her the lamps are lit
  Within thy tower, Seguin!
In vain the harbor-boat shall hail,
  In vain the pilot call;
No hand shall reef her spectral sail,
  Or let her anchor fall.

Shake, brown old wives, with dreary joy,
  Your gray-head hints of ill;
And, over sick-beds whispering low,
  Your prophecies fulfil.
Some home amid yon birchen trees
  Shall drape its door with woe;
And slowly where the Dead Ship sails,
  The burial boat shall row!

From Wolf Neck and from Flying Point,
  From island and from main,
From sheltered cove and tided creek,
  Shall glide the funeral train.
The dead-boat with the bearers four,
  The mourners at her stern,—
And one shall go the silent way
  Who shall no more return!

And men shall sigh, and women weep,
  Whose dear ones pale and pine,
And sadly over sunset seas
  Await the ghostly sign.
They know not that its sails are filled
  By pity's tender breath,
Nor see the Angel at the helm
  Who steers the Ship of Death!

John Greenleaf Whittier

THE PHANTOM SHIP

In Mather's Magnalia Christi,
  Of the old colonial time,
May be found in prose the legend
  That is here set down in rhyme.

A ship sailed from New Haven,
  And the keen and frosty airs,
That filled her sails at parting,
  Were heavy with good men's prayers.

"O Lord! if it be thy pleasure"—
  Thus prayed the old divine—
"To bury our friends in the ocean,
  Take them, for they are thine!"

But Master Lamberton muttered,
  And under his breath said he,
"This ship is so crank and walty
  I fear our grave she will be!"

And the ships that came from England,
  When the winter months were gone,
Brought no tidings of this vessel
  Nor of Master Lamberton.

This put the people to praying
  That the Lord would let them hear
What in his greater wisdom
  He had done with friends so dear.

And at last their prayers were answered:--
  It was in the month of June,
An hour before the sunset
  Of a windy afternoon,

When, steadily steering landward,
  A ship was seen below,
And they knew it was Lamberton, Master,
  Who sailed so long ago.

On she came, with a cloud of canvas,
  Right against the wind that blew,
Until the eye could distinguish
  The faces of the crew.

Then fell her straining topmasts,
  Hanging tangled in the shrouds,
And her sails were loosened and lifted,
  And blown away like clouds.

And the masts, with all their rigging,
  Fell slowly, one by one,
And the hulk dilated and vanished,
  As a sea-mist in the sun!

And the people who saw this marvel
  Each said unto his friend,
That this was the mould of their vessel,
  And thus her tragic end.

And the pastor of the village
  Gave thanks to God in prayer,
That, to quiet their troubled spirits,
  He had sent this Ship of Air.
                    Henry Wadsworth Longfellow

THE *FLYING DUTCHMAN*

When winds are locked along the tropic shore,
And the smooth sea simmers like the roof of Tophet,
A bearded sailor, solemn as a prophet,
Will warn young men of Vanderdecken's oar.

And who was Vanderdecken? Never heard
Of the *Flying Dutchman*, with all canvas full,
Scudding the lazy sea against the lull
Of air that couldn't lift a humming bird?

Three centuries now the *Dutchman* seeks escape
From malice of the wind. He skirts the Horn,
And runs the wastes of water past forlorn
Tristan da Cunha toward the battered Cape

Where the meeting of two oceans weaves a counterpane
Over the churning deep. Sails set for home,
Old Vanderdecken and his sailors comb
Their lengthening beards and seek a port in vain.

Some fear the *Dutchman*'s sails. Let them fear more
The doldrum days when the evil net is cast
Over the winds, and seamen look aghast
At the drip of golden waters from the oar,

Lest it be Vanderdecken come to ask:
"I beg of you, dear friend, to take this letter
To Haarlem, lest my wife think I forget her!"
Aye, duped is he who dares the simple task:

For Vanderdecken cursed upon the wind,
And the wind rose to heaven with the word
Of blasphemy, and Vanderdecken heard
God's judgment on him: "Fool, because thou sinned

"With mortal breath, the winds shall hold in thrall
Thy ship forever. Let no stranger take
Thy tidings homeward, or in folly's sake
The herald shall forget the port of call."

Lloyd's list will tell the names of ships long lost:
Left port and left the world, for all the news
Reported of the captain and the crews—
The *Flying Dutchman* met them with his post.

In eighteen forty-one, Year of Our Lord,
The steamer *President* passed Sandy Hook
For Liverpool. It was the final look
At land for a hundred passengers aboard.

Whether the captain paused for Vanderdecken
And took the fatal letter, none can tell;
But the clerk in Lloyd's pulled on the dismal bell
With one more mystery of the deep to reckon.

When Vanderdecken's men grow bent and old,
He sets a trap for young hands on the stays.
How? I cannot tell, since time betrays
No secrets of his mind. This can be told:

The brig *Marie Celeste* cleared New York
For Genoa, November, seventy-two;
No man has looked on captain or the crew
From that day on;—but rolling like a cork,

With all sails set, they found the idling craft
Caught in the doldrums sou'west of Gibraltar.
If Vanderdecken found them in this halter
Of strangled air, he took them drunk or daft!

My proof? The empty ship—no storm—no war,
No living soul aboard; no corpse, no ghost
To whisper how the forty men were lost—
But Vanderdecken himself could tell you more!

A. M. Sullivan

THE *PALATINE*

Leagues north, as fly the gull and auk,
Point Judith watches with eye of hawk;
Leagues south, thy beacon flames, Montauk!

Lonely and wind-shorn, wood-forsaken,
With never a tree for Spring to waken,
For tryst of lovers or farewells taken,

Circled by waters that never freeze,
Beaten by billow and swept by breeze,
Lieth the island of Manisees,

Set at the mouth of the Sound to hold
The coast lights up on its turret old,
Yellow with moss and sea-fog mould.

Dreary the land when gust and sleet
At its doors and windows howl and beat,
And Winter laughs at its fires of peat!

But in summer time, when pool and pond,
Held in the laps of valleys fond,
Are blue as the glimpses of sea beyond;

When the hills are sweet with the brier-rose,
And, hid in the warm, soft dells, unclose
Flowers the mainland rarely knows;

When boats to their morning fishing go,
And, held to the wind and slanting low,
Whitening and darkening the small sails show,--

Then is that lonely island fair;
And the pale health-seeker findeth there
The wine of life in its pleasant air.

No greener valleys the sun invite,
On smoother beaches no sea-birds light,
No blue waves shatter to foam more white!

There, circling ever their narrow range,
Quaint tradition and legend strange
Live on unchallenged, and know no change.

Old wives spinning their webs of tow,
Or rocking weirdly to and fro
In and out of the peat's dull glow,

And old men mending their nets of twine,
Talk together of dream and sign,
Talk of the lost ship *Palatine*,—

The ship that, a hundred years before,
Freighted deep with its goodly store,
In the gales of the equinox went ashore.

The eager islanders one by one
Counted the shots of her signal gun,
And heard the crash when she drove right on!

Into the teeth of death she sped:
(May God forgive the hands that fed
The false lights over the rocky Head!)

O men and brothers! what sights were there!
White up-turned faces, hands stretched in prayer!
Where waves had pity, could ye not spare?

Down swooped the wreckers, like birds of prey
Tearing the heart of the ship away,
And the dead had never a word to say.

And then, with ghastly shimmer and shine
Over the rocks and the seething brine,
They burned the wreck of the *Palatine*.

In their cruel hearts, as they homeward sped,
"The sea and the rocks are dumb," they said:
"There'll be no reckoning with the dead."

But the year went round, and when once more
Along their foam-white curves of shore
They heard the line-storm rave and roar,

Behold! again, with shimmer and shine,
Over the rocks and the seething brine,
The flaming wreck of the *Palatine!*

So, haply in fitter words than these,
Mending their nets on their patient knees
They tell the legend of Manisees.

Nor looks nor tones a doubt betray;
"It is known to us all," they quietly say;
"We too have seen it in our day."

Is there, then, no death for a word once spoken?
Was never a deed but left its token
Written on tables never broken?

Do the elements subtle reflections give?
Do pictures of all the ages live
On Nature's infinite negative,

Which, half in sport, in malice half,
She shows at times, with shudder or laugh,
Phantom and shadow in photograph?

For still, on many a moonless night,
From Kingston Head and from Montauk light
The spectre kindles and burns in sight.

Now low and dim, now clear and higher,
Leaps up the terrible Ghost of Fire,
Then, slowly sinking, the flames expire.

And the wise Sound skippers, though skies be fine,
Reef their sails when they see the sign
Of the blazing wreck of the *Palatine!*
>> *John Greenleaf Whittier*

THE DHOWS

South of Guardafui with a dark tide flowing
We hailed two ships with tattered canvas bent to the monsoon,
Hung betwixt the outer sea and pale surf showing
Where dead cities of Lybia lay bleaching in the moon.

'Oh whither be ye sailing with torn sails broken?'
'We sail, we sail for Sheba, at Suliman's behest,
With carven silver phalli for the ebony maids of Ophir
From brown-skinned baharias of Arabia the Blest.'

'Oh whither be ye sailing, with your dark flag flying?'
'We sail, with creaking cedar, towards the Northern Star.

The helmsman singeth wearily, and in our hold are
    lying
A hundred slaves in shackles from the marts of Zanzi-
    bar.'

'Oh whither be ye sailing ... ?'
            'Alas, we sail no longer:
Our hulls are wrack, our sails are dust, as any man
    might know.
And why should you torment us ... Your iron keels
    are stronger
Than ghostly ships that sailed from Tyre a thousand
    years ago.'

Francis Brett Young

SIR HUMPHREY GILBERT

Southward with fleet of ice
    Sailed the corsair Death;
Wild and fast blew the blast,
    And the east-wind was his breath.

His lordly ships of ice
    Glisten in the sun;
On each side, like pennons wide,
    Flashing crystal streamlets run.

His sails of white sea-mist
    Dripped with silver rain;
But where he passed there were cast
    Leaden shadows o'er the main.

Eastward from Campobello
  Sir Humphrey Gilbert sailed;
Three days or more seaward he bore,
  Then, alas! the land-wind failed.

Alas! the land-wind failed,
  And ice-cold grew the night;
And nevermore, on sea or shore,
  Should Sir Humphrey see the light.

He sat upon the deck,
  The Book was in his hand;
"Do not fear! Heaven is as near,"
  He said, "by water as by land!"

In the first watch of the night,
  Without a signal's sound,
Out of the sea, mysteriously,
  The fleet of Death rose all around.

The moon and the evening star
  Were hanging in the shrouds;
Every mast as it passed,
  Seemed to rake the passing clouds.

They grappled with their prize,
  At midnight black and cold!
As of a rock was the shock;
  Heavily the ground-swell rolled.

Southward through day and dark,
  They drift in close embrace,
With mist and rain, o'er the open main;
  Yet there seems no change of place.

Southward, forever southward,
  They drift through dark and day;
And like a dream, in the Gulf-stream
  Sinking, vanish all away.

          Henry Wadsworth Longfellow

THE SPECTRE SHIP

When April skies are bright with sun,
And swiftly through the meadows run
The shining brooks and violet blooms
Freight sunny nooks with sweet perfumes,
Along a narrow sandy beach,
That fronts an ever widening reach
Of tossing waves, a ghostly sail
Does battle with a spectral gale.

Up from the horizon it bears,
The sunlight through the great hull glares;
The rigging strains, the masts are bent,
From clew to head the sails are rent;
And on the dark sides, wet and dank,
The mad waves toss the riven plank,
And hoarse command and windy roar
Speed swift along the curving shore.

And all the while, the sunlight gleams
On budding trees, and whispering streams;
The fisher boats drift with the tide;
The gulls each other softly chide;

The wide sea rolls with changing lights
Amid its depths, and sloping heights
Show dimly through the opal haze,
The shimmering green of April days.

When westward shadows fleck the way,
Far out amid the misty gray
That marks the southern water-line,
The streaming sails like white sprays shine;
And swift across the windless deep,
The huge, black ship her course will keep,
Sweep past the beach and disappear,
Fled utterly for one long year.

Her hull is fashioned quaint and old;
Bright is her flag with blazoned gold—
Four lions rampant on a shield,
Set high above an argent field,
Two crossed swords and a double crown,
And underneath a bastioned town,
The arms of one whose restless soul
Was wont to spurn at earth's control.

Three centuries and more ago,
So stories say, when winter's snow
Had melted in the April sun,
And violets to bloom had won,
His ship sped fast before the wind
And left the English cliffs behind,
Love watched the slow years come and wane,
But saw no sail rise up the main.

From out the silence comes no sound,
To tell us of the land she found;
No word has drifted from the deep,
Wherein her oaken timbers sleep;
Only, when in the April skies,
The golden springtime glory lies,
This blazoned flag and ghostly sail
Stream out upon a spectral gale.
Thomas Stephens Collier

THE PHANTOM SHIP

We stood on the haunted island,
　We stood by the haunted bay;
The stars were all over the skyland,
　But the moon had loitered away.

The lights of fisher-boats glimmered,
　The beacon glowed steady and red,
The calm sea icily shimmered
　Like the eye of one who is dead.

Then, all alone on the ocean,
　The ghost of the island came—
The ghost of a vessel in motion,
　The ghost of a vessel of flame.

It shone with vaporous brightness—
　A glamour of tremulous rays;
It was not fire, but the whiteness
　Of a ghost of a perished blaze.

We watched it with all our vision,
  We watched it doubting and dumb;
We had heard of the thing with derision,
  But we surely beheld it come.

We saw it glide o'er the water,
  A phantom of pallid fire;
We saw it tumble and totter
  To ruin, and then flash higher.

Again and again to leeward
  Its ghastly rigging fell o'er;
At last, far away to seaward,
  It foundered, and rose no more.

We had watched it with all our vision,
  We had watched it with eye and glass;
And gone were doubt and derision,
  For surely we saw it pass.

Through many a winter and summer,
  As the sons of the island know,
The gleam of this ghostly comer
  Has prophesied storm and woe—

This ghost of a great three-master
  Which went in the days of yore
To fell and fiery disaster
  Right off the Block Island shore.

J. W. de Forest

OLD SHIPS

There is a memory stays upon old ships,
  A weightless cargo in the musty hold,—
Of bright lagoons and prow-caressing lips,
  Of stormy midnights,—and a tale untold.
They have remembered islands in the dawn,
  And windy capes that tried their slender spars,
And tortuous channels where their keels have gone,
  And calm blue nights of stillness and the stars.

Ah, never think that ships forget a shore,
  Or bitter seas, or winds that made them wise;
There is a dream upon them, evermore;
  And there be some who say that sunk ships rise
To seek familiar harbors in the night,
Blowing in mists, their spectral sails like light.

David Morton

18. "Spin a yarn, Sailor"

SAILOR MAN

He was one who followed
Dreams and stars and ships,
They say the wind had fastened
Strange words upon his lips.

There was something secret
In the way he smiled
As if he could remember
The laughter of a child.

Wayward as a seagull,
Lonely as a hawk
Yet he believed in fairies
And heard the mermaids talk.

Nothing ever held him
Longer than a day,
They speak of him as careless,
And whimsical and gay;

But I think he swaggered
So he could pretend
The other side of Nowhere
Led somewhere in the end.

H. Sewall Bailey

THE YARN OF THE *NANCY BELL*

'T was on the shores that round our coast
  From Deal to Ramsgate span,
That I found alone, on a piece of stone,
  An elderly naval man.

His hair was weedy, his beard was long,
  And weedy and long was he;
And I heard this wight on the shore recite,
  In a singular minor key:

"Oh, I am a cook and a captain bold,
  And the mate of the *Nancy* brig,
And a bo'sun tight, and a midshipmite,
  And the crew of the captain's gig."

And he shook his fists and he tore his hair,
  Till I really felt afraid,
For I couldn't help thinking the man had been drinking,
  And so I simply said:

"Oh, elderly man, it's little I know
  Of the duties of men of the sea,
And I'll eat my hand if I understand
  However you can be

"At once a cook, and a captain bold,
  And the mate of the *Nancy* brig,
And a bo'sun tight, and a midshipmite,
  And the crew of the captain's gig."

"SPIN A YARN, SAILOR!"

Then he gave a hitch to his trousers, which
   Is a trick all seamen larn,
And having got rid of a thumping quid,
   He spun this painful yarn:

" 'T was in the good ship *Nancy Bell*
   That we sailed to the Indian Sea,
And there on a reef we come to grief,
   Which has often occurred to me.

"And pretty nigh all o' the crew was drowned
   (There was seventy-seven o' soul),
And only ten of the *Nancy's* men
   Said 'Here!' to the muster-roll.

"There was me, and the cook, and the captain bold,
   And the mate of the *Nancy* brig,
And the bo'sun tight, and a midshipmite,
   And the crew of the captain's gig.

"For a month we'd neither wittles nor drink,
   Till a-hungry we did feel,
So we drawed a lot, and, accordin', shot
   The captain for our meal.

"The next lot fell to the *Nancy's* mate,
   And a delicate dish he made;
Then our appetite with the midshipmite
   We seven survivors stayed.

"And then we murdered the bo'sun tight,
   And he much resembled pig;
Then we wittled free, did the cook and me,
   On the crew of the captain's gig.

"Then only the cook and me was left,
  And the delicate question, 'Which
Of us two goes to the kettle?' arose,
  And we argued it out as sich.

"For I loved that cook as a brother, I did,
  And the cook he worshipped me;
But we'd both be blowed if we'd either be stowed
  In the other chap's hold, you see.

"'I'll be eat if you dines off me,' says Tom.
  'Yes, that,' says I, 'you'll be,—
I'm boiled if I die, my friend,' quoth I;
  And 'Exactly so,' quoth he.

"Says he: 'Dear James, to murder me
  Were a foolish thing to do,
For don't you see that you can't cook *me*,
  While I can—and will—cook *you!*'

"So he boils the water, and takes the salt
  And the pepper in portions true
(Which he never forgot), and some chopped shalot,
  And some sage and parsley too.

"'Come here,' says he, with a proper pride,
  Which his smiling features tell,
'T will soothing be if I let you see
  How extremely nice you'll smell.'

"And he stirred it round and round and round,
  And he sniffed at the foaming froth;
When I ups with his heels, and smothers his squeals
  In the scum of the boiling broth.

"And I eat that cook in a week or less,
  And—as I eating be
The last of his chops, why, I almost drops,
  For a wessel in sight I see.

"And I never larf, and I never smile,
  And I never lark nor play;
But sit and croak, and a single joke
  I have—which is to say:

"Oh, I am a cook and a captain bold
  And the mate of the *Nancy* brig,
And a bo'sun tight, and a midshipmite,
  And the crew of the captain's gig!"

William S. Gilbert

A SAILOR'S APOLOGY
FOR BOW-LEGS

There's some is born with their legs straight by natur—
And some is born with bow-legs from the first—
And some that should have growed a good deal straighter,
  But they were badly nursed,
And set, you see, like Bacchus, with their pegs
  Astride of casks and kegs.
I've got myself a sort of bow to larboard
  And starboard,
And this is what it was that warped my legs:

'Twas all along of Poll, as I may say,
That fouled my cable when I ought to slip;
   But on the tenth of May,
   When I gets under weigh,
Down here in Hartfordshire, to join my ship.
   I sees the mail
   Get under sail,
The only one there was to make the trip.
   Well, I gives chase
   But as she run
   Two knots to one
There warn't no use in keeping on the race!

Well, casting round about, what next to try on,
   And how to spin,
I spies an ensign with a Bloody Lion,
And bears away to leeward for the inn,
   Beats round the gable,
And fetches up before the coach-horse stable.

Well, there they stand, four kickers in a row,
   And so
I just makes free to cut a brown 'un's cable.
But riding isn't in a seaman's natur;
So I whips out a toughish end of yarn,
And gets a kind of sort of a land-waiter
   To splice me heel to heel
   Under the she-mare's keel,
And off I goes, and leaves the inn a-starn!

   My eyes! how she did pitch!
And wouldn't keep her own to go in no line,
Tho' I kept bowsing, bowsing at her bow-line,

"SPIN A YARN, SAILOR!"

But always making leeway to the ditch,
And yawed her head about all sorts of ways.
    The devil sink the craft!
And wasn't she tremendous slack in stays!
We couldn't no how, keep the inn abaft!
    Well, I suppose
We hadn't run a knot—or much beyond—
(What will you have on it?)—but off she goes,
Up to her bends in a fresh-water pond!
    There I am! all a-back!
So I looks forward for her bridle-gears,
To heave her head round on t'other tack;
    But when I starts,
    The leather parts,
And goes away right over by the ears!

    What could a fellow do,
Whose legs, like mine, you know, were in the bilboes,
But trim myself upright for bringing-to,
And square his yard-arms and brace up his elbows,
    In rig all snug and clever,
Just while his craft was taking in her water?
I didn't like my berth though, howsomdever,
Because the yarn, you see, kept getting tauter.
    Says I—I wish this job was rayther shorter!
The chase had gained a mile
A-head, and still the she-mare stood a drinking:
    Now, all the while

Her body didn't take, of course, to shrinking.
Says I, she's letting out her reefs, I'm thinking;

And so she swelled and swelled,
  And yet the tackle held,
Till both my legs began to bend like winkin'.
My eyes! but she took in enough to founder!
And there's my timbers straining every bit,
  Ready to split,
And her tarnation hull a-growing rounder!

  Well, there—off Hartford Ness,
We lay both lashed and water-logged together,
  And can't contrive a signal of distress.
Thinks I, we must ride out this here foul weather,
Tho' sick of riding out, and nothing less;
When, looking round, I sees a man a-starn:
"Hallo!" says I, "come underneath her quarters!"
And hands him out my knife to cut the yarn.
So I gets off, and lands upon the road,
And leaves the she-mare to her own consarn,
  A-standing by the water.
If I get on another, I'll be blowed!
And that's the way, you see, my legs got bowed!
                                    Thomas Hood

LUCK

*What bring you, sailor, home from the sea—
Coffers of gold and of ivory?*

When first I went to sea as a lad
A new jack-knife was all I had:

And I've sailed for fifty years and three
To the coasts of gold and of ivory:

And now at the end of a lucky life,
Well, still I've got my old jack-knife.
Wilfrid Wilson Gibson

"THE SUN'S OVER THE FOREYARD"

When I was a passenger in the barque *Windrush*
I became aware of a pleasant sea custom.
Along toward noon
The captain's boy used to come politely to me
And whisper
"The captain's compliments, and the sun's over the
    foreyard."
And presently I learned that this meant
Come aft to the poop
And have a drink.
For mariners, men of sound self-control,
Never touch the bottle
Until the sun reaches the yards.

Now that I myself am a seaman
I always ship in square sail,
Never in steam.
In a steamer
The yards are so much higher.
Christopher Morley

SAILOR AND INLAND FLOWER

The stars never had any mystery for me:
In the soft midnight, in the Indian Sea,
I had simply to level my sextant at Arcturus's eye
And he had to tell me where I was; he dared not lie.

I had simply to level my sextant and wonder, "To-night
Where am I, Arcturus, Arcturus bright?"
And he would twirl his silver whiskers and then say:
"You are exactly seventeen hours' steaming from Bombay."
Orion, the Lion, the Crab, and Betelgeuse,
They were all as friendly as farm-hands in the *Fox and Goose*.

But these unwinking wood anemones
That make a Milky Way beneath the trees
Are nothing but secrecies.

They simply shine there, and keep
Themselves in eternal haughtiness and half-sleep,
And I might be in Atlantis, or any haunted place
Out of time and space.

Hamish Maclaren

THE ALARMÈD SKIPPER

Many a long, long year ago,
Nantucket skippers had a plan
Of finding out, though "lying low,"
How near New York their schooners ran.

They greased the lead before it fell,
And then, by sounding through the night,—
Knowing the soil that stuck, so well,
They always guessed their reckoning right.

A skipper gray, whose eyes were dim,
Could tell, by *tasting*, just the spot,
And so below he'd "dowse the glim"—
After, of course, his "something hot."

Snug in his berth, at eight o'clock,
This ancient skipper might be found;
No matter how his craft would rock,
He slept,—for skippers' naps are sound!

The watch on deck would now and then
Run down and wake him, with the lead;—
He'd up, and taste, and tell the men
How many miles they went ahead.

One night, 'twas Jotham Marden's watch,
A curious wag,—the peddler's son,—
And so he mused, (the wanton wretch),
"Tonight I'll have a grain of fun.

"We're all a set of stupid fools
To think the skipper knows by *tasting*
What ground he's on; Nantucket schools
Don't teach such stuff, with all their basting!"

And so he took the well-greased lead
And rubbed it o'er a box of earth
That stood on deck,—a parsnip-bed,—
And then he sought the skipper's berth.

"Where are we now, Sir? Please to taste."
The skipper yawned, put out his tongue,
Then oped his eyes in wondrous haste,
And then upon the floor he sprung!

The skipper stormed, and tore his hair,
Thrust on his boots, and roared to Marden,
*"Nantucket's sunk, and here we are
Right over old Marm Hackett's garden!"*
James T. Fields

A SEA DIALOGUE
(November 10, 1864)

Cabin Passenger *Man at Wheel*

CABIN PASSENGER

Friend, you seem thoughtful. I not wonder much
That he who sails the ocean should be sad.
I am myself reflective. When I think
Of all this wallowing beast, the Sea, has sucked
Between his sharp thin lips, the wedgy waves,

What heaps of diamonds, rubies, emeralds, pearls;
What piles of shekels, talents, ducats, crowns,
What bales of Tyrian mantles, Indian shawls,
Of laces that have blanked the weavers' eyes,
Of silken tissues, wrought by worm and man,
The half-starved workman, and the well-fed worm;
What marbles, bronzes, pictures, parchments, books;
What many-lobuled, thought-engendering brains;
Lie with the gaping sea-shells in his maw,—
I, too, am silent; for all language seems
A mockery, and the speech of man is vain.
O mariner, we look upon the waves
And they rebuke our babbling. 'Peace!' they say,—
'Mortal, be still!' My noisy tongue is hushed,
And with my trembling finger on my lips
My soul exclaims in ecstasy—

MAN AT WHEEL
     Belay!

CABIN PASSENGER
Ah yes! 'Delay,'—it calls, 'nor haste to break
The charm of stillness with an idle word!'
O mariner, I love thee, for thy thought
Strides even with my own, nay, flies before.
Thou art a brother to the wind and wave;
Have they not music for thine ear as mine,
When the wild tempest makes thy ship his lyre,
Smiting a cavernous basso from the shrouds
And climbing up his gamut through the stays,
Through buntlines, bowlines, ratlines, till it shrills
An alto keener than the locust sings,

And all the great Æolian orchestra
Storms out its mad sonata in the gale?
Is not the scene a wondrous and—

MAN AT WHEEL
                        Avast!

CABIN PASSENGER
Ah yes, a vast, a vast and wondrous scene!
I see thy soul is open as the day
That holds the sunshine in its azure bowl
To all the solemn glories of the deep.
Tell me, O mariner, dost thou never feel
The grandeur of thine office,—to control
The keel that cuts the ocean like a knife
And leaves a wake behind it like a seam
In the great shining garment of the world?

MAN AT WHEEL
Belay y'r jaw, y' swab! y' hoss-marine!
            (To the Captain.)
Ay, ay, Sir! Stiddy, Sir! Sou'wes'-b'sou'!
                        Oliver Wendell Holmes

THE CAPTAIN

(A Bridgeport paper on March, 1823, said: "Arrived, schooner FAME, from Charleston, via New-London. While at anchor in that harbour, during the rain storm on Thursday evening last, the FAME was run foul of by the wreck of the Methodist Meeting-house from Norwich, which was carried away in the late freshet.")

"SPIN A YARN, SAILOR!"

Solemn he paced upon that schooner's deck,
And muttered of his hardships:—"I have been
Where the wild will of Mississippi's tide
Has dashed me on the sawyer;— I have sailed
In the thick night, along the wave-washed edge
Of ice, in acres, by the pitiless coast
Of Labrador; and I have scraped my keel
O'er coral rocks in Madagascar seas—
And often in my cold and midnight watch,
Have heard the warning voice of the lee-shore
Speaking in breakers! Ay, and I have seen
The whale and sword-fish fight beneath my bows;
And, when they made the deep boil like a pot,
Have swung into its vortex; and I know
To cord my vessel with a sailor's skill,
And brave such dangers with a sailor's heart;
—But never yet upon the stormy wave,
Or where the river mixes with the main,
Or in the chafing anchorage of the bay,
In all my rough experience of harm,
Met I—a Methodist meeting-house!

* * * * *

Cat-head, or beam, or davit has it none,
Starboard nor larboard, gunwale, stem nor stern!
It comes in such a "questionable shape,"
I cannot even *speak* it! Up jib, Josey,
And make for Bridgeport! There, where Stratford Point,
Long-beach, Fairweather Island, and the buoy,
Are safe from such encounters, we'll *protest!*
And Yankee legends long shall tell the tale,

That once a Charleston schooner was beset,
Riding at anchor, by a Meeting-house.
                        John G. C. Brainard

THE FIGURE-HEAD
(A Salt Sea Yarn)

There was an ancient carver that carved of a saint,
But the parson wouldn't have it, so he took a pot of
    paint
And changed its angel garment for a dashing soldier
    rig,
And said it was a figure-head and sold it to a brig.

The brig hauled her mainsail to an off-shore draught,
Then she shook her snowy royals and the Scillies went
    abaft;
And cloudy with her canvas she ran before the Trade
Till she got to the Equator, where she struck a merry-
    maid.

A string of pearls and conches were all of her togs,
But the flying-fish and porpoises they followed her like
    dogs;
She had a voice of silver and lips of coral red,
She climbed the dolphin-striker and kissed the figure-
    head.

Then every starry evening she'd swim in the foam
About the bows, a-singing like a nightingale at Home;
She'd call to him and sing to him as sweetly as a bird,
But the wooden-headed effigy he never said a word.

And every starry evening in the Doldrum calms
She'd wriggle up the bobstay and throw her tender
    arms
About his scarlet shoulders and fondle him and cry
And stroke his curly whiskers, but he never winked an
    eye.

She couldn't get an answer to her tears or moans,
So she went and told her daddy, told the ancient Davy
    Jones;
Old Davy damned his eyesight and puzzled of his wits,
Then whistled up his hurricanes and tore the brig to
    bits.

Down on the ocean-bed, green fathoms deep,
Where the wrecks lie rotting and great sea-serpents
    creep,
In a gleaming grotto all built of sailors' bones,
Sits the handsome figure-head, listening to Miss Jones.

Songs o' love she sings him the livelong day,
And she hangs upon his bosom and sobs the night
    away,
But he never, never answers, for beneath his soldier
    paint
The wooden-headed lunatic still thinks that he's a
    saint.

Crosbie Garstin

LIKE AN ADVENTUROUS SEA-FARER AM I

Like an adventurous Sea-farer am I,
Who hath some long and dang'rous Voyage beene,
And called to tell of his Discovery
How farre he sayld, what Countries he had seene:
Proceeding from the Port whence he put forth,
Shewes by his Compasse how his Course he steer'd
When East, when West, when South and when by North,
As how the Pole to ev'ry place was rear'd;
What Capes he doubled, of what Continent,
The Gulphes and Straits that strangely he had past,
Where most becalm'd, where with foule Weather spent,
And on what Rockes in perill to be cast.
  Thus in my Love Time calls me to relate
  My tedious Travells and oft-varying Fate.

Michael Drayton

19. Child of the Sea

ALEC YEATON'S SON
Gloucester, August, 1720

The wind it wailed, the wind it moaned,
  And the white caps flecked the sea;
"An' I would to God," the skipper groaned,
  "I had not my boy with me!"

Snug in the stern-sheets, little John
  Laughed as the scud swept by;
But the skipper's sunburnt cheek grew wan
  As he watched the wicked sky.

"Would he were at his mother's side!"
  And the skipper's eyes were dim.
"Good Lord in heaven, if ill betide,
  What would become of him!

"For me—my muscles are as steel,
  For me let hap what may;
I might make shift upon the keel
  Until the break o' day.

"But he, he is so weak and small,
  So young, scarce learned to stand—
O pitying Father of us all,
  I trust him in Thy hand!

"For Thou, who markest from on high
  A sparrow's fall—each one!—
Surely, O Lord, thou'lt have an eye
  On Alec Yeaton's son!"

Then, helm hard-port, right straight he sailed
  Toward the headland light:
The wind it moaned, the wind it wailed,
  And black, black fell the night

Then burst a storm to make one quail,
  Though housed from winds and waves—
They who could tell about that gale
  Must rise from watery graves!

Sudden it came, as sudden went;
  Ere half the night was sped,
The winds were hushed, the waves were spent,
  And the stars shone overhead.

Now, as the morning mist grew thin,
  The folk on Gloucester shore
Saw a little figure floating in,
  Secure on a broken oar!

Up rose the cry, "A wreck! a wreck!
  Pull, mates, and waste no breath!"—
They knew it, though 't was but a speck
  Upon the edge of death!

Long did they marvel in the town
  At God his strange decree,
That let the stalwart skipper drown,
  And the little child go free!

Thomas Bailey Aldrich

A SON OF THE SEA

I was born for deep-sea faring;
I was bred to put to sea;
Stories of my father's daring
Filled me at my mother's knee.

I was sired among the surges;
I was cubbed beside the foam;
All my heart is in its verges,
And the sea wind is my home.

All my boyhood, from far vernal
Bournes of being, came to me
Dream-like, plangent, and eternal
Memories of the plunging sea.

Bliss Carman

SWEET AND LOW

Sweet and low, sweet and low,
   Wind of the western sea,
Low, low, breathe and blow,
   Wind of the western sea!
Over the rolling waters go,
Come from the dying moon, and blow,
   Blow him again to me;
While my little one, while my pretty one sleeps.

Sleep and rest, sleep and rest,
　　Father will come to thee soon;
Rest, rest, on mother's breast,
　　Father will come to thee soon;
Father will come to his babe in the nest,
Silver sails all out of the west
　　Under the silver moon:
Sleep, my little one, sleep, my pretty one, sleep.
　　　　　　　　　　Alfred, Lord Tennyson

LITTLE BILLEE

There were three sailors of Bristol City,
　　Who took a boat and went to sea;
But first with beef, and captain's biscuits,
　　And pickled pork, they loaded she.

There was gorging Jack, and guzzling Jimmy,
　　And the youngest he was little Billee:
Now, when they got as far as the Equator,
　　They'd nothing left but one split pea.

Says gorging Jack to guzzling Jimmy,
　　"I am extremely hungaree."
To gorging Jack says guzzling Jimmy,
　　"We've nothing left: us must eat we."

Says gorging Jack to guzzling Jimmy,
　　"With one another we shouldn't agree:
There's little Bill, he's young and tender,
　　We're old and tough: so let's eat he.

"O Billy! we're going to kill and eat you,
  So undo the button of your chemie."
When Bill received this information
  He used his pocket-handkerchie.

"First let me say my catechism
  Which my poor mammy taught to me."
"Make haste, make haste!" says guzzling Jimmy,
  While Jack pulled out his snickersnee.

So Billy went up to the main-topgallant mast,
  And down he fell on his bended knee:
He scarce had come to the Twelfth Commandment,
  When up he jumps, "There's land I see!

"Jerusalem and Madagascar,
  And North and South Amerikee;
There's the British flag a-riding at anchor,
  With the Admiral Napier, K.C.B."

So when they got aboard of the Admiral's,
  He hanged fat Jack, and flogged Jimmee;
But as for little Bill he made him
  The Captain of a Seventy-three.

William Makepeace Thackeray

A MOTHER'S SONG

Little ships of whitest pearl
With sailors who were ancient kings,
Come over the sea when my little girl
Sings.

And if my little girl should weep,
Little ships with torn sails
Go headlong down among the deep
Whales.

Francis Ledwidge

OVER THE SEA TO SKYE

Sing me a song of a lad that is gone,
   Say, could that lad be I?
Merry of soul he sailed on a day
   Over the sea to Skye.

Mull was astern, Rum on the port,
   Eigg on the starboard bow;
Glory of youth glowed in his soul:
   Where is that glory now?

Sing me a song of a lad that is gone,
   Say, could that lad be I?
Merry of soul he sailed on a day
   Over the sea to Skye.

Give me again all that was there,
   Give me the sun that shone!
Give me the eyes, give me the soul,
   Give me the lad that's gone!

Sing me a song of a lad that is gone,
   Say, could that lad be I?
Merry of soul he sailed on a day
   Over the sea to Skye.

Billow and breeze, islands and seas,
   Mountains of rain and sun,
All that was good, all that was fair,
   All that was me is gone.
Robert Louis Stevenson

ARNOLD, MASTER OF THE *SCUD*

There's a schooner out from Kingsport,
Through the morning's dazzle-gleam,
Snoring down the Bay of Fundy
With a norther on her beam.

How the tough wind springs to wrestle,
When the tide is on the flood!
And between them stands young daring—
Arnold, master of the *Scud*.

He is only "Martin's youngster,"
To the Minas coasting fleet,
"Twelve year old, and full of Satan
As a nut is full of meat."

With a wake of froth behind him,
And the gold green waste before,
Just as though the sea this morning
Were his boat pond by the door,

Legs a-straddle, grips the tiller
This young waif of the old sea;
When the wind comes harder, only
Laughs "Hurrah!" and holds her free.

Little wonder, as you watch him
With the dash in his blue eye,
Long ago his father called him
"Arnold, Master," on the sly,

While his mother's heart foreboded
Reckless father makes rash son.
So today the schooner carries
Just these two whose will is one.

Now the wind grows moody, shifting
Point by point into the east.
Wing and wing the *Scud* is flying
With her scuppers full of yeast.

And the father's older wisdom
On the sea-line has descried,
Like a stealthy cloud-bank making
Up to windward with the tide,

Those tall navies of disaster,
The pale squadrons of the fog,
That maraud this gray world border
Without pilot, chart, or log,

Ranging wanton as marooners
From Minudie to Manan.
"Heave to, and we'll reef, my master!"
Cries he; when no will of man

Spills the foresail, but a clumsy
Wind-flaw with a hand like stone
Hurls the boom round. In an instant
Arnold, Master, there alone

Sees a crushed corpse shot to seaward,
With the gray doom in its face;
And the climbing foam receives it
To its everlasting place.

What does Arnold, Master, think you?
Whimper like a child for dread?
That's not Arnold. Foulest weather
Strongest sailors ever bred.

And this slip of taut sea-faring
Grows a man who throttles fear.
Let the storm and dark in spite now
Do their worst with valor here!

Not a reef and not a shiver,
While the wind jeers in her shrouds,
And the flauts of foam and sea-fog
Swarm upon her deck in crowds,

Flies the *Scud* like a mad racer;
And with iron in his frown,
Holding hard by wrath and dreadnought,
Arnold, Master, rides her down.

Let the taffrail shriek through foam-heads!
Let the licking seas go glut
Elsewhere their old hunger, baffled!
Arnold's making for the Gut.

Cleft sheer down, the sea-wall mountains
Give that one port on the coast;
Made, the Basin lies in sunshine!
Missed, the little *Scud* is lost!

Come now, fog-horn, let your warning
Rip the wind to starboard there!
Suddenly that burly-throated
Welcome ploughs the cumbered air.

The young master hauls a little,
Crowds her up and sheets her home,
Heading for the narrow entry
Whence the safety signals come.

Then the wind lulls, and an eddy
Tells of ledges, where away;
Veers the *Scud*, sheet free, sun breaking,
Through the rifts, and—there's the bay!

Like a bird in from the storm-beat,
As the summer sun goes down,
Slows the schooner to her moorings
By the wharf at Digby town.

All the world next morning wondered.
Largest letters, there it stood,
"Storm in Fundy. A Boy's Daring.
Arnold, Master of the *Scud*."

Bliss Carman

THE SHIP OF RIO

There was a ship of Rio
   Sailed out into the blue,
And nine and ninety monkeys
   Were all her jovial crew.

CHILD OF THE SEA 481

From bos'un to the cabin boy,
    From quarter to caboose,
There weren't a stitch of calico
    To breech 'em—tight or loose;
From spar to deck, from deck to keel,
    From barnacle to shroud,
There weren't one pair of reach-me-downs
    To all that jabbering crowd.
But wasn't it a gladsome sight,
    When roared the deep-sea gales,
To see them reef her fore and aft,
    A-swinging by their tails!
Oh, wasn't it a gladsome sight,
    When glassy calm did come,
To see them squatting tailor-wise
    Around a keg of rum!
Oh, wasn't it a gladsome sight,
    When in she sailed to land,
To see them all a-scampering skip
    For nuts across the sand!

Walter de la Mare

AN OCEAN LULLABY

Our ship is a cradle on ocean's blue billow;
Rest, little spirit, your head on your pillow!
Dream of the dolphin that leaps from the water,
Dream of the flying-fish, dear little daughter;
Dream of the tropic-bird, lone in his flight,—
Where is he sleeping, I wonder, tonight?
Dark is the water with white crests of foam;
Sleep, little mermaid, the sea is your home!

Stars in the heavens are twinkling past number;
Waters are whispering slumber, love, slumber;
Waves are a-murmuring sleep, dearest, sleep!—
And the little one slumbers in peace on the deep.
Sing away wavelets and sigh away low,
Winds of the tropics about us may blow;
Baby is sleeping and mother is singing
And the peace of the evening about us is winging.
Sleep, little mermaid, as onward we roam,
The ship is your cradle, the sea is your home.

Charles Keeler

THE SILKIE O' SULE SKERRIE

An earthly nurrice sits an' sings,
    An' aye she sings: "Bye, lilie-wean;
Little I ken my bairnis' father,
    Far less the land whar maist he's seen."

Then up there rose at her bed-foot,
    And a grumlie guest was he:
"Here I am, thy bairnis' father,
    Tho' I be not sae comelie.

"Upo' the land I am a man,
    A silkie i' yon' sounding sea;
An' when I'm far awa' frae land
    My dwelling is in Sule Skerrie."

"It was nae weel," quoth the young mother,
    "It was nae weel, indeed," quoth she,

"That the Man-Silkie o' Sule Skerrie
   Should cum an' get a bairn ta me!"

Now he has taen a purse o' gowd
   An' he has put it on her knee,
Saying: "Gie thou ta me my little son,
   An' tak thee up thy nurrice-fee.

"An' it sall be on a summer's day,
   When the sun is hot on ev'ry stane,
That I will learn my little young son
   Ta swim in the saut sea faem.

"An' thou sall't marry a proud gunner,
   An' a proud gunner he's sure ta be;
An' the very first shot that he shoots out
   He'll shoot both my young son an' me."
Anonymous

THE MOON-CHILD

A little lonely child am I
   That have not any soul:
God made me as the homeless wave,
   That has no goal.

A seal my father was, a seal
   That once was man:
My mother loved him tho' he was
   'Neath mortal ban.

He took a wave and drowned her,
  She took a wave and lifted him:
And I was born where shadows are
  In sea-depths dim.

All through the sunny blue-sweet hours
  I swim and glide in waters green:
Never by day the mournful shores
  By me are seen.

But when the gloom is on the wave
  A shell unto the shore I bring:
And then upon the rocks I sit
  And plaintive sing.

I have no playmate but the tide
  The seaweed loves with dark brown eyes:
The night-waves have the stars for play,
  For me but sighs.

Fiona Macleod

From VIRGILIA

What was I back in the world's first wonder?—
  An elf-child found on an ocean-reef,
A sea-child nursed by the surge and thunder,
  And marked for the lyric grief.

So I will go down by the way of the willows,
  And whisper it out to the mother Sea,
To the soft sweet shores and the long bright billows,
  The dream that cannot be.

There will be help for the soul's great trouble,
  Where the clouds fly swift as the foot of fear,
Where the high gray cliff in the pool hangs double,
  And the moon is misting the mere.

'Twas down in the sea that your soul took fashion,
  O strange Love born of the white sea-wave!
And only the sea and her lyric passion
  Can ease the wound you gave.

I will go down to the wide wild places,
  Where the calm cliffs look on the shores around:
I will rest in the power of their great grave faces
  And the gray hush of the ground.

On a cliff's high head a gray gull clamors,
  But down at the base is the Devil's brew,
And the swing of arms and the heave of hammers,
  And the white flood roaring through.

There on the cliff is the sea-bird's tavern,
  And there with the wild things I'll find a home,
Laugh with the lightning, shout with the cavern,
  Run with the feathering foam.

I will climb down where the nests are hanging,
  And the young birds scream to the swinging deep,
Where the rocks and the iron winds are clanging,
  And the long waves lift and leap.

I will thread the shores to the cavern hollows,
  Where the edge of the wave runs white and thin;
I will sing to the surge and the foam that follows
  When the dark tides thunder in.

I will go out where the sea-birds travel,
　　And mix my soul with the wind and sea;
Let the green waves weave and the gray rains ravel,
　　And the tides go over me.

The sea is the mother of songs and sorrows,
　　And out of her wonder our wild loves come;
And so it will be thro' the long tomorrows,
　　Till all our lips are dumb.

She knows all sighs and she knows all sinning,
　　And they whisper out in her breaking wave:
She has known it all since the far beginning,
　　Since the grief of that first grave.

She shakes the heart with her stars and thunder
　　And her soft low word when the winds are late;
For the sea is Woman, the sea is Wonder—
　　Her other name is Fate!

There is daring and dream in her billows breaking—
　　In the burst of her beauty our griefs forget:
She can ease the heart of the old, old aching,
　　And put away regret.

Edwin Markham

ROUGHCHIN, THE PIRATE

　Sometimes when I wake up I lie
　　　And make believe I'm out at sea
　And that the ceiling is the sky
　　　Ever so far up over me.

CHILD OF THE SEA

Our cribs are each a little boat,
  Brother's and mine, upon the main
Where side by side they quietly float
  All in a sea of counterpane.

And through the door, in father's room,
  His big brass bedstead is a brig,
Stealthily creeping through the gloom
  With long low lines and rakish rig.

Then, when I've kept quiet fearful long,
  My heart just going pit-a-pat,
All of a sudden, loud and strong,
  I holler out "What ship is that?"

The answer comes in hollow tones
  "We're eight hours out from Bedtime Land—
This is the good ship *Lazybones*
  With Captain Roughchin in command."

And pulling out on the steamer trunk
  He fires a pillow across my bow—
"Lay to," he shouts, "or you'll be sunk—
  All hands ahoy to board her now!"

Up the side of my boat he climbs,
  I wriggle and yell, I squirm and roar,
But my neck he scratches seven times
  With the great rough chin I named him for.

But brother leaps from off his deck—
  A dirk in his teeth he breasts the wave
And Roughchin the Pirate, stabbed in the neck,
  Sinks like lead in a feathery grave.

Then mother makes believe to scold
   And chases father out the door,
And says our breakfast will be cold
   If we play pirate any more.

Arthur Boswell

EAST COAST LULLABY

Day has barred her windows close, and gangs wi' quiet feet;
Nicht, wrapt in coat o' gray, steals saftly doon the street;
Birdies deep in feathered nest bid the warld adieu—
Lullaby and lullaloo; sleep, lammie, noo.

One by one the glimmerin' een aboot the harbor dark
Wink an' blink an' fa' to gloom; scarce is left a spark.
Ne'er a thing but wind and waves'll moan the lang nicht through—
Lullaby and lullaloo; sleep, lammie, noo.

Frae the sea the wind blaws wild like a pibroch shrill;
Grant the Lord there's naucht to fear, naucht o' wae or ill!
When ye're grown my heart'll ache, sonnie, just for you—
Lullaby and lullaloo; sleep, lammie, noo.

Will ye sail awa' at dawn to net the herrin' fine?
Will ye track the monster whale yon where northlichts shine?

Mither-heart's a bonnie star, steady, clear and true—
Lullaby and lullaloo; sleep, lammie, noo.
Lady Lindsay

GREYPORT LEGEND

They ran through the streets of the seaport town;
They peered from the decks of the ships where they
    lay;
The cold sea-fog that came whitening down
Was never as cold or white as they.
  "Ho, Starbuck and Pinckney and Tenterden
  Run for your shallops, gather your men,
  Scatter your boats on the lower bay!"

Good cause for fear! In the thick midday
The hulk that lay by the rotting pier,
Filled with the children in happy play,
Parted its moorings and drifted clear;
  Drifted clear beyond reach or call—
  Thirteen children there were in all—
  All adrift in the lower bay!

Said a hard-faced skipper, "God help us all!
She will not float till the turning tide!"
Said his wife, "My darling will hear *my* call,
Whether in sea or Heaven she bide."
  And she lifted a quavering voice and high,
  Wild and strange as a sea-bird's cry,
  Till they shuddered and wondered at her side.

The fog broke down on each laboring crew,
Veiled each from each and the sky and shore;
There was not a sound but the breath they drew,
And the lap of water and creak of oar;
    And they felt the breath of the downs, fresh blown
    O'er league of clover, and cold grey stone,
    But not from the lips that had gone before.

They come no more. But they tell the tale,
That, when fogs are thick on the harbor reef,
The mackerel fishers shorten sail,
For the signal they know will bring relief,—
    For the voices of children, still at play
    In a phantom hulk that drifts alway
    Through channels whose waters never fail.

It is but a foolish shipman's tale,
A theme for a poet's idle page,
But still when the mists of doubt prevail,
And we lie becalmed by the shores of age,
    We hear from the misty troubled shore
    The voice of the children gone before,
    Drawing the soul to its anchorage.

Bret Harte

20. The Voice of the Sea

SONG OF THE SEA

The song of the sea was an ancient song
In the days when the earth was young:
The waves were gossiping loud and long
Ere mortals had found a tongue:
The heart of the waves with wrath was wrung
Or soothed to a siren strain,
As they tossed the primitive isles among,
Or slept in the open main.
Such was the song and its changes free,
   Such was the song of the sea.

The song of the sea took a human tone
In the days of the coming of man;
A mournfuller meaning swelled her moan,
And fiercer her riots ran:
Because that her stately voice began
To speak of our human woes;
With music mighty to grasp and span
Life's tale and its passion-throes.
Such was the song as it grew to be;
   Such was the song of the sea.

The song of the sea was a hungry sound
As the human years unrolled;
For the notes were hoarse with the doomed and
      drowned,
Or choked with a shipwreck's gold:

Till it seemed no dirge above the mould
So sorry a story said,
As the midnight cry of the waters old
Calling above their dead.
Such is the song and its threnody;
   Such is the song of the sea.

The song of the sea is a wondrous lay,
For it mirrors human life:
It is grave and great as the judgment-day,
It is torn with the thought of strife:
Yet under the stars it is smooth, and rife
With love-lights everywhere,
When the sky has taken the deep to wife
And their wedding day is fair—
Such is the ocean's mystery,
   Such is the song of the sea.

Richard E. Burton

SONNET ON THE SEA

It keeps eternal whisperings around
   Desolate shores, and with its mighty swell
   Gluts twice ten thousand caverns, till the spell
Of Hecate leaves them their old shadowy sound.
Often 'tis in such gentle temper found
   That scarcely will the very smallest shell
   Be moved for days from whence it sometime fell,
When last the winds of heaven were unbound.
Oh ye! who have your eye-balls vexed and tired,
   Feast them upon the wideness of the Sea;

Oh ye! whose ears are dinned with uproar rude,
Or fed too much with cloying melody,—
Sit ye near some old cavern's mouth, and brood
Until ye start, as if the sea-nymphs quired!

John Keats

HARP IN THE RIGGING

There is a harp set above us
In the wind between our moving masts:
The north wind
Flies into it silver-fingered,
The west wind sweeps
Over and over it sounding deep-toned bells:
The stars
Look down and brush it with their gold eyelashes.
Our harp is never silent.

Hamish Maclaren

GRAY SHORE

I spoke the sea, that reaches green
And avid fingers in between
The capes, the gray capes of the world:

Will there be suns?
I asked; and will the gray tides flee
When morning banners shake above the sea?
Hush! said the sea;

So many hopes there are that fly
And clamor in the painted sky!
Hush! said the sea, and hush.

Will there be winds?
I asked—a shrill wind sent for me
To blow me high and set me free?
Hush! said the sea;
The winds do naught but prowl
Upon my deeps, and howl, and howl.
Hush! said the sea, and hush.

Will I have peace?
I asked—when sleep at last will come
With shadowy breasts to bear me home?
Hush! said the sea;
There come so many moaning things
With weeping eyes and trailing wings—
Hush! said the sea, and hush.

James Rorty

THE SOUND OF THE SEA

Always, here where I sleep, I hear the sound of the sea,
  Rolling along the dunes, along the desolate places,
    Full of a vague rumor of dreams and remembered faces—
Always, here where I sleep, I hear the sound of the sea.

So have I heard it sound, for thirty summers or more,
  Sighing up through the meadows, between the unanswering houses,

Up through the dewy fields where the dark herd
    sleepily browses—
So have I heard it sound, for thirty summers or more.

Under quivering stars, or stars that were clouded and
    scattered,
    All through my moments of joy and pain, of sleep-
        ing and dreaming,
    Ever that quiet murmur sorrowfully was stream-
        ing—
Under quivering stars, or stars that were clouded and
    scattered.

Out of that somber voice swept on the wings of time,
    Shall I not, bending down from the starry trellis of
        heaven,
    Look on this empty room, these meadows shining
        and even—
Out of that somber voice swept on the wings of time!

Beyond what glittering stars and in what ultimate re-
    gions,
    Drifted along with the night, shall I look back and
        ponder
    On the forgotten sound, the earth, and the ancient
        wonder—
Beyond what glittering stars and in what ultimate re-
    gions!

John Hall Wheelock

BY THE SEA

It is a beauteous evening, calm and free;
The holy time is quiet as a nun
Breathless with adoration; the broad sun
Is sinking down in its tranquillity;

The gentleness of heaven is on the Sea:
Listen! the mighty being is awake,
And doth with his eternal motion make
A sound like thunder—everlastingly.
William Wordsworth

LOST SHIPS

"Where have you hidden them?" I asked the sea,
And from its rim an answer came to me
   In lazy tumblings like purple wheat
    Upon the ivory shore-line at my feet,
But scarfed in magic by the silver foam,
I lost the message it was bringing home.

"Where are the galleons," I cried afar,
"The Argosies, the barks, the men-of-war,
   The battened pinnaces that rode the bay,
    The souls and ingots that you warped away?"
A white shape rose above the curving sea,
But fog swept through ere it could signal me.

Yet on I waited till the world was night,
Then gleamed the shape again in fog-drenched light,

It was the lodestar risen from the sea,
It was the lurestar come to answer me.
And lest I hear its beckoning reply,
I fled under a hill that hid the sky.

Thomas Hornsby Ferril

THE FULL SEA ROLLS AND THUNDERS

The full sea rolls and thunders
  In glory and in glee.
O, bury me not in the senseless earth
  But in the living sea!

Ay, bury me where it surges
  A thousand miles from shore,
And in its brotherly unrest
  I'll range for evermore.

William Ernest Henley

A SEA LYRIC

There is no music that man has heard
  Like the voice of the minstrel Sea,
Whose major and minor chords are fraught
  With infinite mystery,—
For the Sea is a harp, and the winds of God
  Play over his rhythmic breast,
And bear on the sweep of their mighty wings
  The song of a vast unrest.

There is no passion that man has sung
  Like the love of the deep-souled Sea,
Whose tide responds to the Moon's soft light
  With marvelous melody,—
For the Sea is a harp, and the winds of God
  Play over his rhythmic breast,
And bear on the sweep of their mighty wings
  The song of a vast unrest.

There is no sorrow that man has known,
  Like the grief of the wordless Main,
Whose titan bosom forever throbs
  With an untranslated pain,—
For the Sea is a harp, and the winds of God
  Play over his rhythmic breast,
And bear on the sweep of their mighty wings
  The song of a vast unrest.
                    William Hamilton Hayne

THE SONNET'S VOICE
(A Metrical Lesson by the Seashore)

Yon silvery billows breaking on the beach
Fall back in foam beneath the star-shine clear,
The while my rhymes are murmuring in your ear
A restless lore like that the billows teach;
For on these sonnet-waves my soul would reach
From its own depths, and rest within you, dear,
As, through the billowy voices yearning here,
Great nature strives to find a human speech.
A sonnet is a wave of melody:

From heaving waters of the impassion'd soul
A billow of tidal music one and whole
Flows in the "octave"; then returning free,
Its ebbing surges in the "sestet" roll
Back to the deeps of Life's tumultuous sea.
Theodore Watts-Dunton

THE SOUND OF THE SEA

The sea awoke at midnight from its sleep,
   And round the pebbly beaches far and wide
   I heard the first wave of the rising tide
   Rush onward with uninterrupted sweep;
A voice out of the silence of the deep,
   A sound mysteriously multiplied
   As of a cataract from the mountain's side,
   Or roar of winds upon a wooded steep.
So comes to us at times, from the unknown
   And inaccessible solitudes of being,
   The rushing of the sea-tides of the soul;
And inspirations, that we deem our own,
   Are some divine foreshadowing and foreseeing
   Of things beyond our reason or control.
Henry Wadsworth Longfellow

SHADOWS OF SAILS

ROYALS!

Over them all, we sit aloft and sing
  To space. How faintly to us come your calls.
We are gods, and the centre of the ring:
  We chuckle when you vail us to the squalls.

THE ETERNAL SEA

TOPGALLANT SAILS!
We are the passage makers!
Hang on to us, and we
Will crown you record breakers
All down God's regal sea.

UPPER TOPSAILS!
Hoist us with song! and sweat our leeches taut.
  We know the Westerlies. We have been curbed
In reefs: a many battles we have fought.
  Belay! not ours the wish to be disturbed.

LOWER TOPSAILS!
First set! and, when storms blow,
  Last furl'd—at times, sore torn.
Goose-winged! ah, Christ! we know
  The passage of the Horn.

FORESAIL!
I am the driver and I lift her head.
  I am the Fores'l! give my sheets full scope.
My course is East—but leave my gaskets shed—
  I'll reach the dawn, and bind with faith your hope.

John Anderson

LAND'S END
(Point Lobos, California)

Here rage the furies that have shaped the world,
Here where a beaked old headland splits the sea
And white Niagaras of the surf are hurled

THE VOICE OF THE SEA

In crashing enmity
Against the rocks' worn giant filigree.
Above the thunder where the wave and shore
Merge and re-merge in fountain-bursts of spray,
The weird continual half-yelping roar
Of congregated seals rings out all day
From islets wet and gray.
And pelicans in heavy lines flap by,
And gulls skim low beneath the precipice,
And hunchback cypresses, limb-twisted, lie
On the blunt slope and in the hoarse abyss,
And here and there a skeleton tree that stares,
Like agony petrified, with ashen bole
And boughs, where life with all her struggles and cares
Incarnates her writhing soul.

Step to the gnarled cliff-edge; some Siren power
Will urge you, pull you doomward... down and down
There where in turquoise pools the kelp lies brown,
And where tall rollers charge in shower on shower
Of fierce erupting white, and the salt cascade
Drenching the misty shoals, and waterfalls
Replenished with every breaker, look on walls
Of inlets paved with jade.
Wild as the earth's beginning! lone and grand
This universe of reef and cave and foam,
As when scale-armored dragons clawed the sand
And the fish-lizard made the brine its home!
Hear! in each billow clamoring at the rock
Voices of Masters throned aloof from man,
Lords of the deep for whom the great world-clock
Ticks not in years, but by a Cyclops' span

Of epochs and of eons Hear the moan
Of time that stretches out to timelessness,
And power that trumpets of the shock and stress
Of planets forged in wars of storm and stone!

Ranging the headland's verge,
For but an hour I come, a transient thing,
Yet from this tumult and this beat and surge
Of elemental frenzies I shall bring
Back to the soberer world a brooding sense
Of some fresh wonder and magnificence,
The overtones of some age-hallowed glory,
When on this furrowed cypress promontory
Gods speak in the torn waves' droning eloquence.
Stanton A. Coblentz

THE ENDURING MUSIC

This shell, this slender spiral in the hand,
Held to the ear, shall still evoke the sound
Of the sea's sandals running on the sand,
The voice of foam, whose music is profound.
The drift of water falling against stone,
Or the spume-fingered breakers when they raced
Are heard here still, the sound of sea alone
Falling upon the ear and without haste.

The tides that washed the shores of Greece are here,
The rush of waters around Zanzibar,
Held quietly against the waiting ear,
One hears across some far and distant bar

The waves of lost Atlantis, dim and deep,
Whose waters are the crystal tides of sleep.

Harold Vinal

SEA WORDS

I love sea words—
The salt of them, the tang of them, the roughness on the tongue.
In them is strength, the vigor of the storm
And pull of tides, the waters' surge and run.
Peak-purchase, gammonshackle:—
What taste of brine is on the lips that speak such words as these!
Who would not hold it play to work a buntline cringle?
To frap the royal slings?
How should the muscles ripple and be glad
To reeve a spurling-line, haul taut head-earings,
Ease off the lee main brace!
Who, brailing in a stormsail, could forbear to sing?

"Clue up the royals!
Free the yard arm gasket!
Main topsail haul!
Wear ship and stand by halyards!"
How the stormy winds of these commands beat on the spirit—
Beat and break in spindrift!
Sea words may be beautiful.
Mistral: we speak the enchanted syllables
And all about us creep and curl delicate sea vapors.

Albatross: we are winged with joy and light.
Lagoon: the restless ocean suddenly
Is studded with quiet stars.
Adarris, larboard, lee, ballow and martingale;—
These words are gentle. The wash of a liquid moon
    against lean bows
Is in them, and sea stillness and sea wonder.
Mary Sinton Leitch

THE SEA'S VOICE

I

Around the rocky headlands, far and near,
  The wakened ocean murmured with dull tongue,
  Till all the coast's mysterious caverns rung
  With the waves' voice, barbaric, hoarse and drear.
Within this distant valley, with rapt ear,
  I listened, thrilled, as though a spirit sung,
  Or some grey god, as when the world was young
  Moaned to his fellow, mad with rage or fear.
Thus in the dark, ere the first dawn, methought,
  The sea's deep roar and sullen surge and shock
  Broke the long silence of eternity,
And echoed from the summits where God wrought,
  Building the world, and ploughing the steep rock
  With ploughs of ice-hills, harnessed to the sea.

II

The sea is never quiet, east and west,
  The nations hear it, like the voice of fate,
  Within vast shores its strife makes desolate,

Still murmuring, 'mid storms that to its breast
Return, as eagles screaming to their nest.
  Is it the voice of worlds and isles that wait,
  While old earth crumbles to eternal rest,
  Or some hoar monster calling to his mate?
O ye, that hear it moan about the shore,
  Be still and listen: that loud voice hath sung,
  Where mountains rise, where desert sands are blown;
And when man's voice is dumb, for evermore
  'Twill murmur on, its craggy shores among,
  Singing of gods, and nations overthrown.
William Prescott Foster

THE SHELL'S SONG

I stood upon a shore, a pleasant shore,
Where a sweet clime was breathed from a land
Of fragrance, quietness, and trees, and flowers.
Full of calm joy it was, as I of grief;
Too full of joy and soft delicious warmth;
So that I felt a movement in my heart
To chide, and to reproach that solitude
With songs of misery, music of our woes;
And sat me down, and took a mouthèd shell
And murmur'd into it, and made melody—
O melody no more! for while I sang,
And with poor skill let pass into the breeze
The dull shell's echo, from a bowery strand
Just opposite, an island of the sea,
There came enchantment with the shifting wind,
That did both drown and keep alive my ears.

I threw my shell away upon the sand,
And a wave fill'd it, as my sense was fill'd
With that new blissful golden melody.

John Keats

THE BUOY-BELL

How like the leper, with his own sad cry
Enforcing his own solitude, it tolls!
That lonely bell set in the rushing shoals,
To warn us from the place of jeopardy!
O friend of man! sore-vexed by ocean's power,
The changing tides wash o'er thee day by day;
Thy trembling mouth is filled with bitter spray,
Yet still thou ringest on from hour to hour;
High is thy mission, though thy lot is wild—
To be in danger's realm a guardian sound;
In seamen's dreams a pleasant part to bear,
And earn their blessing as the year goes round;
And strike the key-note of each grateful prayer,
Breathed in their distant homes by wife or child!

Charles Tennyson Turner

FRUTTA DI MARE

I am a sea-shell flung
Up from the ancient sea;
Now I lie here, among
Roots of a tamarisk tree;
No one listens to me.

I sing to myself all day
In a husky voice quite low,
Things the great fishes say
And you must need to know;
All night I sing just so.

But lift me from the ground
And hearken at my rim,
Only your sorrow's sound
Amazed, perplexed and dim,
Comes coiling to the brim;

For what the wise whales ponder
Awaking out from sleep,
The key to all your wonder,
The answers of the deep,
These to myself I keep.

Geoffrey Scott

THE SEA LIMITS

Consider the sea's listless chime:
   Time's self it is, made audible,—
   The murmur of the earth's own shell.
Secret continuance sublime
   Is the sea's end: our sight may pass
   No furlong further. Since time was,
This sound has told the lapse of time.

No quiet, which is death's,—it hath
   The mournfulness of ancient life,
   Enduring always at dull strife.

As the world's heart of rest and wrath,
  Its painful pulse is in the sands.
  Lost utterly, the whole sky stands,
Grey and not known, along its path.

Listen, alone beside the sea,
  Listen alone among the woods;
  Those voices of twin solitudes
Shall have one sound alike to thee:
  Hark where the murmurs of thronged men
  Surge and sink back and surge again,—
Still the one voice of wave and tree.

Gather a shell from the strewn beach
  And listen at its lips: they sigh
  The same desire and mystery,
The echo of the whole sea's speech.
  And all mankind is thus at heart
  Not anything but what thou art:
And Earth, Sea, Man, are all in each.
Dante Gabriel Rossetti

SONNETS ON THE SEA'S VOICE

I

Since ocean rolled and ocean winds were strong,
  That voice on all the narrow shores is found,
  Unchanging, immemorial, profound,
A sorrowing the caverned cliffs prolong,

THE VOICE OF THE SEA

Where foam is choral and where thunders throng,
   Or where the sands, uncharted or renowned,
   Tremble forever to its elder sound,
The ground note of the planet's undersong.

What man shall hear that utterance, alone,
   That dirge of life, that music not of man,
   Nor know how brief a term our seasons span
     And what a mystery our hearts denote,
That hear from strands eternally unknown
     The pulse of chords tremendous and remote?

II

The wind has loosed its armies on the west,
   And ocean joined that huge hostility;
   Armored in jade, the legions, swinging free,
Hurl rank on rank against the headland's breast.
Within the thunders of that old unrest,
   The doom of gods that were and gods to be
   Seems sounded by the trumpets of the sea—
The music of an everlasting quest.

That cry was, when the sapphire deeps began,
   And still the hosts of wind and sea renew
Their ancient menace in the heart of man,
   As, consonant, the voices of that war
Meet in one Voice on the Eternal blue:
   "Time was, Time is, and Time shall be no more!"

George Sterling

THE MYSTERIOUS MUSIC OF OCEAN

   Lonely and wild it rose,
That strain of solemn music from the sea,
As though the bright air trembled to disclose
   An ocean mystery.

   Again a low, sweet tone,
Fainting in murmurs on the listening day,
Just bade the excited thought its presence own,
   Then died away.

   Once more the gush of sound,
Struggling and swelling from the heaving plain,
Thrilled a rich peal triumphantly around,
   And fled again.

   O boundless deep! We know
Thou hast strange wonders in thy gloom concealed,
Gems, flashing gems, from whose unearthly glow
   Sunlight is sealed.

   And an eternal spring
Showers her rich colors with unsparing hand,
Where coral trees their graceful branches fling
   O'er golden sand.

   But tell, O restless main!
Who are the dwellers in thy mold beneath,
That thus the watery realm cannot contain
   The joy they breathe?

Anonymous

21. Hail and Farewell

SAY THAT HE LOVED OLD SHIPS

Say that he loved old ships; write nothing more
  Upon the stone above his resting place;
And they who read will know he loved the roar
  Of breakers white as starlight, shadow lace
Of purple twilights on a quiet sea,
  First ridge of daybreaks in a waiting sky,
The wings of gulls that beat eternally
  And haunt old harbors with their silver cry.
Speak softly now, his heart has earned its rest,
  This heart that knew each alien star by name,
Knew passion of the waves against his breast
  When clouds swept down the sea and lightning's flame
Tore skies asunder with swift finger tips;
  Write nothing more; say that he loved old ships.
Daniel Whitehead Hicky

A BALLAD OF THE CAPTAINS

Where are now the Captains
  Of the narrow ships of old—
Who with valiant souls went seeking
  For the Fabled Fleece of Gold;
In the clouded Dusk of Ages,
  In the Dawn of History,
When the ringing songs of Homer
  First re-echoed o'er the Sea?

*Oh, the Captains lie a-sleeping
Where great iron hulls are sweeping
　Out of Suez in their pride;
And they hear not, and they heed not,
And they know not, and they need not
　In their deep graves far and wide.*

Where are now the Captains
　Who went blindly through the Strait,
With a tribute to Poseidon,
　A libation poured to Fate?
They were heroes giant-hearted,
　That with Terrors, told and sung,
Like blindfolded lions grappled,
　When the World was strange and young.

*Oh, the Captains brave and daring,
With their grim old crews are faring
　Where our guiding beacons gleam;
And the homeward liners o'er them—
All the charted seas before them—
　Shall not wake them as they dream.*

Where are now the Captains
　From bold Nelson back to Drake,
Who came drumming up the Channel
　Haling prizes in their wake?
Where are England's fighting Captains
　Who, with battle flags unfurled,
Went a-rieving all the rievers
　O'er the waves of all the world?

*Oh, these Captains, all confiding
In the strong right hand, are biding
 In the margins, on the Main;
They are shining bright in story,
They are sleeping deep in glory,
 On the silken lap of fame.*

Where are now the Captains
 Who regarded not the tears
Of the captured Christian maidens
 Carried, weeping, to Algiers?

Yes, the swarthy Moorish Captains,
 Storming wildly 'cross the Bay,
With a dead hidalgo's daughter
 As a dower for the Dey?

*Oh, those cruel Captains never
Shall sweet lovers more dissever,
 On their forays as they roll;
Or the mad Dons curse them vainly,
As their baffled ships, ungainly,
 Heel them, jeering, to the Mole.*

Where are now the Captains
 Of those racing, roaring days,
Who of knowledge and of courage,
 Drove the clippers on their ways—
To the furthest ounce of pressure,
 To the latest stitch of sail,
'Carried on' before the tempest
 Till the waters lapped the rail?

Oh, the merry, manly skippers
Of the traders and the clippers,
  They are sleeping East and West,
And the brave blue seas shall hold them,
And the oceans five enfold them
  In the havens where they rest.

Where are now the Captains
  Of the gallant days agone?
They are biding in their places,
  And the Great Deep bears no traces
Of their good ships passed and gone.
  They are biding in their places,
Where the light of God's own grace is,
  And the Great Deep thunders on.

Yea, with never port to steer for,
And with never storm to fear for,
  They are waiting wan and white,
And they hear no more the calling
Of the watches, or the falling
  Of the sea rain in the night.

E. J. Brady

HOW'S MY BOY?

"Ho, sailor of the sea!
  How's my boy—my boy?"
"What's your boy's name, good wife,
  And in what good ship sailed he?"

"My boy John—
 He that went to sea—
 What care I for the ship, sailor?
 My boy's my boy to me!

"You come back from sea,
 And not know my John?
 I might as well have asked some landsman,
 Yonder down in the town.
 There's not an ass in all the parish
 But knows my John!

"How's my boy—my boy?
 And unless you let me know
 I'll swear you are no sailor,
 Blue jacket or no—
 Brass buttons or no, sailor,
 Anchor and crown or no—
 Sure his ship was the '*Jolly Briton*' "—
"Speak low, woman, speak low!"

"And why should I speak low, sailor,
 About my own boy John?
 If I was loud as I am proud
 I'd sing him over the town!
 Why should I speak low, sailor?"—
"That good ship went down."

"How's my boy—my boy?
 What care I for the ship, sailor—
 I was never aboard her.

Be she afloat or be she aground,
Sinking or swimming, I'll be bound
Her owners can afford her!
I say, how's my John?"—
"Every man on board went down,
Every man aboard her."

"How's my boy—my boy?
What care I for the men, sailor?
I'm not their mother—
How's my boy—my boy?
Tell me of him and no other!
How's my boy—my boy?"

Sydney Dobell

OPIUM CLIPPERS

Where are the opium ships—gulls of the Indian seas?
Where are the clippers that mated the gale?
Ships of the baleful flower, stealing from Singapore,
Mocking the brigs of war slow on their trail?

Where is the *Waterwitch?* Where does the *Kelpie* flit?
Where scuds the *Falcon*—under what stars?
Where is the *Antelope*—who, when the pirates swarmed,
Sailed with the yellow thieves hung to her spars?

Where are the men of iron, filling the topsail yards
While yet the ocean seethes from the typhoon—
Skippers who held their ships dearer than dancing girls
In Shanghai taverns or dives of Rangoon?

Where went the *Ariel?* Where sails the wild *Dayrell?*
Where is the beauty that knew not it sinned?
Search for the rainbow that painted the stormy mist
"Where flies the spindrift? Where went the wind?"
                                        Daniel Henderson

EPITAPH FOR A SAILOR BURIED ASHORE

He who but yesterday would roam
  Careless as clouds and currents range,
In homeless wandering most at home,
  Inhabiter of change;

Who wooed the West to win the East,
  And named the stars of North and South,
And felt the zest of Freedom's feast
  Familiar in his mouth;

Who found a faith in stranger-speech,
  And fellowship in foreign hands,
And had within his eager reach
  The relish of all lands—

How circumscribed a plot of earth
  Keeps now his restless footsteps still,
Whose wish was wide as ocean's girth,
  Whose will the water's will!
                            Charles G. D. Roberts

A SEA DIRGE

Full fathom five thy father lies;
   Of his bones are coral made:
Those are pearls that were his eyes:
   Nothing of him that doth fade,
   But doth suffer a sea-change
   Into something rich and strange.
   Sea-nymphs hourly ring his knell.
         Ding-dong.
Hark! now I hear them,—ding-dong, bell.
             William Shakespeare

CROSSING THE BAR

Sunset and evening star,
   And one clear call for me!
And may there be no moaning of the bar,
   When I put out to sea,

But such a tide as moving seems asleep,
   Too full for sound and foam,
When that which drew from out the boundless deep
   Turns again home.

Twilight and evening bell,
   And after that the dark!
And may there be no sadness of farewell,
   When I embark;

HAIL AND FAREWELL 523

For tho' from out our bourne of Time and Place
  The flood may bear me far,
I hope to see my Pilot face to face
  When I have crost the bar.

Alfred, Lord *Tennyson*

THE OLD CONSERVATIVE
(On the Battery)

I saw the old man pause, then turn his head,
Stumbling a little as with vertigo,
His lips pursed out, his squally, red-rimmed eyes
Sweeping the wide periphery of the bay.
Dumb with unspeakable thoughts, at last he turned
And, with an angry flirt of his thick stick,
Growled, "Ar-r-r!" and, clumping, hobbled out of sight.

"Here once I saw proud clipper ships, bound in
From Java Head and up around the Horn,
Brail up their tripping skirts like dainty maids.
I heard the hawse-pipes roar, and saw the ships
Turn noses to the wind like hunting dogs
Still eager for the chase, though once more home.
Brown men swarmed on the foot-ropes; 'Harbor furl!'
Mates roared from decks; and shanty-men, perched high
Upon the knight-heads, to the click of pawls
Lined out their shanties for the singing crews.
I had no need of house-flags then to know

Each slender beauty as she opened out
Beyond the slope of Bay Ridge like a cloud.
I knew them all, the temperamental dears,
Each meeting trouble in her own sweet way;
One springing up the tall seas with a laugh,
One burrowing in pillows of white foam,
Like any other sulky, crying girl,
But human, mind you. There in quiet docks
Tall ships drove jib-booms far above the street
Where brown-faced sailors stood about in groups
And talked of brawls and mates, but most of girls—
Of slim, dark girls who poled the bum-boats down
The river at Manila in the dawn;
Or others that in crowded Singapore
Laughed from black doorways, but wore daggers, too.
South Street was like a foreign market then,
Where sailormen hawked parrots from Brazil,
And Malay creeses, rolls of China silk,
And full-rigged ships in bottles, curious things;
Or, grouped about the apple-women's carts,
They bought broadsides of sentimental songs,
And proudly bragged of things no one believed.
And sometimes through the huddled throng would stalk,
In black broadcloth and high silk stocks, grim men
With cold, unseeing eyes—masters of ships
Who might have had a knife between the ribs
But for that something, majesty or law,
That hedged them in. And mostly good men, too.
But give a dog a bad name—well, you know.
The street's half gutter now, and desolate,
With all that good salt water flooding past

Without a sail. For see our harbor now!
There goes a liner, just a huge café,
With dancing girls, and officers in white,
And dock-rat crews of pantry-serving boys,
And not a soul of all on board who knows
A quarter gasket from the futtock-shrouds;
And there a hog-backed tramp, listed to port,
Slobbered with iron-rust and ashy grit,
And smearing God's own blue with her foul smoke;
There a tin wagon run by gasoline.

Oh, why not play one vast joke on the Flood—
And dump old Ararat into the sea,
And make the 'vasty deep' a boulevard
For motors and joy-riders! All it's worth."
L. Frank Tooker

THE MEETING OF THE SHIPS

When, o'er the silent seas alone,
For days and nights we've cheerless gone,
Oh, they who've felt it know how sweet,
Some sunny morn a sail to meet!

Sparkling at once is every eye,
"Ship ahoy! ship ahoy!" our joyful cry;
While answering back the sounds we hear,
"Ship ahoy! ship ahoy! what cheer? What
 cheer?"

Then sails are backed; we nearer come:
Kind words are said of friends and home;
And soon, too soon, we part with pain,
To sail o'er silent seas again.

Thomas Moore

WOODEN SHIPS

They are remembering forests where they grew,—
  The midnight quiet, and the giant dance;
And all the murmuring summers that they knew
  Are haunting still their altered circumstance.
Leaves they have lost, and robins in the nest,
  Tug of the goodly earth denied to ships,
These, and the rooted certainties, and rest,—
  To gain a watery girdle at the hips.

Only the wind that follows ever aft,
  They greet not as a stranger on their ways;
But this old friend, with whom they drank and laughed,
  Sits in the stern and talks of other days
When they held high bacchanalias still,
  Or dreamed among the stars on some tall hill.

David Morton

"CAP'N"

Far from the sea in his grey later days,
  A dweller where the salt winds never came,
  Where sunsets never sank with crash of flame,
He was an exile in the human maze

Of valley lives. A friendly pathway strays
   Up grave Pine Hill, and there, with some strange aim,
   He climbed—perhaps to hear pine voices frame
Their ancient choruses of old sea ways.

The valley saw him daily mount the height,
   And from the grey cliff face the soaring sky;
   And there a ghostly galleon paused a while,
At some far hail across the verge of night
   Swift veering through the dusk, and anchored nigh,
   And bore him joyous from his lonely isle.
                        Arthur Wallace Peach

THE OLD SAILOR

A white cloud drifts to meet a sail at sea
   Come in from ports that one may yearn to know,
   And here beside the road a slanted tree
   Seems peering down on splendors tossed below.
Beneath the shade a deeper shadow stirs,
   A vagabond gives voice unto his dream,
   He says, "My ship had wider sails than hers;
   But see, still distant, how they strain and gleam."
Now in his rags as tattered as the sails,
   Blown in on rocks of some disastrous shore,
   He walks a road beside the sea and hails
The ships that left him strong of arm no more.
   At farms, a little inland, where he begs
   He blusters still and walks with seaman's legs.
                        Glenn Ward Dresbach

THE CAPTAIN OF ST. KITTS

Once a rover of the sea, captain of a barkentine
Bearing chests of camphor wood and parrots from Azores,
How he stamped his wooden leg, swearing like a picaroon
When the decks were all awash and hell loose out of doors.
Strange, he scans an old gazette, smokes his pipe and snores.

Cargoes of green tea and spice, sandalwood from India,
Heavy tusks of elephants, amber in the hold;
Slipping past old pirate junks, cruising in the Yellow Sea
When the sudden typhoon raged, a panther black and cold.
Strange, that he should be ashore, on a cane and old.

Trampling on the esplanade, gazing past the Spanish Fort,
Stiff as any ramming rod, though he has had his day,
Waiting for a phantom ship, sunk along of Barbary—
For his snowy barkentine to anchor in the bay.
Strange, the past should come again when a man is gray.

Beulah May

TOM BOWLING

Here, a sheer hulk, lies poor Tom Bowling,
  The darling of our crew;
No more he'll hear the tempest howling,
  For death has broach'd him to.
His form was of the manliest beauty,
  His heart was kind and soft,
Faithful, below, he did his duty;
  But now he's gone aloft.

Tom never from his word departed,
  His virtues were so rare,
His friends were many and true-hearted,
  His Poll was kind and fair:
And then he'd sing so blithe and jolly,
  Ah, many's the time and oft!
But mirth is turned to melancholy,
  For Tom is gone aloft.

Yet shall poor Tom find pleasant weather,
  When He, who all commands,
Shall give, to call life's crew together,
  The word to pipe all hands.
Thus Death, who kings and tars despatches,
  In vain Tom's life has doff'd,
For, though his body's under hatches,
  His soul has gone aloft.

Charles Dibdin

'NEVER MORE, SAILOR'

Never more, Sailor,
Shalt thou be
Tossed on the wind-ridden,
Restless sea.
Its tides may labour;
All the world
Shake 'neath that weight
Of waters hurled:
But its whole shock
Can only stir
Thy dust to a quiet
Even quieter.
Thou mock'dst at land
Who now art come
To such a small
And shallow home;
Yet bore the sea
Full many a care
For bones that once
A sailor's were.
And though the grave's
Deep soundlessness
Thy once sea-deafened
Ear distress,
No robin ever
On the deep
Hopped with his song
To haunt thy sleep.

Walter de la Mare

SEA BURIAL

Lower him gently, gently, now, into the quiet deep,
   Let the long furrow of the sea fall softly, slowly over him;
Let the broad veils of purple mist, the wide gray swells of sleep,
   Like a thick mantle cover him.

Only the wind shall comfort him, only the low-voiced tide
   Shall speak to him of his heart's desire, under each passing prow;
Only a dream of stars at dusk, when Heaven's wheel spins wide,
   Shall break his slumber now.

Only the beat of shoal-wise surf, a lone gull's distant cry,
   Shall whisper low of his heart's lost dream, through the undertow of the years;
Only the swift green tongues of flame, sweeping the northern sky
   Shall touch his soul to tears.

Lower him gently, gently now, into those aisles of night;
   Let the long ripples stretch slim hands of crested foam to cover him;
Leave him at last to sea-dark sleep, with one clear Harbour light
   Bright as the pole star over him.

Robina Monkman

BREAK, BREAK, BREAK

Break, break, break,
   On thy cold gray stones, O Sea!
And I would that my tongue could utter
   The thoughts that arise in me.

O, well for the fisherman's boy,
   That he shouts with his sister at play!
O, well for the sailor lad,
   That he sings in his boat on the bay!

And the stately ships go on
   To their haven under the hill;
But O for the touch of a vanish'd hand,
   And the sound of a voice that is still!

Break, break, break,
   At the foot of thy crags, O Sea!
But the tender grace of a day that is dead
   Will never come back to me.
              Alfred, Lord Tennyson

PASA THALASSA THALASSA
"The sea is everywhere the sea."

I

Gone—faded out of the story, the sea-faring friend I remember?
Gone for a decade, they say: never a word or a sign.

HAIL AND FAREWELL

Gone with his hard red face that only his laughter
  could wrinkle,
Down where men go to be still, by the old way of the
  sea.

Never again will he come, with rings in his ears like a
  pirate,
Back to be living and seen, here with his roses and
  vines;
Here where the tenants are shadows and echoes of
  years uneventful,
Memory meets the event, told from afar by the sea.

Smoke that floated and rolled in the twilight away from
  the chimney
Floats and rolls no more. Wheeling and falling, instead,
Down with a twittering flash go the smooth and in-
  scrutable swallows,
Down to the place made theirs by the cold work of the
  sea.

Roses have had their day, and the dusk is on yarrow
  and wormwood—
Dusk that is over the grass, drenched with memorial
  dew;
Trellises lie like bones in a ruin that once was a garden,
Swallows have lingered and ceased, shadows and echoes
  are all.

II

Where is he lying tonight, as I turn away down to the
  valley,

THE ETERNAL SEA

Down where the lamps of men tell me the streets are alive?
Where shall I ask, and of whom, in the town or on land or on water,
News of a time and a place buried alike and with him.

Few now remain who may care, nor may they be wiser for caring,
Where or what manner the doom, whether by day or by night;
Whether in Indian deeps or on flood-laden fields of Atlantis,
Or by the roaring Horn, shrouded in silence he lies.

Few now remain who return by the weed-weary path to his cottage,
Drawn by the scene as it was—met by the chill and the change;
Few are alive who report, and few are alive who remember,
More of him now than a name carved somewhere on the sea.

"Where is he lying?" I ask and the lights in the valley are nearer;
Down to the streets I go, down to the murmur of men.
Down to the roar of the sea in a ship may be well for another—
Down where he lies tonight, silent, and under the storms.

Edwin Arlington Robinson

THE OLD QUARTERMASTER

Next week they're goin' to lay me off because
 I'm gettin' old.
Well, maybe I've it comin' after forty years
 at sea,
An' partin' ain't so bitter hard from liners
 white an' gold,
For bred-in-sail seafarin' men like what they
 used to be.

I stand my trick—I take the wheel, all trimmed
 with patent gear;
Electro-gadget compasses an' iron mikes an'
 such,
An' babe-faced youngsters come to me an'
 tell me how to steer
This forty thousand tons of steel, respondin'
 to a touch.

The school I learned *my* steerin' in was no
 steam heated suite,
With no shore station radios to tell you
 where you are.
Lashed to a five foot buckin' helm in blindin'
 Cape Horn sleet,
Or ghostin' through the tropic night, the
 mast-head on a star.

I knew as much as all this lot when I was
 half their age;

A man to turn a handle there or push a
    button here,
A man to close an' open valves, a man to
    watch a gauge,
An' show the pretty passengers their scientific
    gear.

Fine art in trimmin' sail to wind, to coax another
    knot,
Of crackin' on for full-sail breeze, or shortenin'
    to the gale,
Is gone with all the ships that's gone, an'
    like to be forgot,
Except by ancient crabs like me, who served
    their time in sail.

Gordon Grant

CLIPPER SHIPS

O Clipper Ships! where are, where are ye now?
    The Trades yet ply, still boom the Westerlies.
O wasted winds! when ne'er a clipper bow
    Remains of all the dear dead yesterdays.

O moonlit nights! when sails in shadows drows'd,
    While cradled keel slid o'er the slumb'rous swells!
O tempest dark! when shrill the cry arous'd
    All hands to furl the topsails at eight bells.

Shall we not hear again the slatting sail,
    Freed from the loosen'd gaskets' taut array?
Nor stand to catch, through dizzy heights, the hail—
    "All clear aloft! Sheet home and hoist away!"

O cheery crews! what port laid ye aboard?
  After salt stress, did ye find peace and ease?
They know you now, and tardy fame award
  Your careless ruling of the furrow'd seas.

O Clipper Ships! where are, where are ye now?
  I cry the long degrees through foul and fair!
The Trade Winds sigh, "We speed no clipper bow;"
  The hollow-roaring Forties echo, "Where?"
                                        John Anderson

SAILS

In the growing haste of the world must this thing be:
The passing of sails forever from the sea?
Fewer always the sails go out to the West;
More and huger the steamers howl to the star—
    Trailing their smoke afar,
Staining the deep and the heavens' patient breast.
    Mighty are these we have tamed—
Giants electric, monsters of gas and of steam,
    Titans unknown tho' named.
But oh! for a younger sea and the sails' glad gleam,
    And the clean horizon's call
And the Powers of the air man never shall tame at all!
    Was it not well with the world
    And well with the heart,
When ships went forth to lands untraced on a chart?—
    When dauntless wings were furled
In wonderful havens, virgin then of a mast,
    At islands without a past,
Girt around with an alien ocean's foam,
    Over the world from home?

THE ETERNAL SEA

    Splendid now in my dream
    The snows of the clipper gleam,
Towers of marble, glorious, tall in the sun—
Hurling south to the hurricanes of the Horn.
    O pinions, wrenched and torn
    By the north Atlantic's breath,
On homing whalers, three years' cruising done.
(Captain! captain! what of the seas of Death?)
O colored sails of the little fishing-boats,
From a thousand turquoise harbors venturing,
    Under the tropic day!
    Grey canvases that bring
The shapely sealers to San Francisco Bay,
    Where the steel-walled cruiser floats.

    But I hear a naiad sing,
And softer now in my vision the vans of silk
Glimmer on eastern shallops, by dusk adrift
On waters of legend; and webs as white as milk
Are wafting a murdered queen to her island tomb,
    Where the cypress columns lift.
    And ghostly now on the gloom
The shrouded spars of the Flying Dutchman go
    To harbors that none shall know;
Foamless the ripples of her passing die
    Across the dark, and then from the dark, a cry!

O light of the sea-solitude! O sails!
    Must you pass even so
To the realms of fantasy and the olden tales?
Ports of oblivion, hidden far from the sun,
At your anchorage shall every one be furled,
These wings of man's adventure around the world—

Like the old beauties dying, one by one?
Ever the clouds return: shall these come back
   On the wind's uncharted track—
Braving again the deep's immortal wrath?
O wings of man's adventure in old years!
   Here at an ocean's brink
   Whence the great, increasing quest
   On the everlasting path
Draws yet the heart and the hand to the sea's frontiers
   And spaces scornful of rest,
Under the night's first star I watch you sink,
In the world's twilight fading, fading West.

George Sterling

SHIPS THAT PASS IN THE NIGHT

Ships that pass in the night, and speak each other in passing,
Only a signal shown and a distant voice in the darknesss;
So on the ocean of life we pass and speak one another,
Only a look and a voice, then darkness again and a silence.

Henry Wadsworth Longfellow

ACKNOWLEDGMENTS
(To original edition)

The editor of THE ETERNAL SEA and Coward-McCann, Inc., are grateful to the following publishers, authors, literary executors, and estates for their kind permission to reprint various poems in this volume. Where the selections are in copyright all care has been taken to give full acknowledgment. Should unavoidable omissions have occurred, these will gladly be corrected in later editions if the information is addressed to the publisher, 2 West 45th Street, New York 19, N. Y.

Thanks are given to:

Bill Adams for "Shore Roads of April," "Stowaway," "Peg-leg's Fiddle," and "The Homeward Bound" from *Fenceless Meadows* by Bill Adams, published by Frederick A. Stokes Company.

Mrs. Maggie Y. Allison for "Derelict" by Young E. Allison.

American Poetry Magazine for "Sailor Man" by H. Sewall Bailey.

John Anderson for "Shadows of Sails" and "Clipper Ships" from *Shadows of Sails* by John Anderson, published by Brown, Son & Ferguson, Ltd., Glasgow.

D. Appleton-Century Company, Inc., for "Homeward Bound" and "The Sea-King" reprinted from *The Call of the Sea* by L. Frank Tooker, copyright 1902 by The Century Co., 1930 by Violette S. Tooker, by permission of D. Appleton-Century Company, Inc., also for "Down Among the Wharves" by Eleanore Myers Jewett, reprinted from *St. Nicholas Magazine*, copyright 1922 by The Century Co., by permission of D. Appleton-Century Company, Inc., also for "The Cod-Fisher" reprinted from *Cape Cod Ballads* by Joseph C. Lincoln, copyright 1910 by D. Appleton and Company, 1938 by Joseph C. Lincoln, by permission of D. Appleton-Century Company, Inc.

The Atlantic Monthly for "Hakluyt Unpurchased" by Franklin McDuffee; the editor of this anthology also thanks the author of the poem, whom he was unable to trace through the author's English publisher. *The Atlantic Monthly* also for "A Sea Lyric" by William Hamilton Hayne.

Mrs. F. A. Barbour and Mr. Charles Wharton Stork for "Roughchin, the Pirate" by Arthur Boswell, originally published in *Contemporary Verse Magazine*.

The late Henry Bellamann for "The Deeper Seas" from *Cups of Illusion* by Henry Bellamann, published by Houghton Mifflin Company, 1923, and for "The Gulf Stream" from *The Upward Pass* by Henry Bellamann, published by Houghton Mifflin Company, 1928.

ACKNOWLEDGMENTS

The Bobbs-Merrill Company for "Song of the Sea" from *Collected Poems of Richard Burton*, copyright 1931, used by special permission of the publishers, The Bobbs-Merrill Company.

Albert and Charles Boni, Inc. and the author for "At the Edge of the Bay" from *Ships and Lovers* by Thomas Caldecot Chubb.

Bostick & Thornley, Inc., and the author, for "O Mariners!" from *Rain on the Marsh* by Archibald Rutledge, published 1940 by Bostick & Thornley, Inc., Columbia, South Carolina.

Bradbury, Agnew & Co., Ltd., London, the Proprietors of *Punch*, for "The Figure-Head (A Salt Sea Yarn)" by Crosbie Garstin.

Brandt & Brandt for "Exiled" from *Second April*, published by Harper & Brothers, copyright, 1921, by Edna St. Vincent Millay.

The Canadian Poetry Magazine and the author for "Sea Burial" by Robina Monkman, published in *The Canadian Poetry Magazine*.

Jonathan Cape Ltd., London, for "Dreams of the Sea" and "The Sailor to His Parrot" from *Collected Poems* by W. H. Davies, published by Jonathan Cape, Ltd., London.

The Caxton Printers, Ltd., and the author for "A Ship Comes In (Salem: 1825)" and "Waterfront (Salem)" from *Captain's Walk* by Oliver Jenkins, published by The Caxton Printers, Ltd., Caldwell, Idaho; used by special permission of the copyright owners.

The Christian Science Monitor and the author, in each case, for "Last Cargo" by Silence Buck Bellows; for "Sea Town" by Frances Frost; for "A Sailor's Song" by Hazel Harper Harris; for "Out from Gloucester" by Harlan Trott; for "The Enduring Music" by Harold Vinal; and for "Nor'easter" by Bianca Bradbury.

The Cloister Press, San Francisco, and the author for "The Ship" from *From a Rose Jar* by Louise A. Doran.

Stanton A. Coblentz for "Calm" from his volume *The Merry Hunt and Other Poems*, published by Bruce Humphries, Inc.

C. C. Cockrell, Publisher, Dallas, Texas, and the author for "A Sailor's Song" from *Winds of the Morning* by Hazel Harper Harris.

The Commonweal and the author for permission to use "Cap'n" by Arthur Wallace Peach.

Coward-McCann, Inc. and the author for "Pirates" from *Compass Rose* by Elizabeth Coatsworth, copyright 1929 by Coward-McCann, Inc., also Coward-McCann, Inc. for "The Ships of Arcady" and for "A Mother's Song" from *The Complete Poems of Francis Ledwidge*.

L. Effingham de Forest for "The Sea-Maiden" and "The Phantom Ship" by J. W. de Forest.

Dodd, Mead & Company, Inc., for "The Sea Gipsy" by Richard Hovey, "Coromandel Fishers" by Sarojini Naidu, "The Men Behind the Guns" by John Jerome Rooney, "The Moon-Child" by Fiona Macleod and "The Sonnet's Voice" by Theodore Watts-Dunton; also for "A Son of the Sea," "Arnold, Master of the *Scud*," and "The Ships of Saint John" from *Bliss Carman's Poems*; also Dodd, Mead & Company, Inc., and the author for "Whale" from *Golden Fleece* by

ACKNOWLEDGMENTS 543

William Rose Benét. All these selections reprinted by permission of Dodd, Mead & Company, Inc.

Miss Elizabeth Dodge and Miss Mary D. Dodge for "Thrustararorum" and "Spirit of Freedom, Thou Dost Love the Sea" by Dr. Henry Nehemiah Dodge.

Doubleday and Company, Inc., for "To the Man-of-War Bird" from *Leaves of Grass* by Walt Whitman, copyright 1924 by Doubleday, Doran and Company, Inc.

Francis E. Falkenbury for his poem "South Street," originally published in *McClure's Magazine*.

Thomas Hornsby Ferril for "Lost Ships," published in the former *Denver Times*.

Francis Alan Ford for "Song of the Gulf Stream" from *The Gorilla of Hospital Cay and Other Sea Ballads* by Francis Alan Ford, privately printed, 1939, by Central Printing Company, Little Rock, Arkansas.

Victor Gollancz, Ltd., London, for "The Dolphins," "Sailor and Inland Flower" and "Harp in the Rigging" from *Sailor with Banjo* by Hamish Maclaren. Thanks are also given the author whom correspondence addressed in care of his English publisher has failed to trace.

Mrs. Barbara Ayrton Gould, M.P., and Messrs. Victor Gollancz, Ltd., for "The Sea-Captain" from *Collected Poems of Gerald Gould*.

Harper & Brothers for "The Return," "Sunrise at Sea," and "To a Seamew" from *The Poems of Algernon Charles Swinburne*; also for "Sea-Change" from *Collected Poems, 1918-1938* by Genevieve Taggard, published by Harper & Brothers, copyright, 1938, by Harper & Brothers; also for "Wayfarers" from *Poems* by Dana Burnet, copyright, 1915, by Harper & Brothers.

George G. Harrap & Company, Ltd., London, for "Hymn to the Sea" from *The Poems of Sir William Watson 1878-1935*; also for "A Ballad of the Captains" from *The House of the Winds* by E. J. Brady, published by George G. Harrap & Company, Ltd., London.

William Heinemann, Ltd., London and Toronto, for "The Return," "Sunrise at Sea," and "To a Seamew" from *The Poems of Algernon Charles Swinburne,* published by William Heinemann, Ltd., London.

Henry Holt and Company, Inc., and the author, in each case, for "The Ship of Rio" from *Peacock Pie* by Walter de la Mare, and for "Never More, Sailor" from *Collected Poems of Walter de la Mare;* also for "Say That He Loved Old Ships" from *Bright Harbor* by Daniel Whitehead Hicky; also for "The Old Sailor" from *Selected Poems* by Glenn Ward Dresbach. All the above selections from volumes published by Henry Holt and Company, Inc.

Houghton Mifflin Company for "A Tropical Morning at Sea" from *The Hermitage and Later Poems*, by Edward Rowland Sill, published by Houghton Mifflin Company; also for "Of Little Faith" from *Rowen* by Harold T. Pulsifer, published by Houghton Mifflin Company, 1937, copyright 1937 by Harold T. Pulsifer, and whose permission to reprint is also acknowledged; also for "The Fisherman" from Abbie

ACKNOWLEDGMENTS

Farwell Brown's *Songs of Sixpence*, and "Pirate Treasure" from Abbie Farwell Brown's *The Silver Stair*, which selections are used by permission of the publishers, Houghton Mifflin Company. Also Houghton Mifflin Company for the selections from *The Poetical Works of Henry Wadsworth Longfellow*, *The Poetical Works of Oliver Wendell Holmes*, *Poems by Ralph Waldo Emerson*, *The Poetical Works of Thomas Bailey Aldrich*, *The Poetical Works of Bret Harte*, *Poems by John Greenleaf Whittier*, *Complete Poetical Works of Bayard Taylor*, *Poems of Harriet Prescott Spofford*; all of these selections are used by permission of, and special arrangement with the Houghton Mifflin Company, the authorized publishers.

John Howell, San Francisco, for "The Gardens of the Sea," "Sonnets on the Sea's Voice," and "Sails" from the works of George Sterling.

Bruce Humphries, Inc., and the author, in each case for "Sea" from *Statement: Poems* by Don Gordon, copyright, 1943, by Bruce Humphries, Inc., also for "Nantucket Whalers" and "Opium Clippers" from *Frontiers* by Daniel Henderson, copyright, 1934, by Bruce Humphries, Inc.

Percy Hutchison for his poem "Columbus."

Mrs. Ormeida Keeler and Mr. Harry Robertson for "Black Sailor's Chanty," "Cleaning Ship" and "An Ocean Lullaby" from *A Wanderer's Songs of the Sea* by Charles Keeler.

Kegan Paul, Trench, Trubner & Co., Ltd., London, and the author, for "A Christmas Dawn at Sea" from *At Dawn* by Evan Morgan.

Alfred A. Knopf, Inc., The Macmillan Company of Canada Limited, and the author for "The Way of Cape Race" and "Sea Gulls," reprinted from *Collected Poems* by E. J. Pratt, by permission of Alfred A. Knopf, Inc., and the Macmillan Company of Canada Limited. Alfred A. Knopf, Inc., and the author for "Elegy (On a Dead Mermaid Washed Ashore at Plymouth Rock)" from *The Collected Poems of Robert Hillyer*, published 1933 by Alfred A. Knopf, Inc., copyright 1933 by Robert Hillyer.

J. B. Lippincott Company for "Seagulls on the Serpentine," reprinted by permission of the publisher, J. B. Lippincott Company, from *Dick Turpin's Ride* by Alfred Noyes, copyright, 1927, by J. B. Lippincott Company; also for "The Sun's Over the Foreyard" and "Thoughts in the Gulf Stream" from *Translations from the Chinese*, copyright, 1922, by Christopher Morley, published by the J. B. Lippincott Company.

Little, Brown & Company for "The Sea's Spell" from *The Wings of Icarus* by Susan Marr Spalding, reprinted by permission of Little, Brown & Company; also for "Gulf Stream" from *Verses* by Susan Coolidge, reprinted by permission of Little, Brown & Company.

Longmans, Green & Co., Inc., and the author, for "The *Ark* and the *Dove*" from *God's Ambuscade—A Book of Poems* by Daniel Sargent, published 1935 by Longmans, Green & Co., London, New York, Toronto; also for "Epitaph for a Sailor Buried Ashore" from

ACKNOWLEDGMENTS

Songs of the Common Day by Charles G. D. Roberts, published by Longmans, Green & Co., 1893.

The Lookout for poem "The Lookout" by William Collins, winner of first prize in marine poetry contest conducted by the Seamen's Church Institute of New York.

Mrs. B. R. C. Low for "Due North" from *The House That Was and Other Poems* by Benjamin R. C. Low.

Archibald MacLeish for "Alien" from his volume *The Happy Marriage*, published by Houghton Mifflin Company.

The Macmillan Company, New York, for "Sea-Fever" from *Poems* by John Masefield; the two selections from "Dauber" from *The Story of a Round-House and Other Poems* by John Masefield; for "Calm Morning at Sea" from *Collected Poems* by Sara Teasdale; for "The Secret of the Deeps" from *Poems, Comprising Poems of the Unknown Way, and Horizons and Landmarks* by Sidney Royse Lysaght; for "The Sea Bird to the Wave" from *Wild Earth and Other Poems* by Padraic Colum; for "Fisherman's Luck" from *The Golden Room* by Wilfrid Wilson Gibson and "Luck" from *Collected Poems* by Wilfrid Wilson Gibson; for "Escapade" from *Windward Rock* by Kenneth Leslie; for "The Dolphins," "Sailor and Inland Flower" and "Harp in the Rigging" from *Sailor with Banjo* by Hamish Maclaren; for "The Ballad of O'Bruadir" from *The Dark Breed—A Book of Poems* by F. R. Higgins; for "Legend" from *Hesperides* by Ridgely Torrence, copyright, 1925, by The Macmillan Company; for "Gray Shore" from *Children of the Sun and Other Poems* by James Rorty. All the above selections used by permission of The Macmillan Company, Publishers.

Virgil Markham for the excerpt from "Virgilia" by Edwin Markham.

Beulah May for her poem "Deprecating Parrots," published originally in *Shards Magazine.*

Theodore Maynard for "The Ships" from his volume *Poems* published by Frederick A. Stokes Company, 1919.

McClelland and Stewart Limited, for permission to use "Old Ship Riggers" and "The Old Figurehead Carver" from book *Song of a Blue Nose* by H. A. Cody; also for "Off Rivière du Loup" from the *Collected Poems of Duncan Campbell Scott*, by permission of McClelland and Stewart Limited.

Methuen & Co., Ltd., and the author for "In the Trades" and "Pictures" from *Sea Songs and Ballads* by C. Fox Smith, and for "What the Old Man Said (A Yarn of Dan's)" from *Full Sail* by C. Fox Smith.

Miss Juanita Miller for "Columbus" by Joaquin Miller.

The Mosher Press for "Ships with Your Silver Nets" from *Sky-Rider* by Wade Oliver; also for "Sunken Gold" from *Sonnets of the Wingless Hours* by Eugene Lee-Hamilton.

Captain Francis Newbolt, Executor, for "Sailing at Dawn" and "Drake's Drum" used by permission from *Poems New and Old* by

ACKNOWLEDGMENTS

Sir Henry Newbolt, published by Messrs. John Murray, Ltd., London.

The New York Herald-Tribune and the author for "The Old Quartermaster" by Gordon Grant.

The New York Times and the author, in each case, for "They Who Possess the Sea" by Marguerite Janvrin Adams, and for "Sea Hunger" by John Hanlon Mitchell.

The Notebook, Cleveland, Ohio, and the author for "Chameleon" by Gordon LeClaire, published originally in *The Notebook*.

N. S. Olds for his poem "Rivets" which originally appeared in *Scribner's Magazine*.

The Delegates of the Oxford University Press for permission to use "A Passer-By" and "Upon the Shore" from *The Poetical Works of Robert Bridges*.

Oxford University Press, London, for "Frutta di Mare" from *Poems* by Geoffrey Scott, and for "Homeward Bound" by D. H. Rogers from *Oxford Book of Australasian Verse*, chosen by Walter Murdoch, published by Oxford University Press, London, 1918.

Poetry: A Magazine of Verse and the author for "May-Day at Sea" by John F. Finerty.

Princeton University Press and the translator for "The Sea-Farer" from *Old English Elegies* by Charles W. Kennedy, pp. 55-63 (Princeton University Press, Princeton, New Jersey, 1936).

Promenade Magazine and the author for "Waters of the Sea" by Cecil Goldbeck.

G. P. Putnam's Sons and the author, in each case, for "Old Ships," "Ships in Harbour," "Wooden Ships" and "Mariners" from *Ships in Harbour* by David Morton; also for "Sea Words" from *Spider Architect* by Mary Sinton Leitch, published by G. P. Putnam's Sons, 1937.

G. P. Putnam's Sons, D. E. Kilgour, and The Ryerson Press, Toronto, Canada, for permission to use "The Song of the Derelict" and "The Harvest of the Sea" from *In Flanders Fields and Other Poems* by John McCrae. G. P. Putnam's Sons also for permission to reprint "When the Great Gray Ships Come In" by Guy Wetmore Carryl.

Reynolds Printing, New Bedford, Mass., and William H. Tripp, Curator of The New Bedford Whaling Museum, for "The Whaleman's Song" and "A Song of the Hatteras Whale" from *There Goes Flukes!* by William H. Tripp, published by Reynolds Printing, 1938.

Mr. Laban Lacy Rice, Mr. C. A. Gerst, and D. Appleton-Century Company, Inc., for "To the Afternoon Moon, at Sea," "Nights on the Indian Ocean" and "Submarine Mountains" from *A Sea Lover's Scrip* by Cale Young Rice, published by D. Appleton-Century Company, Inc.

Rinehart and Company, Inc., and the author for "Southward Sidonian Hanno" and the excerpt from "Saga of Leif the Lucky," from *Earth Moods and Other Poems* by Hervey Allen, copyright, 1925, and reprinted by permission of Rinehart and Company, Inc., Publishers.

ACKNOWLEDGMENTS 547

THE RUDDER, The Magazine for Yachtsmen for permission to reprint "The Clipper," "The Main-Sheet Song" and "Making Land" by Thomas Fleming Day.

The Ryerson Press, Toronto, for "Sea Hunger" from *Songs* by John Hanlon Mitchell; also for "The Harvest of the Sea" and "The Song of the Derelict" from *In Flanders Fields and Other Poems* by John McCrae. By permission of The Ryerson Press, Toronto, Canada.

The Saturday Evening Post and the author, in each case, for "Figurehead" by Dorothy Paul, and for "The Last Gloucesterman" by Gordon Grant.

Charles Scribner's Sons for "Ode to the Mediterranean" from *Poems* by George Santayana, copyright, 1923, by Charles Scribner's Sons; for "Christmas at Sea" and "Over the Sea to Skye" from *Poems and Ballads* by Robert Louis Stevenson, copyright, 1895, by Charles Scribner's Sons; for "The Tornado" from *Hesperus, and Other Poems* by Charles de Kay, copyright, 1880, by Charles Scribner's Sons; for "A Hymn to the Sea" from *The Poems of Richard Henry Stoddard,* copyright, 1880, by Charles Scribner's Sons; for "Dawn on Mid-Ocean," "Sea-Voyage," "The Fish-Hawk" and "The Sound of the Sea" from *Poems, 1911-1936* by John Hall Wheelock, copyright, 1936, reprinted by permission of the author and Charles Scribner's Sons; for "The Sea is His" from *Poems* by Edward Sandford Martin, copyright, 1914, by Charles Scribner's Sons; for "A Song of the Wave" from *The Song of the Wave, and Other Poems* by George Cabot Lodge, copyright, 1898, by Charles Scribner's Sons; for "Homecoming in Storm" from *Songs of Unrest* by Bernice Lesbia Kenyon, copyright, 1923, by Charles Scribner's Sons; for "Clouds" from *Songs and Poems* by John Jay Chapman, copyright, 1919, by Charles Scribner's Sons; for "The Full Sea Rolls and Thunders" from *Poems* by William Ernest Henley, copyright, 1898, by Charles Scribner's Sons; for "Pasa Thalassa Thalassa" from *The Town Down the River* by Edwin Arlington Robinson, published by Charles Scribner's Sons, and for excerpt from "The Marshes of Glynn" from *Poems* by Sidney Lanier, published by Charles Scribner's Sons.

Martin Secker & Warburg, Ltd., London for "Jonah and the Whale" from *The Frozen Ocean* by Viola Meynell, published by Martin Secker, Ltd., 1930, and for "The Old Ships" from *Collected Poems of James Elroy Flecker.*

A. M. Sullivan for "The *Flying Dutchman*" and "The Whale and the *Essex.*"

Katherine Kelley Taylor for "Flying Fish" from her volume *The Sea Gull's Daughter and Other Poems,* published by The William Feather Company, Cleveland, Ohio, copyright, 1937, by Katherine Kelley Taylor.

Wilfrid Thorley for "Norse Sailor's Joy" from his volume *Londoner's Chariot,* published 1925 by Jonathan Cape, Ltd., London.

John Curtis Underwood for "The Wave" from *The Iron Muse* by

ACKNOWLEDGMENTS

John Curtis Underwood, published by G. P. Putnam's Sons, copyright, 1910, by John Curtis Underwood.

VerseCraft and the author for "Land's End (Point Lobos, California)" by Stanton A. Coblentz, published in *VerseCraft*.

The Virginia Quarterly Review for "The Old Conservative (On the Battery)" by L. Frank Tooker, published in *The Virginia Quarterly Review*, July 1925.

Voices: A Journal of Poetry, The Kaleidograph Press and the author for "Flying Fish," originally published in *Voices* and included in volume *Finger at the Crossroads* by J. Corson Miller, published 1942 by the Kaleidograph Press.

The Washington Post and the author for "Winged Mariner" by Grace Clementine Howes.

Messrs. A. P. Watt and Son, Mrs. George Bambridge, Doubleday and Company, Inc., and The Macmillan Company of Canada Limited for "Frankie's Trade" from *Rewards and Fairies* by Rudyard Kipling, copyright, 1910, by Rudyard Kipling, and for "The Last Chantey" and "The Coastwise Lights" from *The Seven Seas* by Rudyard Kipling, copyright, 1896, by Rudyard Kipling.

Westward Magazine, Florence R. Keene and the author for "The Captain of St. Kitts" by Beulah May, published originally in *Westward* and included in volume *Buccaneer's Gold* by Beulah May, published by The Fine Arts Press, Santa Ana, Calif.

James T. White & Company and the author for "If I Could Grasp a Wave from the Great Sea" from *The Sea and April* by John Richard Moreland, published 1928.

Wings, a Quarterly of Verse and the author for "Tranquil Sea" by Claire Aven Thomson.

Mrs. Charles D. Woodberry for "A Life" by George Edward Woodberry.

Yale University Press for "The Heritage" from *Sea Moods and Other Poems* by Edward Bliss Reed.

Yankee Magazine and the author for "Hydrographic Report" by Frances Frost.

Francis Brett Young, W. Collins Sons & Co., Ltd., and E. P. Dutton & Co., Inc., for "Five Degrees South" and "The Dhows" from *Poems 1916-1918* by Francis Brett Young, published and copyright by E. P. Dutton & Co., Inc., New York.

Miss Nancy McIntosh and Macmillan & Co., Ltd., for "The Yarn of the Nancy Bell" from *The Bab Ballads* by Sir W. S. Gilbert.

INDEX OF AUTHORS AND TITLES

ADAMS, B. (1879-   )
  Shore Roads of April, 20
  Stowaway, 65
  Peg-leg's Fiddle, 77
  The Homeward Bound (Landfall), 222
ADAMS, M. J. (Contemporary)
  They Who Possess the Sea, 15
ALDRICH, T. B. (1836-1907)
  Outward Bound, 254
  Alec Yeaton's Son, 471
ALLEN, H. (1889-   )
  Southward Sidonian Hanno, 72
  From "Saga of Leif the Lucky," 227
ALLEN, W. B. (1855-1938)
  Thalatta, 284
ALLISON, Y. E. (1853-1932)
  Derelict, 378
ANDERSON, J. (1879-   )
  Shadows of Sails, 501
  Clipper Ships, 536
ANONYMOUS
  A Perilous Life, 374
  A Song of the Hatteras Whale, 367
  An Old Seaport (Evening Sketch), 268
  Brand Fire New Whaling Song Right from the Pacific Ocean, 362
  "Round Cape Horn," 265
  The Ballad of Sir Patrick Spens, 326
  The Birth of Venus, 213
  The Coast of Peru, 351
  The Fisher's Life, 309
  The Mysterious Music of Ocean, 512
  The Pirate of High Barbary, 393
  The Seafarer (Translated from the Anglo-Saxon by Prof. C. W. Kennedy), 11
  The Silkie o' Sule Skerrie, 482
  The Whale, 359
  The Whaleman's Song, 366
  The Yankee Man-of-War, 313
  There She Blows! 355
  We'll Go to Sea No More, 308
ARNOLD, G. (1834-1865)
  Jubilate, 229
ARNOLD, M. (1822-1888)
  Dover Beach, 176
  The Forsaken Merman, 398
ATHERSTONE, E. (1788-1872)
  Sunrise at Sea, 140

BAILEY, H. S.
  Sailor Man, 451
BEDDOES, T. L. (1802-1849)
  To Sea, To Sea! 75
BELLAMANN, H. (1882-1945)
  The Deeper Seas, 72
  The Gulf Stream, 134
BELLOWS, S. B. (Contemporary)
  Last Cargo, 425
BENET, W. R. (1886-   )
  Whale, 369
BEST, C. (circa 1600)
  Looke How the Pale Queene, 212
BOSWELL, A.
  Roughchin, the Pirate, 486
BRADBURY, B. (Contemporary)
  Nor'easter, 122
BRADY, E. J. (1869-   )
  A Ballad of the Captains, 515

INDEX OF AUTHORS AND TITLES

BRAINARD, J. G. C. (1796-1828)
  The Deep, 403
  Sonnet to the Sea-Serpent, 412
  The Captain, 464
BRIDGES, R. (1844-1930)
  A Passer-By, 57
  Upon the Shore, 135
BROWN, A. F. (1875-1927)
  The Fisherman, 291
  Pirate Treasure, 390
BROWNE, W. (1590-1645)
  The Sirens' Song, 404
BROWNELL, H. H. (1820-1872)
  The River Fight, 320
BURNET, D. (1888-   )
  Wayfarers, 257
BURTON, R. E. (1861-1940)
  Song of the Sea, 493
BYRON, Lord (1788-1824)
  Apostrophe to the Ocean, 145
  Song of the Corsairs, 381

CAEDMON (7th Century)
  Far and Wide She Went, 284
CAMOENS, L. (1524-1579)
  Waterspout, 112
CAMPBELL, T. (1777-1844)
  The Beatific Sea, 160
  Mighty Sea! Cameleon-like Thou Changest, 205
  Ye Mariners of England, 329
CAMPION, T. (1567-1619)
  A Hymne in Prayse of Neptune, 397
CARMAN, B. (1861-1929)
  The Ships of Saint John, 259
  A Son of the Sea, 473
  Arnold, Master of the *Scud*, 477
CARRYL, G. W. (1873-1904)
  When the Great Gray Ships Come In, 337
CHAPMAN, G. (1560-1634)
  The Master Spirit, 189
  The Pilot, 193
  Homeric Hymn to Neptune, 410

CHAPMAN, J. J. (1862-1933)
  Clouds, 429
CHAUCER, G. (1328-1400)
  The Shipman, 253
CHUBB, T. C. (1899-   )
  At the Edge of the Bay, 17
CLARKE, C. R.
  Song of the Mariner's Needle, 54
CLARKE, J. F. (1810-1888)
  White-Capped Waves, 132
CLOUGH, A. H. (1819-1861)
  Where Lies the Land? 79
  Qua Cursum Ventus, 177
COATSWORTH, E. (Contemporary)
  Pirates, 392
COBLENTZ, S. A. (1896-   )
  Calm, 139
  Land's End (Point Lobos, California), 502
CODY, H. A. (1872-   )
  Old Ship Riggers, 30
  The Old Figurehead Carver, 32
COLLIER, T. S. (1842-1893)
  The Spectre Ship, 444
COLLINS, W. (Contemporary)
  The Lookout, 192
COLUM, P. (1881-   )
  The Sea Bird to the Wave, 271
COOLIDGE, S. (1845-1905)
  Gulf Stream, 208
COOPER, J. F. (1789-1851)
  My Brigantine, 68
CORNWALL, B. (1787-1874)
  The Sea—in Calm, 125
  Is My Lover on the Sea? 199
  The Stormy Petrel, 272
COWPER, W. (1731-1800)
  On the Loss of the *Royal George*, 339
CRABBE, G. (1754-1832)
  The Winter Storm at Sea, 119
CUNNINGHAM, A. (1784-1842)
  A Wet Sheet and a Flowing Sea, 66
  The Mariner, 217

DANA, R. H. (1787-1879)
The Little Beach Bird, 282
DAVIES, Sir J. (1569-1626)
The Sea Danceth, 200
DAVIES, W. H. (1870-   )
Dreams of the Sea, 14
The Sailor to His Parrot, 273
DAY, T. F. (1861-1927)
The Clipper, 67
The Main-Sheet Song, 75
Making Land, 231
DE FOREST, J. W. (1826-1906)
The Sea-Maiden, 405
The Phantom Ship, 446
DE KAY, C. (1848-1935)
The Tornado, 108
DE LA MARE, W. (1873-   )
The Ship of Rio, 480
'Never More, Sailor,' 530
DIBDIN, C. (1745-1814)
Jack's Fidelity, 206
Tom Bowling, 529
DOBELL, S. T. (1824-1874)
How's My Boy? 518
DODGE, H. N. (1843-1937)
Spirit of Freedom, Thou Dost Love the Sea, 24
Thrustararorum, 305
DONNE, J. (1573-1631)
The Storm, 114
DORAN, L. A. (Contemporary)
The Ship, 235
DRAYTON, M. (1563-1631)
Like an Adventurous Sea-Farer Am I, 468
DRESBACH, G. W. (1889-   )
The Old Sailor, 527

EMERSON, R. W. (1803-1882)
Sea-Shore, 4

FALCONER, W. (1730-1769)
All Hands Unmoor! 77
Shortening Sail, 91
High O'er the Poop the Audacious Seas Aspire, 105

FALKENBURY, F. E. (1882-   )
South Street, 263
FENNER, C. G. (1822-1847)
Gulf-Weed, 178
FERRIL, T. H. (1896-   )
Lost Ships, 498
FIELDS, J. T. (1816-1881)
Ballad of the Tempest, 85
The Alarmèd Skipper, 461
FINERTY, J F. (Contemporary)
May-Day at Sea, 127
FLECKER, J. E. (1884-1915)
The Old Ships, 427
FORD, F. A. (1898-   )
Song of the Gulf Stream, 129
FOSTER, W. P.
The Sea's Voice, 506
Icebergs, 141
FROST, F. (Contemporary)
Hydrographic Report, 109
Sea Town, 250

GARSTIN, C. (1887-1930)
The Figure-Head (A Salt Sea Yarn), 466
GAY, J. (1688-1732)
Black-Eyed Susan, 201
GIBSON, W. W. (1878-   )
Fisherman's Luck, 292
Luck, 458
GILBERT, W. S. (1836-1911)
The Yarn of the *Nancy Bell*, 452
GOLDBECK, C. (1897-   )
Waters of the Sea, 208
GORDON, D.
Sea, 150
GOULD, G. (1885-1936)
The Sea-Captain, 211
GRANT, G. (1875-   )
The Last Gloucesterman, 293
The Old Quartermaster, 535
GRAY, B. (1826-1886)
Ships at Sea, 236

HARRIS, H. H. (Contemporary)
A Sailor's Song, 229

INDEX OF AUTHORS AND TITLES

HARTE, B. (1839-1902)
To a Sea-Bird, 278
Greyport Legend, 489
HAYNE, W. H. (1856-1929)
A Sea Lyric, 499
HEMANS, F. (1794-1835)
Where is the Sea? 21
Casabianca, 331
HENDERSON, D. (1880-   )
Nantucket Whalers, 353
Opium Clippers, 520
HENLEY, W. E. (1849-1903)
The Full Sea Rolls and Thunders, 499
HICKY, D. W. (1903-   )
Say That He Loved Old Ships, 515
HIGGINS, F. R. (1896-1941)
The Ballad of O'Bruadir, 377
HILLYER, R. (1895-   )
Elegy (On a Dead Mermaid Washed Ashore at Plymouth Rock), 421
HOLMES, O. W. (1809-1894)
The Chambered Nautilus, 172
Old Ironsides, 315
The Ballad of the Oysterman, 298
A Sea Dialogue, 462
HOOD, T. (1798-1845)
A Sailor's Apology for Bow-Legs, 455
HOVEY, R. (1864-1900)
The Sea Gipsy, 5
HOWES, G. C. (Contemporary)
Winged Mariner, 279
HUGHES, J. (1677-1720)
The Court of Neptune, 417
HUTCHISON, P. (Contemporary)
Columbus, 387

INGELOW, J. (1830-1897)
Sea-Nurtured, 22

JENKINS, O. (Contemporary)
A Ship Comes In (Salem: 1825), 252
Waterfront (Salem), 428

JEWETT, E. M.
Down Among the Wharves, 249

KEATS, J. (1795-1821)
He Saw Far in the Concave Green of the Sea, 413
Sonnet on the Sea, 494
The Shell's Song, 507
KEELER, C. (1871-1937)
Black Sailor's Chanty, 120
Cleaning Ship, 243
An Ocean Lullaby, 481
KENYON, B. L. (Contemporary)
Homecoming in Storm, 230
KINGSLEY, C. (1819-1875)
The Three Fishers, 289
The Last Buccaneer, 382
KIPLING, R. (1865-1936)
Frankie's Trade, 96
The Last Chantey, 147
The Coastwise Lights, 224

LAMB, C. (1775-1834)
The Triumph of the Whale, 374
LANIER, S. (1842-1881)
From "The Marshes of Glynn," 195
LECLAIRE, G. (1905-   )
Chameleon, 209
LEDWIDGE, F. (1891-1917)
The Ships of Arcady, 426
A Mother's Song, 475
LEE-HAMILTON, E. (1845-1907)
Sunken Gold, 411
LEITCH, M. S. (Contemporary)
Sea Words, 505
LESLIE, K. (1892-   )
Escapade, 294
LINCOLN, J. C. (1870-1944)
The Cod-Fisher, 290
LINDSAY, Lady
East Coast Lullaby, 488
LODGE, G. C. (1873-1909)
A Song of the Wave, 184
LONGFELLOW, H. W. (1807-1882)
The Secret of the Sea, 6
The Building of the Ship, 34
The Building of the Long Serpent, 50

INDEX OF AUTHORS AND TITLES

The Equinox (From "Seaweed"), 107
The Wreck of the *Hesperus*, 115
My Lost Youth, 262
The *Cumberland*, 332
A Dutch Picture, 388
The Phantom Ship, 433
Sir Humphrey Gilbert, 442
The Sound of the Sea, 501
Ships That Pass in the Night, 539

Low, B. R. C.
Due North, 69

Lysaght, S. R.
The Secret of the Deeps, 170

Macaulay, Lord (1800-1859)
The Last Buccaneer, 385

MacDonald, G. (1824-1905)
The Earl o' Quarterdeck, 343

MacLaren, H. (1901-   )
The Dolphins, 364
Sailor and Inland Flower, 460
Harp in the Rigging, 495

MacLeish, A. (1892-   )
Alien, 275

Macleod, F. (1855-1905)
The Moon-Child, 483

Markham, E. (1852-1940)
From "Virgilia," 484

Marryat, F. (1792-1848)
The Captain Stood on the Carronade, 335

Martin, E. S. (1856-1939)
The Sea is His, 173

Masefield, J. (1878-   )
Sea-Fever, 3
Rounding the Horn (From "Dauber"), 86
The Clipper Loitered South (From "Dauber"), 130

May, B. (Contemporary)
Deprecating Parrots, 283
The Captain of St. Kitts, 528

Maynard, T. (1890-   )
The Ships, 238

McCrae, J. (1872-1918)
The Harvest of the Sea, 294
The Song of the Derelict, 428

McDuffee, F.
Hakluyt Unpurchased, 23

McKay, J. T.
Making Port, 241

Melville, H. (1819-1891)
Father Mapple's Hymn (From "Moby Dick"), 360
The Stone Fleet, 361

Meredith, W. T.
Farragut, 318

Meynell, V.
Jonah and the Whale, 357

Millay, E. St. V. (Contemporary)
Exiled, 8

Miller, J. (1841-1913)
Columbus, 58

Miller, J. C. (1883-   )
Flying Fish, 277

Miller, T. (1807-1874)
The Sea-Deeps, 420

Milton, J. (1608-1674)
The Ark, 47
Over All the Face of Earth Main Ocean Flowed, 187
And God Created the Great Whales, 365

Mitchell, J. H. (1897-   )
Sea Hunger, 16

Mitchell, W. (1826-1908)
Tacking Ship Off Shore, 62
Reefing Topsails, 99
The Cheer of the *Trenton* (A Samoan Memory—1889), 341

Monkman, R. (Contemporary)
Sea Burial, 531

Moore, T. (1779-1852)
The Meeting of the Ships, 525

Moreland, J. R. (1880-   )
If I Could Grasp a Wave from the Great Sea, 180

Morgan, E. (1893-   )
A Christmas Dawn at Sea, 179

INDEX OF AUTHORS AND TITLES

MORLEY, C. (1890-   )
The Sun's Over the Foreyard, 459
Thoughts in the Gulf Stream, 217
MORRIS, W. (1834-1896)
Song of the Argonauts, 81
MORTON, D. (1886-   )
Mariners, 15
Ships in Harbour, 257
Old Ships, 448
Wooden Ships, 526

NAIDU, S. (1879-   )
Coromandel Fishers, 303
NEWBOLT, Sir H. (1862-1938)
Sailing at Dawn, 70
Drake's Drum, 334
NOYES, A. (1880-   )
Seagulls on the Serpentine, 285

OLDS, N. S. (1875-   )
Rivets, 48
OLIVER, W. (1890-   )
Ships with Your Silver Nets, 297

PAUL, D. (Contemporary)
Figurehead, 210
PEACH, A. W. (1886-   )
"Cap'n," 526
PEARCE, J.
Heaving the Lead, 226
PERCIVAL, J. G. (1795-1856)
The Coral Grove, 406
PITT, W. (1778-1839)
Sailor's Consolation, 103
POE, E. A. (1809-1849)
Annabel Lee, 214
POLLOK, R. (1798-1827)
Ocean, 193

PRATT, E. J. (1883-   )
The Way of Cape Race, 111
Sea Gulls, 275
PRENTICE, G. D. (1802-1870)
The Ocean, 161

PSALM CVII, 23-30, 169
PULSIFER, H. T. (1886-   )
Of Little Faith, 203

READ, T. B. (1822-1872)
The Flag of the *Constellation*, 347
REED, E. B. (1872-1940)
The Heritage, 19
RICE, C. Y. (1872-1943)
To the Afternoon Moon, at Sea, 138
Nights on the Indian Ocean, 194
Submarine Mountains, 418
RICH, H.
The Skipper-Hermit, 295
ROBERTS, C. G. D. (1860-1943)
Epitaph for a Sailor Buried Ashore, 521
ROBINSON, E. A. (1869-1936)
Pasa Thalassa Thalassa, 532
ROGERS, D. H.
Homeward Bound, 244
ROONEY, J. J. (1866-1934)
The Men Behind the Guns, 316
RORTY, J. (1890-   )
Gray Shore, 495
ROSSETTI, D. G. (1828-1882)
The Sea Limits, 509
RUTLEDGE, A. (1883-   )
O Mariners! 180

SANTAYANA, G. (1863-   )
Ode to the Mediterranean, 9
SARGENT, D. (1890-   )
The *Ark* and the *Dove*, 239
SARGENT, E. (1813-1880)
A Life on the Ocean Wave, 60
Sunrise at Sea, 136
A Summer Noon at Sea, 137
Tropical Weather, 139
Evening in Gloucester Harbor, 251
SCOTT, D. C. (1862-   )
Off Rivière du Loup, 234

INDEX OF AUTHORS AND TITLES 555

Scott, G. (1885-1929)
Frutta di Mare, 508
Scott, Sir W. (1771-1832)
Mermaids and Mermen, 414
Sedley, Sir C. (1663-1701)
Love Still Has Something of the Sea, 199
Shakespeare, W. (1564-1616)
Methought I Saw a Thousand Fearful Wrecks, 412
A Sea Dirge, 522
Shea, J. A. (1802-1845)
The Ocean, 181
Shelley, P. B. (1792-1822)
The Trackless Deeps, 153
Unfathomable Sea! 160
Sill, E. R. (1841-1887)
A Tropical Morning at Sea, 125
Simms, W. G. (1806-1870)
Night Storm, 98
Smith, C. F. (Contemporary)
In the Trades, 59
What the Old Man Said (A Yarn of Dan's), 102
Pictures, 255
Southey, R. (1774-1843)
A Calm Sea, 132
Homeward Bound, 233
Spalding, S. M. (1841-1908)
The Sea's Spell, 205
Spenser, E. (1552-1599)
Sonnet: Lyke as a Ship, 204
Port After Stormie Seas, 225
Now Strike Your Sailes Ye Jolly Mariners! 245
Next Unto Him Was Neptune Pictured, 407
Spofford, H. P. (1835-1921)
Godspeed, 79
Sterling, G. (1869-1926)
The Gardens of the Sea, 416
Sonnets on the Sea's Voice, 510
Sails, 537
Stevenson, R. L. (1850-1894)
Christmas at Sea, 88
Over the Sea to Skye, 476

Stoddard, C. W. (1843-1909)
Albatross, 281
Stoddard, R. H. (1825-1903)
A Hymn to the Sea, 151
Sullivan, A. M. (1896-   )
The Whale and the *Essex*, 372
The *Flying Dutchman*, 435
Swinburne, A. C. (1837-1909)
The Return, 18
Sunrise at Sea, 128
To a Seamew, 276

Taggard, G. (Contemporary)
Sea-Change, 201
Taylor, B. (1825-1878)
Storm Song, 111
Taylor, K. K. (Contemporary)
Flying Fish, 285
Teasdale, S. (1884-1933)
Calm Morning at Sea, 131
Tennyson, A. (1809-1892)
From "Ulysses," 61
Sweet and Low, 473
Crossing the Bar, 522
Break, Break, Break, 532
Thackeray, W. M. (1810-1863)
Little Billee, 474
Thaxter, C. (1836-1894)
As Happy Dwellers by the Seaside Hear, 216
Thomson, C. A. (Contemporary)
Tranquil Sea, 133
Thomson, J. (1700-1748)
Sea-Birds, 286
Thorley, W. (1878-   )
Norse Sailor's Joy, 240
Tooker, L. F. (1855-1925)
Homeward Bound, 221
The Sea-King, 384
The Old Conservative (On the Battery), 523
Torrence, R. (1875-   )
Legend, 408
Trott, H. (1907-   )
Out from Gloucester, 310
Trowbridge, J. T. (1827-1916)
At Sea, 183

INDEX OF AUTHORS AND TITLES

TURBERVILLE, G. (1540-1610)
The Pine to the Mariner, 53
TURNER, C. T. (1808-1879)
The Buoy-Bell, 508

UNDERWOOD, J. C. (1874-   )
The Wave, 164

VINAL, H. (1891-   )
The Enduring Music, 504

WATSON, SIR W. (1858-1935)
Hymn to the Sea, 154
WATTS-DUNTON, T. (1832-1914)
The Sonnet's Voice (A Metrical Lesson by the Seashore), 500
WHEELOCK, J. H. (1886-   )
Dawn on Mid-Ocean, 169
Sea-Voyage, 190
The Fish-Hawk, 279
The Sound of the Sea, 496
WHITMAN, W. (1819-1892)
To the Man-of-War Bird, 271
WHITTIER, J. G. (1807-1892)

The Ship-Builders, 27
The *Three Bells*, 104
The Fishermen, 300
The Dead Ship of Harpswell, 430
The *Palatine*, 437
WILLIAMS, S. (1841-1868)
Deep Sea Soundings, 188
WILSON, A. (1766-1813)
The Fisherman's Hymn, 304
WILSON, J. (1785-1854)
Calm as the Cloudless Heaven, 142
WOODBERRY, G. E. (1855-1930)
A Life, 80
WORDSWORTH, W. (1770-1850)
Where Lies the Land to Which Yon Ship Must Go? 64
By the Sea, 498
WYATT, SIR T. (1503-1542)
The Lover Like to a Ship Tossed on the Sea, 215

YOUNG, F. B. (1884-   )
Five Degrees South, 134
The Dhows, 441

INDEX OF FIRST LINES

A cheer and salute for the Admiral, and here's to the Captain bold 316
A holy stillness, beautiful and deep 137
A lady loved a swaggering rover 390
A life on the ocean wave 60
A little lonely child am I 483
A lofty ship from Salcombe came 393
A perilous life, and hard as life may be......................... 374
A schipman was ther, wonyng fer by weste...................... 253
A song I sing of my sea-adventure 11
A thousand miles from land are we 272
A thundering sound he hears 77
A weary weed, tossed to and fro 178
A wet sheet and a flowing sea 66
A white cloud drifts to meet a sail at sea 527
Ah! what pleasant visions haunt me 6
All day long till the west was red 241
All in the Downs the fleet was moored 201
Almighty Wisdom made the land 173
Always, here where I sleep, I hear the sound of the sea 496
An earthly nurrice sits an' sings 482
And God created the great whales, and each 365
And lo! the sea that fleets about the land 200
And oft, while wonder thrill'd my breast, mine eyes 112
Around the rocky headlands, far and near 506
As happy dwellers by the seaside hear 216
As I came down to the long street by the water, the sea-ships
    drooped their masts like ladies bowing...................... 263
As I sail home to Galveston 229
As I sunk the lobster-pots 292
As ships becalmed at eve, that lay 177
As the proud horse with costly trappings gay 91
As threads spilling dew-drops 364
Ask any question in this town 265
At anchor in Hampton Roads we lay 332
At length a reverend sire among them came 47
Ay, tear her tattered ensign down! 315

Behind him lay the gray Azores 58
Beneath the low-hung night cloud 104
Beneath the ocean's sapphire lid 416
Beneath thy spell, O radiant summer sea 205

INDEX OF FIRST LINES

Break, break, break 532
Bright shine the golden summits in the light 132
"Build me straight, O worthy Master!" 34

Come all ye bold sailors 351
Come, dear children, let us away 398
Consider the sea's listless chime 509

Day has barred her windows close, and gangs wi' quiet feet 488
"Death is a voyage," I heard it lightly told 180
Deep in the wave is a coral grove 406
Deeper than the narwhal sinketh 420
"Don't you take no sail off 'er," the Ol' Man said............ 102
Down among the wharves—that's the place I like to wander! 249
Down on your knees, boys, holystone the decks 243
Drake he's in his hammock an' a thousand mile away 334

Enough: you have the dream, the flame........................ 69

Far and wide she went, her own will she sought 284
Far from the sea in his grey later days 526
Far over the billows unresting forever 284
Farragut, Farragut 318
Fathoms deep beneath the wave 414
Fifteen men on the Dead Man's Chest— 378
For Demerara bound with cod she flies 294
For England when with favoring gale 226
For now are wider ways, profounder tides 72
For one carved instant as they flew 275
For thirty year, come herrin'-time 295
Friend, you seem thoughtful. I not wonder much 462
From Java, Sumatra, and old Cathay 252
From out his castle on the sand 384
From the drear North, a cold and cheerless land.............. 19
Full fathom five thy father lies 522

Give me a spirit that on life's rough sea 189
Gone—faded out of the story, the sea-faring friend I remember? .. 532
Grant, O regal in bounty, a subtle and delicate largess 154
Gray distance hid each shining sail 229
Great Ocean! strongest of creation's sons 193

Hail and farewell! Lo, I am the last of a glorious fleet of sail ... 293
Has a love of adventure, a promise of gold 366
He saw far in the concave green of the sea 413
He sported round the watery world 357
He was one who followed 451
He who but yesterday would roam 521

INDEX OF FIRST LINES 559

Her sails are strong and yellow as the sand	67
Here, a sheer hulk, lies poor Tom Bowling	529
Here in this inland garden	275
Here rage the furies that have shaped the world	502
High o'er the poop the audacious seas aspire	105
Ho! burnish well, ye cunning hands	54
Ho, let her rip—with her royal clew a-quiver	59
"Ho, sailor of the sea!"	518
How beautiful!—from his blue throne on high	161
How do you know that May has come	127
How like the leper, with his own sad cry	508
Hurrah! the seaward breezes	300
I am a sea-shell flung	508
I am fevered with the sunset	5
I am in love with the sea, but I do not trust her yet	211
I crossed the gangway in the winter's raining	65
I have a feeling for those ships	361
I have done my bit of carving	32
I have not known a quieter thing than ships	257
I have seen old ships sail like swans asleep	427
I have ships that went to sea	236
I heard my ancient sea-blood say	80
I heard, or seemed to hear, the chiding Sea	4
I know not why I yearn for thee again	14
I leave behind me the elm-shadowed square	254
I love all waves and lovely water in motion	134
I love sea words—	505
I must down to the seas again, to the lonely sea and the sky	3
I said, when the word came, "She will break	203
I saunter by the shore and lose myself	151
I saw the old man pause, then turn his head	523
I spoke the sea, that reaches green	495
I stood upon a shore, a pleasant shore	507
I was born for deep-sea faring	473
I was not meant to stand in a sea-edge garden	210
I will go back to the great sweet mother	18
If ever a sailor was fond of good sport	206
If I could grasp a wave from the great sea	180
In dim green depths rot ingot-laden ships	411
In Mather's Magnalia Christi	433
In the growing haste of the world must this thing be	537
Io! Paean! Io! sing	374
Is my lover on the sea	199
It is a beauteous evening, calm and free	498
It is the midnight hour;—the beauteous sea	142
It keeps eternal whisperings around	494

It was a tall young oysterman lived by the harbor-side 298
It was many and many a year ago 214
It was the schooner *Hesperus* 115
I've a pal called Billy Peg-leg, with one leg a wood leg 77

Leagues north, as fly the gull and auk 437
Leif was a man's name 227
Lightest foam, straightest spray 208
Like an adventurous Sea-farer am I 468
Likeness of heaven! 181
Lion-hunger, tiger-leap! 111
Little ships of whitest pearl 475
Lo, as the sun from his ocean bed rising 355
Lonely and cold and fierce I keep my way 208
Lonely and wild it rose 512
Look what immortal floods the sunset pours 125
Looke how the pale Queene of the silent night 212
Love still has something of the Sea 199
Low lies the land upon the sea 192
Lower him gently, gently, now, into the quiet deep 531
Lyke as a ship, that through the Ocean wyde 204

Man is a fool and a bag of wind! 23
Man is a torch borne in the wind; a dream 193
Many a long, long year ago 461
Mariner, what of the deep? 188
Memory, out of the mist, in a long slow ripple 285
Men who have loved the ships they took to sea 15
Methought I saw a thousand fearful wrecks 412
Midocean like a pale blue morning-glory 131
Mighty Sea! Cameleon-like thou changest 205
My brigantine! 68
My galley chargèd with forgetfulness 215
My grandfather's hands were wise and hard 48

Neptune, the mighty Marine God, I sing 410
Nereid, Grand Turk, Good Intent 428
Never more, Sailor 530
Next unto him was Neptune pictured 407
Next week they're goin' to lay me off because I'm gettin' old ... 535
Nights on the Indian Ocean 194
Nooked underneath steep, sterile hills that rise 268
Now, landsmen, list! There is no sight more fair 240
Now strike your sailes ye jolly Mariners 245
Now we're afloat upon the tropic sea 139

O bitter sea, tumultuous sea 81

INDEX OF FIRST LINES 561

O Clipper Ships! where are, where are ye now? 536
"O man of little wit 53
O Muse! by thee conducted down, I dare 417
O ship incoming from the sea 234
O'er the glad waters of the dark-blue sea 381
Of Neptunes Empyre let us sing 397
Of thee the Northman by his beachèd galley 9
Off Portland: wind east, visibility eight 109
Often I think of the beautiful town 262
Oh blythely shines the bonnie sun 308
Oh England is a pleasant place for them that's rich and high 382
Oh, what is abroad in the marsh and the terminal sea? 195
Old Horn to All Atlantic said 96
Old ocean was infinity of ages ere we breathed 160
On and on 271
On the large highway of the awful air that flows 279
Once a rover of the sea, captain of a barkentine 528
One by one the pale stars die before the day now 70
One night came on a hurricane 103
Our anchors drag and our cables surge 341
Our brows are wreathed with spindrift and the weed is on our
   knees 224
Our ship is a cradle on ocean's blue billow 481
Out in a dark, lost kingdom of their own 122
Out of the air a time of quiet came 130
Out of the darkness of time and the stress of an impulse unending 164
Out where the white waves whisper 310
Over all the face of earth main ocean flow'd 187
Over the shining pavement of the sea 235
Over them all, we sit aloft and sing 501

Pallidly sleeping, the Ocean's mysterious daughter 421
Pirates, after all, were usually 392
"Pull, men, for, lo, see there they blow! 362

Rain, with a silver flail 369
Rise, brothers, rise; the wakening skies pray to the morning light . 303
Roll on, thou deep and dark blue Ocean—roll! 145
Rushing along on a narrow reach 75

Sauntering hither on listless wings 278
Say that he loved old ships; write nothing more 515
Sea is wild marble waiting a stonecutter's hand, chaos crying for
   symmetry 150
Searching my heart for its true sorrow 8
She comes, majestic with her swelling sails 233

INDEX OF FIRST LINES

Ships that pass in the night, and speak each other in passing 539
Ships with your silver nets 297
Shu-lin was a parrot who sat on the shoulder 283
Simon Danz has come home again 388
Since ocean rolled and ocean winds were strong 510
Sing me a song of a lad that is gone 476
Sky in its lucent splendor lifted 125
So tame, so languid looks this drowsing sea 139
Solemn he paced upon that schooner's deck 464
"Some likes picturs o' women," said Bill, "an' some likes 'orses best" 255
Sometimes when I wake up I lie 486
South of Guardafui with a dark tide flowing 441
Southward Sidonian Hanno lashed his slaves 72
Southward with fleet of ice 442
Spirit of freedom, thou dost love the sea 24
Steer hither, steer your wingéd pines 404
Sunlight falls happily upon this sea 133
Sunset and evening star 522
Sweet and low, sweet and low 473

Take care, O wisp of a moon 138
The bending sails shall whiten on the sea 238
The boy stood on the burning deck 331
The captain stood on the carronade—"First lieutenant," says he .. 335
The clouds are scudding across the moon 111
The earth grows white with harvest; all day long 294
The fisherman goes out at dawn 291
The flashing of an arc that bright and briefly 285
The fore-royal furled, I pause and I stand 231
The full sea rolls and thunders 499
The gay sea-plants familiar were to her 22
The great ship spreads her wings, her plumes are flying 79
The interminable ocean lay beneath 140
The king sits in Dunfermline town 326
The night was made for cooling shade 183
The ocean stood like crystal. The soft air 213
The ocean thunders in the caverned sky 230
The osprey sails about the sound 304
The quick sea shone 128
The ribs and terrors in the whale 360
The sea awoke at midnight from its sleep 501
The sea is calm tonight 176
The seagull's narrow sails of feather lift 279
The sheets were frozen hard, and they cut the naked hand 88
The sky is ruddy in the east 27

INDEX OF FIRST LINES 563

The song of the sea was an ancient song	493
The south and west winds joined, and, as they blew	114
The stars never had any mystery for me	460
The stars of the morn	347
The tireless flight of a pursuing gull	179
The very pulse of ocean now was still	251
The wail of a waking wind in a wide-flung wheat field	16
The weather leech of the topsail shivers	62
The wild and plunging seas have smote our sides	387
The wind it blew and the ship it flew	343
The wind it wailed, the wind it moaned	471
The winds were yelling, the waves were swelling	385
Then came the cry of "Call all hands on deck!"	86
There is a harp set above us	495
There is a memory stays upon old ships	448
There is no music that man has heard	499
There is no sorrow anywhere	221
There lies the port; the vessel puffs her sail	61
There was a lily and rose sea-maiden	405
There was a ship of Rio	480
There was an ancient carver that carved of a saint	466
There were three sailors of Bristol City	474
There's a schooner out from Kingsport	477
There's beauty in the deep	403
There's some is born with their legs straight by natur—	455
There's the gals at the bar, there's the beer	222
They are remembering forests where they grew,—	526
They come again those monsters of the sea	141
They ran through the streets of the seaport town	489
They say a tropic river threads the seas	134
They that go down to the sea in ships, that do business in great waters	169
They were met in the Last Inn's tap-room, where the road strikes hands with the sea	257
They who possess the sea within their blood	15
They will take us from the moorings, they will tow us down the Bay	244
This cruising caballero of the deep	277
This is a salt steep-cobbled town	250
This is the breed that followed the tails	353
This is the ship of pearl, which, poets feign	172
This is the song of the wave! The mighty one!	184
This shell, this slender spiral in the hand	504
This tempest sweeps the Atlantic!	98
Thorberg Skafting, master-builder	50
Those trackless deeps, where many a weary sail	153
Thou foul-mouthed wretch! Why dost thou choose	273

INDEX OF FIRST LINES

Thou little bird, thou dweller by the sea 282
Thou who hast slept all night upon the storm 271
Three fishers went sailing away to the West 289
Three hand-spike raps on the forward hatch 99
Through the faintest filigree 426
Thus said the Lord in the Vault above the Cherubim 147
Time cannot age thy sinews, nor the gale 281
"Tis a hundred years," said the bosun bold 359
'Tis of a gallant Yankee ship that flew the stripes and stars 313
To an ebbing tide, all sail apeak 367
To eastward ringing, to westward winging, o'er mapless miles of
    sea 337
To sea, to sea! The calm is o'er 75
To what dark purpose was the will employed 190
Toll for the brave! 339
'T was on the shores that round our coast 452
'T was Yesterday He made me and Tomorrow I shall die 129

Under the sea, which is their sky, they rise 418
Unfathomable Sea! whose waves are years! 160

Veiled are the heavens, veiled the throne 169
View now the winter storm! Above—one cloud 119

We sailed by the old world's tideways, down through the long sea-
    lanes 170
We stood on the haunted island 446
We were crowded in the cabin 85
Welter upon the waters, mighty one— 412
What! After your six-month drowsing and indolent sleeping 17
What are the voices that harass their dreaming? 425
What bring you, sailor, home from the sea— 458
What do I see and hear of an April morning? 20
What flecks the outer gray beyond 430
What if some little paine the passage have 225
What joy attends the fisher's life! 309
What time I hear the storming sea 305
What was I back in the world's first wonder?— 484
When April skies are bright with sun 444
When Captain O'Bruadir shook a sword across the sea 377
When descends on the Atlantic 107
When I had wings, my brother 276
When I have lain an hour watching the skies 429
When I was a passenger in the barque *Windrush* 459
When, o'er the silent seas alone 525
When storms go growling off to lonely places 372
When the *Ark* and *Dove* within the glassy wave 239